THE LONGING OF THE SOUL

THE LONGING
OF THE SOUL

Rabia Christine Brodbeck

TUGHRA
BOOKS

New Jersey

Published by Tughra Books
345 Clifton Avenue
Clifton, NJ, 07011, USA

www.tughrabooks.com

Library of Congress Cataloging-in-Publication Data

Brodbeck, Rabia Christine.
The longing of the soul / Rabia Christine Brodbeck.
pages cm.
ISBN 978-1-59784-322-5 (alk. paper)
1. Prayer--Islam. I. Title.
BP184.3.B76 2014
297.3--dc23
2014006769

ISBN: 978-1-59784-322-5

Contents

Introduction ix

The Pillars of Islam 1

The Essence of Islamic Worship 5

The Effectiveness of Supplication 9

The Secret Essence of Repetition in Worship, Supplication, and Remembrance 17

The Qualities of Humility and Modesty 19

Divine Beauty and Perfection 27

    The Wealth of the Inner Dimensions of Islamic Worship Rituals 36

The Holy Qur'an as a Pure Form of Worship 63

Salah (The Ritual Prayer) 71

    The Night of the Ascension and Servanthood 75

    The Daily Prayers 80

    Salah and the Saints of Islam 85

    The Ritual Prayer: A Sacred Communication 88

    Surah Al-Fatiha 89

    The Postures of *Salah* 93

    Reflections on the Ritual Prayer 102

    Performing the True Prayer 106

    Supplications 114

Zakah (The Prescribed Purifying Alms) 119

    Tears 128

    Ahl al-Bayt: The Prophet's Family and the Blessed Companions 134

    Supplications 143

    Supplication with the Tongue of Impotence 145

    The Inner Witness to the Events of the Present World 147

The Fasting and the Holy Month of Ramadan 155

    Supplications 181

Hajj (The Pilgrimage) 185

    Supplications 216

Introduction

Ail praise be to Allah, we are given to drink from the purest source, the Divine Word, along with the words of His Prophet, the Companions and other saintly believers.

The Islamic canon law, the *Sharia*, literally means "pathway to be followed," or "path to the water hole." The Islamic law is, therefore, the Divinely granted, pure source of water to be drunk, or rather the true way to be followed, throughout the lives of the believers. The law consists of rules and commandments from the All-Holy regarding worship and conduct and the rules of how to govern human behavior in society. This book deals exclusively with the meaning and essence of worship in Islam, including especially the Daily Prayers (*Salah*), the Prescribed Purifying Alms (*Zakah*), fasting during the month of Ramadan (*Sawm*), the pilgrimage to Mecca (*Hajj*). These are the acts of worship a Muslim has to fulfill in his life. These are coming from the pure source.

While researching the soul of Islamic acts of worship, sources have been drawn from the verses of the Holy Qur'an, from the *Sunnah*, the actions, words, and tacit approvals of Prophet Muhammad, peace and blessings be upon him, from his esteemed Companions and disciples, and from all the great saints of Islam and secondarily the venerable followers, lovers and saints of the Prophet, who nurtured the religious worship duties with admiration and love for the Almighty Creator.

Thus this book does not aim to represent a guideline for the proper performance of religious rituals. This book tries to reawaken the sacred sensibilities we have lost. The essential goal lies in the attempt to bring back the love we have lost in terms of the acts of worship the All-Merciful enjoined us to fulfill, the joy of obedience to His command, and the pleasure of having faith in Him. I believe that it is the need of our time to regain the wealth of the inner dimensions of the sacred worship duties, to be of active help to fulfill the religious duties with love and beauty again in order to reawaken the worshipping hearts for the sweet smell of the Hereafter.

This book represents an attempt to shed light on the inexhaustible treasures within ourselves. The seed of eternal love, which is granted by the All-Merciful, grows within the deepest interior of man. It is the raison d'être of our sacred origin; it is the wealth of human goodness. The real love is the love for the Divine. In this sense, this writing is an attempt to revive the treasury of eternal lights within our hearts: It tries to regain the lost treasury of the human spirit. It tries to encourage the internalization of all this in the worshipper's personality in order to beautify his inner self.

This book is an attempt to rediscover the treasury of the *ihram*, the sacred state of a pilgrim. The *ihram* symbolizes the internal, human condition of modesty, poverty, need and loving surrender. It represents the state of desirelessness, wishlessness and complete submission. The five pillars of the sacred law are given for no other reason. In this respect, I carry the strong conviction that it is time to distance ourselves from the long lasting external concerns of the Muslim communities with the questions of outer loose garments or *hijab* and begin an inward research of the treasury of keeping the sacred state of *ihram* throughout our lives. I believe that the Muslim communities, as well as the secular societies with their rational argumentations, opinions, and reasoning to express their hostilities towards the religion of Islam have to begin to shift from the purely political, social, outward, legal concerns, from the purely rational approaches, to the eternal concerns of our master, the beloved of our hearts, Prophet Muhammad, peace and blessings be upon him. I believe it is time to put discussions at rest. Dealing with events of political, religious and social nature exclusively on the official, formal, outward level means to ignore their problems. Rumi says: "*The first to employ this silly reasoning in the face of the Lights of God was Iblis. He said, 'Without doubt fire is better than earth, and I am made of fire, while Adam is made from dark-colored clay.' Satan stirs up a doubt and throws these blind men down on their heads. Did not God show you mercy and bounty, the staff of your rational argument would break!*" Reasoning and rational analysis of reality happens through the absence of a universal consciousness, the absence of love and through the loss of the dimensions of inwardness. Muhyiddin ibn Arabi demonstrates with his penetrating clarity of vision the required attitude we should adapt as believing servants for the Lord of all the worlds and for the mercy for all the worlds: *"Whoever theorizes his religion offends against the Way of God and peace. Heretic! Deviate toward the Law! Do not complicate. All this learned talk is ignorance. Station and state, discard it. It is not discussion; Religion is what my Lord said or what he said—the master guide, the Messenger, peace and blessings be upon him, for he said not a word!"*

The reason for the lack of excitement for Islamic worship rituals is due to the lack of vision of Divine beauty during the practices. The reason for the inability to witness beauty is due to the lack of sacred awareness. It is the awareness of the sacred reality that allows the manifestations of the Divine Attributes and Names within ourselves; sincere devotion to God will give rise to the radiance of the jewels of human character. An important fact for the loss of inspiration and pleasure during devotional activities is actually the loss of the sensation of the sacred thirst. We lost the need and longing for our Supreme Creator, which means we lack the need to turn to Him, to plead with Him, to converse with Him, and to take refuge in Him. That is to say, we lack the need for the truth. The sacred thirst is precisely the thirst of the soul of man yearning for its Creator. Being deprived of the need and wish for the Almighty means consequently not being able to feel and hear the soul's desire, its sacred thirst pleading for the Water of life, longing to unify with his Supreme Majesty. In other words, the holy attraction is not felt. This is the reason for dry, mechanical and lifeless worship; the devotee lost the sacred sensibilities which enable him to feel the inner richness of the Prayer rituals.

All of creation needs inspiration for its survival. All levels of existence from the mineral, vegetation, animals to earth and the heavenly bodies in the universe follow the sacred, harmonious order. Allah the Almighty gave inspiration to all of His creation. The trees are inspired to bear fruits, the cow is inspired to give milk, the flower is inspired to produce luminous colors, and the stars are inspired to shine with beams of sparkling lights for thousands of years. Allah says to the bees in the Holy Qur'an: *"Your Lord inspired the bee. 'Take for yourself dwelling-place in the mountains, and in the trees, and in what they (human beings) may build and weave'"* (an-Nahl, 16:68). Allah has given them the inspiration to pluck the sustenance from flowers in order to produce honey. All the millions of different kinds of animals have inherited the inspiration to live and perform duties for their survival. Unfortunately this life energy, this heightened joy and enthusiasm is severely lowered and decayed, that is to say, the majority of human beings lost sacred inspirations within their lives, within their families, with their friends and working colleagues. Consequently, they lose inspiration within their Prayers. Allah the Almighty says in Surah Ar-Rahman: *"The stars and the trees both prostrate (before God in perfect submission to His laws)* (ar-Rahman 55:6). *"All that are in the heavens and on the earth entreat Him (in their needs). Every (moment of every) day, He is in a new manifestation (with all His Attributes and Names as the Divine Being)"* (ar-Rahman 55:29). These verses are of such artistic beauty; they reveal the infinite wonders and treasures of Allah's creation, His grace and favors given to humanity. The earth is a place where honey and milk flow in abundance. All existence turns by the Breath of the All-Merciful. The whole of creation is immersed in continuous worship of its Lord. The earth and humankind is entrusted with the knowledge of God. The whole universe is receiving God's glory. All things are one with Him, all things are in harmony with Him. That is to say, all existence shows evidence of God Most High. To be blind to the wonders of His creation is equal to being ignorant and ungrateful. If the herbs and trees bow in adoration, should not the human being endowed with intelligent speech, capacity of understanding, faculties of seeing, hearing, tasting be utterly appreciative of His endless gifts. The question, *"Then which of the favors of your Lord will you deny?"*, is repeated thirty-one times in Surah Ar-Rahman. Allah reminds us to acknowledge His uncountable bounties and gifts. He reminds us to open the eyes of our hearts and to wake up from the darkness of unconsciousness. We have to see that our Merciful Creator invites us to the highest pleasure of God-consciousness. He invites us to see the infinite beauty of the treasures of His creation. He calls us for admiration, for love. He bestows the delight of Divine inspirations to His believing servants. When will we wake up from the sleep of unconsciousness and begin to see the worth, honor and elevation given on us?

People are generally mistaken that the teaching of the religion means simply obeying the orders of Allah and refraining from what He has forbidden. So they fear His punishment and worship Him in order to receive credit for the good deeds in hopes of Paradise. This is in fact the lowest level of human existence. To look at man exclusively on the moral level, judging him in terms of right and wrong, good and bad, permissible and forbidden, obedience and disobedience decreases man's value into the narrowness of a black-and-white existence... Especially in the religion of Islam, we can learn from and through beauty. Rumi comments: *"All goals are Your Beauty. The lovers' teacher is the Beloved's Beauty. Their book and lesson are His Face. Where do angels find food? From the beauty of God's Presence... The moon and planets seek nourishment from the world's sun."*

The main wisdom I discovered through turning every day to the Creator in worship is this; there is a treasury of Divine beauty within ourselves, a source of eternal life. It is the hidden treasure we carry within ourselves. Praying makes us aware of the sacred reality within ourselves. Praying to the Almighty has to be an expression of one's love, admiration and longing towards the Only One. So, praying becomes food for the heart. The secret for successful worship lies therefore in the desire we have for Him, in the wish to become intimate with Him, in the degree of our yearning to communicate with Him, and in the profoundness of our longing in order to be raised to the level of real friendship with Him. This is the crucial point where real worship starts, where the door of sacred communication to the Lord of all the worlds opens, where the flames of love from the worshipper to the Worshipped become ignited. The secret for true worship lies in offering ourselves like a slave to its Owner, for He is the Sought and the Seeker, He is the Desired and the Desirer, He is the Lover and the Beloved.

Islam holds intention above action. There is the example of the ant going on *Hajj* and the bird carrying one drop of water in his tiny mouth, desiring to extinguish the fire of the tyrant Nimrod for Prophet Abraham (Ibrahim), peace be upon him. Both of these little creatures seem to have faced a goal impossible to accomplish from the rational point of view. But in God's view, their intention was of stainless and luminous purity, and thus they are able to touch the deepest interior of our hearts. If we do not learn to see with the eyes of compassion, with the eyes of humility, if we do not share the mercy and compassion of Allah for His creation, we will remain in a no man's land, in a meaningless, empty, purposeless life. Our hearts will turn into a dry desert where nothing can grow. Observing the present events on the worldly stage, our tongue is tied in impotence, our hearts are shattered into pieces, the eye-water continuously pouring down our cheeks in the face of all the injustice, the human misery, the human tragedies, the internal wars, the terror, the calamities we are witnessing. Therefore I carry the strong conviction that each believer has to demonstrate the very best intention within his life, namely, he has to carry in his mouth some drop of water as a bird and fly towards the fire with the desire to extinguish it. If each individual would act with this pure intention the fire of tyranny would certainly be extinguished. Once oppression and tyranny are eliminated, our world will turn into a rose-garden, as Nimrod's fire turned into a green garden for Prophet Abraham, peace be upon him. If each believer in this world would take a glass of water and pour it out in the same place, an ocean would emerge and the tyrant Pharaoh with his armies would all be drowned in it.

Furthermore, this book is an attempt to make us aware of some of the greatest losses, namely the feelings of humility, compassion, mercy, shame, modesty, and true love. In the absence of these supreme character features, we will miss the reality of intimacy. There is knowledge of God as opposed to familiarity with God. There is knowledge of the Qur'an as opposed to familiarity with the Qur'an. There is knowledge of the religion and there is the sacred awareness of the religion. There is the word "Allah" and there is the power of the Holy Presence of Allah. When true believers read the Qur'an, they witness the reality of intimacy. We can make a principle distinction; formal, systematic, and traditional learning as opposed to internalizing and realizing religious knowledge into love. It is the borderline between the illusionary man and the attainment of intimacy with God.

Abdul Qadir al-Jilani comments: "*The true believer belongs entirely to God. Not a single atom of his being belongs to creatures. God is in charge of both his outer and his inner dimension. He makes no movement except because of Him, and he does not come to rest except because of Him—for he has his being entirely because of Him, from Him, and in Him.*"

Allah says in a Divine *hadith*: "*My servant, if you wish to enter the sanctuary of My intimacy, do not pay attention to this world or the higher world of the angels, not even to the higher realms where you may receive My Divine Attributes.*"

The Sufi saint Ahmad Sam'ani describes: *"God addresses His crea-tures: "O Ridwan, Paradise belongs to you! O Malik, Hell belongs to you! O Cherubim, the Throne belongs to you! O you with the burnt heart, you who carry the seal of My love! You belong to Me, and I belong to you."*

Bahauddin Walad is expressing the burning heart of his sacred aspi-rations: *"You have brought me up by ways of manifest doors, so give me my daily bread from Yourself. Since you have not let me do without the secondary causes, I want beauties, I want blessings, I want audition, I want esteem, I want power, and I want will. God inspired into me: Drink from Me without end, like a bee from flowers, so that all parts may become honey. For We are the life-giver, and life-giving takes place only through happiness and objects of desire. We are the death-giver, and death-giving takes place only through separation from happiness and objects of desire. As much as happiness goes, annihilation appears."*

The religion of Islam teaches the knowledge of humility. The attain-ment of the consciousness of humility will enhance the highest spiritual station. It is man's consciousness of responsibility, namely the need for servanthood. The honor of the universe, the mercy for all the worlds, dem-onstrated to all humanity that the knowledge of the Almighty is a mercy for all living souls, that sacred awareness will bring beauty and blessings, that the Divine revelations of the Holy Qur'an are pearls of wisdom which have a healing effect and cure our spiritual wounds. They bring remedy for broken hearts, they offer comfort to the distressed, they nourish human needs, and they bring spiritual salvation to all living souls.

Furthermore, I wish to highlight the following fact while being moti-vated and inspired by the All-Merciful One to write this book. The read-er might conclude that I give too many examples. The majority of believ-ers might not be able to follow the examples of the noble Companions of the blessed Prophet. But the crucial point is this: If we do not reflect through the light of Prophethood, through the light of the Holy verses of the Qur'an, through the light of the noble traditions, the *Hadith*, through the light of the *Sunnah* of the Messenger, we will be unable to learn and to see, we will not be able to open up the horizon of sacred awareness. For the abandoning the sacred obligations means to break away from the light of Muhammad. Abandoning religion means to deny the com-mands of God and to deny the reality of Divine Mercy. If believers do not think and reason within the light of Prophethood and the light of the

Holy Qur'an, there will be chaos, confusion, and disharmony. It is through the light of guidance of Prophet Muhammad, peace and blessings be upon him, his family, and the Companions that we learn about the value, meaning, and the place and honor of the human being, because they are a manifestation of realized love. Through their enlightened examples, we are able to gain awareness of who we are, of our true human nature, the way God meant us to be. We are the manifestation of His Attributes and Names. We carry the hidden treasure within ourselves implanted at the time of creation. We are created as representatives of Allah on earth, which means that we are honored for the noblest station of vicegerency. It represents the highest rank in the spiritual hierarchy. The Qur'an states, "*Remember (when) your Lord said to the angels: 'I am setting on the earth a vicegerent'*" (al-Baqarah 2:30).

Furthermore this book concentrates on one of the worst problems the modern societies face today: the loss of unity, or *tawhid*. Humanity lost the highest goal of true belief expressed in the words of our noble Prophet Muhammad, peace and blessings be upon him, who said: "*The believers are brothers and sisters, and men of knowledge are like a single soul.*" The Holy Qur'an states: "*Your creation and your resurrection are as but a single soul*" (Luqman 31:28). "*Humankind were (in the beginning) one community (following one way of life without disputing over provision and other similar things. Later on, differences arose and) God sent Prophets as bearers of glad tidings (of prosperity in return for faith and righteousness) and warners (against the consequences of straying and transgression)*" (al-Baqarah 2:213). We can observe that chaotic and destructive events are shattering modern societies into pieces. Unfortunately, modern societies have lost mystery, grace, vision, charm and love which means, they have lost their touch with their origins, their roots, the true purpose of life. Consequently, human beings have lost the dimension of inwardness, they have lost meaning and value, respectively, and they have lost the sensitivity which makes them into human beings, which means that they have lost the sacredness of all life.

We can observe wide-spread political and economic corruption and instability, sectarian violence, terror, and internal civil wars. Said Nursi gives us great insight about the moderation in Islamic thought: "*Too much or too little of anything is not good. Moderation is the middle way. O Sunnis, who are people of truth and Alawis whose way is love of the Proph-*

et's family! Quickly put an end to this meaningless, disloyal, unjust and harmful dispute between you... Since you are believers in Divine unity, it is essential to leave aside unimportant matters which necessitate division while there are a hundred fundamental sacred bonds between you which command brotherhood and unity."

Togetherness, embracement, love, sharing, brotherhood, communal life, are all necessary elements for human survival. What is felt is felt through each other. Through the light of Divine unity there is brotherhood. Through the union of shared brotherhood there is the treasury of the community of Muhammad. As an individual of the world's population we have to see each other as one soul, one family, one community, one body, one brotherhood and sisterhood. We have to leave all differences, distinctions between people, nationalities, communities, social status, and rank and unite in the love of universal brotherhood. What unify people are eternal values inherent in everyone. As believers we have to realize the unity of God's Names and Attributes. If human life is devoid of His Attributes, human beings will become stranger to each other, misunderstand each other, and get distant to each other. The true brotherhood is the brotherhood of milk because it unites those who drink. Without being able to share the food of the lovers of God, without sitting down with them on the banquet of heaven, without unifying with the lovers and tasting the sweetness of faith, without having inhaled the sweet taste of the Hereafter within a loving brotherhood, without having shared wonderment, admiration, affection, without having shared the running tears for our blessed master with his abundant lovers, we cannot reach the honor of being part of the Muhammad's community. We have to melt and get lost in the longing of the noble Prophet for his community. We have to get lost and melt in the love God has for His beloved.

Due to the loss of unity, oneness, brotherhood, we can observe that modern life has lost language. We have lost the capacity to reflect. We have lost speech, and we have lost the ability to share. We lack sacred communication and mutual understanding. We have lost true friendship, true brotherhood. All of this means that we have lost the qualities of modesty and humility, the capacity to shed tears, the perfume of intimate friendship, the silence of the heart's speech, the living grace of spirituality. In other words, we have lost the secret of love, which is the need for the truth. The whole drama of human life on the planet shows a grave misery; it is the separation of hearts. This fact is a sign for the greatest of all losses; the separation from our beloved Lord of all the worlds. For to live a religious life means enjoyment from nourishment and healing through light. I believe that it is the essential duty for all believers to share radical healing and enlightenment with all beings. The greatest spiritual fulfillment human beings are able to experience in this world is the current of love from heart to heart. In this respect, a friend of God, Terzi Osman, narrated in one of his talks: "*Once I saw the Messenger of Allah in my dream and I said to him; 'Do not show yourself in my dreams anymore!*" The people who were present asked him: "*Why, why, how much we all desire to see him!*" He responded: "*I told the beloved of God; O my Prophet, send me to your followers who yearn for you, who feel passionate love for you, who are looking for you in this world, send me to those honored servants whom you bless with your sacred presence. Make me know them, make me friends with them!*" In other words, the friend of God asked the blessed Messenger not just to appear in his dream, but to make his sacred presence felt within his life and share it with all of his lovers. Today, believers miss the desire to see the sacred beauty of the glory of the universe within themselves and within their fellow beings, which means, we miss the grace and beauty of sacred friendship.

Prophet Abraham, upon him be peace, said: "*Only the brotherhood of milk is important, which unites those who drink, because they have acquired the same knowledge.*" Rumi says: "*Man must cleanse all ulterior motives from his faculty of discernment and seek companions in religion. Religion is to seek companions.*" Religion is to establish an experimental relationship of taste from heart to heart and thus taste the sweet perfumes of intimate friendship. The essence of the religion is to be in love with the lovers who are in love with the reason of creation, the honor of the universe, Prophet Muhammad, peace and blessings be upon him. Religion means to share the taste of healing, to share the joy of enlightenment, to share the bliss of the Divine secrets shining from the pure surface of the heart, to share to intoxication of the heavenly sound: "*Am I not your Lord?*", to share the enjoyment of Divine nourishment, to share one's innermost thoughts, to share the state of the eye of certainty, to share the bliss of union with those who drink. This way we can join the sea of saints: "*Know well that the friends (saintly servants) of God—they will have no fear (both in this world and the next, for they will always find*

My help and support with them), nor will they grieve" (Yunus 10:62), and experience the greatest bliss of the reality, as expressed in these *hadiths*: *"The believer is the mirror of his fellow brother,"* and *"Neither My Earth nor My Heavens can contain Me, but the heart of a believing servant."* Divine friendship is to mirror God, to mirror God's Perfection. Rumi says: *"Those with mirror-like hearts do not depend on fragrance and color; they behold the beauty in the moment. They have cracked open the shell of knowledge and raised the banner of the eye of certainty. Thought is gone in a flash of light"* (*Masnawi*, I/3492–3494).

The peak of blissful experience is to become a fellow of those Companions of the Prophet who swore the obey him. Such exalted companionship means to dwell in union in the realm of the souls with one's Creator, *"Alastu bi Rabbikum?—Am I not your Lord?),"* and answer continuously: *"Bala!"—"Yes indeed You are our Lord!"* (al-A'raf 7:172) while living in this world. Such exalted Companionship demands to live together and to die together, which means to share each other's heartache. As Rumi says: *"The lovers who are each other's spirit, die in their mutual love. The water of love soothes their aching livers; they all come and die in that heartache."*

The human being carries within himself the seeds of universal love, the greatest force in the universe. So shouldn't we feel the need to love and embrace each other? It is actually not enough to love each other. Love has to be proved by respecting each other, by helping each other, by being an inspiration for each other, a guidance for each other, by admiring each other, by exchanging sacred knowledge with each other, by serving each other, by being patient, forgiving and compassionate towards each other. In short, love has to be proved by our behavior, offering service to the ones in need under all circumstances. Love is expressed through the exchange of these qualities. For what comes from the heart can enter hearts, for what shines from the souls will shine to the other souls, culminating in the absolute spiritual fulfillment of the blessed master's *hadith*: *"The believer is the mirror of his fellow brother."* That is to say, the seekers on the path of truth will receive the honor to share the membership of the most honored of all communities, the community of Muhammad. This feeling overpowers all other feelings. They will melt in the holy bliss becoming one single soul. Only the truth unites!

In modern societies people flee from what is best for them and they desire what is worst for them. The modern man generally lives a life in the opposite direction of belief, opposite of the Divine order of the universe. He lives in a paradox. His values are turned upside down, because he has let go eternity in exchange of the world. He has preferred his selfish desires over the beauty of Divine goodness. He has deformed the truth into falseness. Instead of confronting himself with himself, he becomes a stranger to himself, which means he becomes a stranger towards his Supreme Creator. His whole life gives witness to the reversed direction, away from sacred reality. In other words, he desires the world to such a degree that he becomes deaf, blind and sore. He loses the ability of distinction between right and wrong, good and bad, beneficial and harmful. His greatest mistake lies in taking his miserliness as happiness, his imprisoning as freedom, his lowness as elevation. He has mistaken his miserliness for his salvation. An excellent description of the modern man is given by Rumi. In one of his discourses he is asking his followers: *"When do you give up being happy in this hellish prison of this world?"* The ultimate wisdom we should attain in our earthly lives; what makes you free is the abundance of what imprisons you. We have to ask ourselves: Who depends on whom? Who serves who? Who is the slave of whom? Who is in control of whom? Who is the owner of whom? Who is the ruler of whom? Who is in charge? We can mention a basic fact: either you rule your body, or your body rules you. Either your ego controls you control your ego. Either you govern your own human kingdom or you become slave in your own kingdom. Either you are in control of your subconsciousness, or the subconsciousness will control you. The danger we continuously encounter within our lives is that we will be convicted by our own actions if we are not the leader of all our affairs. The human being is endowed with a will power, with the ability of discrimination, with rulership, and with ownership. All of these faculties give man an intuitive perception of himself. Whatever problem, calamity the human being in his life encounters is due to his not mastering and controlling his own self. Whereas the greatest victory a human being is able to achieve in this world is to know his own self. Our blessed master says in a tradition: *"When you know yourself, you know your Lord."* If our desire to know ourselves is sincere, it will be paired with Allah's desire to be known. Our need to know ourselves will meet the Divine Will's Desire to be known. Our efforts will close the circle. All truths are present at all times and at all places for those who have eyes to see. Search for yourself in everything and search for everything in yourself. When we have knowledge of God, we perceive His sacred manifestations in all things. He, who knows himself, knows his Lord means; he who knows his impotence, his nothingness, knows his Lord. In the religion of Islam, nothingness becomes our capital, our elevation, our honor, because human perfection is paradoxically reached through non-existence. In other words, when God awakens the servant towards helplessness, need, poverty, destitution, nothingness, He makes us aware of our capital. This means, when we realize our nothingness, we realize our total need for Him. Respectively, when we recognize our nothingness and God's Totality, we will be able to attain true knowledge of Him and ourselves and we will have established the perfect relationship with the Exalted Creator. The majority of believers, do not know how to look at their own selves, how to investigate their own selves, respectively they do not know how to study themselves. What is self? What is ego? The problem is that we do not understand the reality of our heart, soul, body, psyche, and mind. What value do we have to give to our emotions, feelings, sensations? How do we deal with our pain, worries, and anxieties? What value has the intellect, mind, and contemplation in relation to the flesh of our bodies and in relation to the soul? One of the essential truths we know is that our greatest enemy is within ourselves: our carnal soul.

Islam embraces the whole life. But what is actually happening today in most Islamic countries is that mundane, profane life has embraced Islam. It is the virus of modernization; its weapon is the secularization of life brainwashing people to believe that the accumulation of wealth in this world is the ultimate Paradise. At the dawn of Islam, the life of believers was penetrated by religion. Today life is penetrated by materialism. Rumi said that health and wealth are the biggest obstacles between man and God. There is no other reason for neglecting Prayers in one's life than the attachment to the world and the involvement in the world. Perfect faith is only reached when one divorces one's self from the world. Khadija made the following statement when she started to know our blessed master: *"After I fell in love with the honor of the universe, for me the existence of the world ended. Concerning the world, there is only service left."* May the Almighty not let us drown in the insensitivities of modern societies.

Ignorance and heedlessness create insensitivity, and insensitivity, in turn, creates unawareness and so on ad infinitum. In today's modern societies we experience a great lack of the longing for the Truth. Man does not hear the call of his Lord anymore. He suffers from insensitivities, from a lack of sacred thirst, from a lack of sacred awareness, and therefore he suffers from a lack of sacred attraction. Thus; it is time for an awakening for the glorious all-compassing Truth! It is time to hear that Voice of all voices: *"The Water is asking; is there nobody to drink from Me?"* All people of this world are invited by His Majesty every moment of their lives. The remedy of all spiritual sicknesses is the need for the Divine, the longing for the Truth. Without need God gives nothing. The only need is the need for the search for God! Let us not head into our own ruins of moral decay. Let's supplicate to our Lord and ask Him to increase our need towards Him and help us become aware of our dependence towards Him! It is related in a tradition: *"He who sleeps contentedly while his neighbors sleep hungry did not believe in my message."* Without crushing under the truth of these words and taking the appropriate actions, we lack humanity.

Our Supreme Creator fashioned the human being superior to the rest of creation. Man is the goal of Allah's creation. The Qur'an states: *"Assuredly We have honored the children of Adam"* (Isra 17:70). The fact is; we are in infinite depth towards our Creator having been honored to belong to the community of Muhammad. Having received the greatest of all heavenly scriptures, the Holy Qur'an, having been nurtured with the illumination, goodness, mercy, blessings of His uncountable saints, friends and lovers, let's regain the flow of the human breath unsullied by the dirt of the world. Let's regain the water of life, the brilliance of sacred awareness, the infinite expansion of the breast. Let's regain the honor, elevation, and worth bestowed on human beings. The Qur'an states: *"Is he (who derives lessons from God's acts in the universe, and so) whose breast God has expanded to Islam, so that he follows a light from his Lord (is such a one to be likened to one whose heart is closed up to any remembrance of God and, therefore, to Islam)? So woe to those whose hearts are hardened against the remembrance of God (and who learn nothing from His signs and Revelations)! Those are lost in obvious error"* (az-Zumar 39:22). Rumi calls his followers: *"Be aware! O you who are like a drop, sacrifice yourself without hesitation so that you may buy a sea in return for a drop"* (Masnawi, IV/2619). We have to wake up from our sleep of ignorance induced by worldly narcosis and return back to experience the truth of the words from the Lord of all the worlds, "*I created every-thing for you; I created you for Myself*" (Divine *hadith*) and we must try to make this wisdom into the guiding principle of our lives.

Only through selflessness believers will become an empty recepta-cle for Allah's gentleness and mercy. Only with the help of the awe of the mystery of God's Essence they will be able to free themselves from the imprisonment of his egos and the evil forces of Satan. When the heart is full of selfish attributes, there will be no room for Allah's Grace. Man has received the light of his spirit from God at the time of his creation and he needs this light in order to see and hear. A believing life should be spent in fear to lose closeness to the Almighty God. Believers should always be busy with their personal failures and feel regret and repent. The essen-tial duty is to love and fear Allah; to love to do what He commands us to do, respectively showing love in obedience towards Him and feeling fear to lose His agreement, His contentment.

To conclude, we lack the realization of love in our lives. In terms of religion, we lost *zuhd*, seclusion, *khalwat*, retreat, *itikaf*, solitude in the last ten days of Ramadan, we lost *Tahajjud*, the Supererogatory Night Prayer, we lost the treasury of *sajdah,* prostration, we lost the *miraj,* the ascension of the spirit, we lost *ihram,* the sacred state, we lost *jihad*, striving in God's cause and for humanity's good. This shows that we lost the treasury of intimacy with our Lord of all the worlds. In the end of times, to keep one's faith will be as difficult as to carry burning coals in the palm of one's hands. If one drops it, one's faith will leave. May we not burn in the fire of modern times!

May all worshipping believers reach the ultimate spiritual fulfill-ment, namely to arrive at the door of intimate conversation with our Lord of Majesty and Bounty. There they will drink from the hand of the intimacy of the Almighty, "*Their Lord will favor them with the service of a pure drink*" (Insan 76:21), and they will reach the sacred state of "*Know well that the friends (saintly servants) of God—they will have no fear (both in this world and the next, for they will always find My help and support with them), nor will they grieve*" (Yunus 10:62).

The Pillars of Islam

The All-Glorious Creator gave His creatures a miraculous prescription for the salvation of humankind: the sacred law, the *Sharia*, consisting of five pillars, which are the worship duties imposed on the Muslim believers. As it is said, this book deals primarily with the obligatory worship rituals, the five pillars of Islam, and only secondarily with the rules governing human behavior in society. The five pillars of the *Sharia* represent the foundation for all the worship activities given by Allah. Within it lies the inner wealth of the religion Islam. The *Sharia* symbolizes submission to the Will of God. A believer's life without the five pillars of the religion is like a house without a foundation, walls, windows, and roof. Without the source of strength of the religious obligations, the life of a believer will become disordered and lose its spiritual value and meaning.

The *Sharia* has to be understood as the foundation for the spiritual realization for the human being. If it is lived and understood correctly, all further levels of spiritual development can be attained which are the *Sharia, Tariqa, Haqiqa* and *Marifa*. The *Sharia* is inextricably interrelated with all of the proceeding spiritual degrees from the simple conformity to the sacred law up to the *Marifa*, the station of sacred wisdom, or spiritual knowledge, representing the attainment of the highest secrets of the truth. These four stages of sacred perfection of man can be compared to that of a tree; the *Sharia* rules are the roots, *Tariqa* the trunk, *Haqiqa* the branches, *Marifa* are the fruits. Another spiritual hierarchy in the religion of Islam is given in a Prophetic tradition, defining three stages; *al-Islam* (external submission to the Law), *al-iman* (internal conviction), and *al-ihsan* (the perfection consisting of "acting and praying as if seeing God, and being conscious of that He sees you though you do not see Him"). Further, three degrees of spiritual development are described as; the "Lore of Certainty", *ilm al-yaqin*, leading into the "Eye of Certainty," *ayn al-yaqin*, to the "Truth of Certainty," *haqq al-yaqin*. On his journey, in the first stage, man accomplishes the knowledge of the law of the religion and he proceeds stages by stages until he reaches at the end of his voyage the ultimate level of the awareness of the truth. The traveler on the way of truth completes his journey by the observance of the *Sharia*. Though, the return of the believer is an absolute necessity in order to reach perfection. He will then have the vision of the truth during his ritual acts of worship, because he has realized the Presence of Allah the Almighty in his heart. He will then experience "the light of the eye," the spiritual delight of our blessed master during the performance of the ritual Prayer. In other words, the obligatory Prayers enable the worshipper to descend back towards his origin in order to approach the mystery of the glory of the universe, and the mystery of his status. In that sense, the *Sharia* is the foundation of unity. The simple conformity to the sacred law leads into spiritual perfection. In his exclusive interpretations Muhyiddin ibn Arabi comments: "*It is in your fall that your elevation comes, and it is in your earth that your heaven is found.*" The worshipper's gradual extinction generates in the same time his elevation; he is raised by Allah, as he lowers himself. Thus, the ritual worship duties of the religion of Islam represent a Divine recipe for human resurrection. More precisely, the religion of Islam demonstrates that the worth and honor of a human being does not lie in the perfection of knowledge, rather in the degree of love he shows in his submission to Allah's commandments and in the degree of his struggle to achieve the highest ethics of character. Thus it is through living a life of joy of devotion and loving servanthood towards His creation, that a believer can realize the highest levels of human development.

The first pillar represents the profession of faith, *Al-Kalimah al-Shahadah*. One bears witness that there is no deity but Allah and that Muhammad is His servant and Messenger. Additionally one pronounces the six principles of faith: to believe in Allah, His angels, His Holy Books, His Prophets, the Day of Judgment, and the Divine Destiny and decree (both good and evil are created by Allah; the creation of evil is not evil, doing an evil act is evil). Without pronouncing and believing in one's heart the profession of faith and the articles of faith, one cannot be considered as a believing Muslim, one cannot be considered to belong to the religion. In the initial stages of spiritual development, one pronounces the profession of faith, one bears witness to the oneness and unity of

God with one's tongue. In the ultimate sense, it gives witness that nothing other than God exists independently. The believers negate everything other than God and affirm the absolute Presence of their Supreme Creator. They renounce everything other than God, the love for the transient world, the love for mortal things, for all idols, so that God is seen as the Ever-Living and Self-Subsisting One. In the last stages of one's spiritual development, one has sacrificed one's whole self in loving surrender towards one's Lord, one has become an instrument of His Will. One has passed the three degrees of spiritual development, from the "Lore of Certainty" *ilm al-yaqin*, through the "Eye of Certainty" *ayn al-yaqin*, to the "Truth of Certainty" *haqq al-yaqin*. Especially with the testimony of faith we can observe how much the first pillar represents a means for spiritual growth, how much it generates a spiritual becoming. It is actually through a sincere performance of the four pillars throughout one's life. In other words, *Salah*, *Sawm*, *Zakah*, and *Hajj* and enable the believer to accomplish and realize the sincere faith within his own life. More precisely, in the first step, one pronounces the *Shahadah* with one's tongue and enters the religion as a believer and in the last stages of spiritual development; this affirmation of faith will become a reality within one's life. One has extinguished in one's heart all and everything what is not for the sake of Allah the Almighty. Such a believer reaches the heights of true belief; he enters the Majestic Presence, the palace of the Divine Mercy.

The sacred law is not separate from the one who brought the sacred law to humanity, the honor of the universe, our beloved Prophet. Allah sent him to the world not only as a Messenger, but also as a servant. He sent him for the perfection of good character and as a mercy for all creatures. The essence of the sacred law bears our blessed master's noble character, his unique compassion, and his abundant servanthood. It is thus the Prophet himself who represents the *Sharia*, because the sacred pillars mirror his servanthood. This means that the treasury of the Surah Al-Fatiha, the prostration, the *Tahajjud*, the call to Prayer, the ascension (*miraj*), the pilgrimage, fasting, almsgiving, and self-sacrifice are all symbolized by the noble Prophet himself. We have to see that the sacred law is a mercy for the whole world. A true master becomes the servant of its people; a true master becomes the healer of its people. It is only with servanthood that one can earn mastership, perfection, spiritual ranks, leadership and authority. It is through the essence of servanthood that our Prophet owned the highest station and was raised to become Allah's beloved one.

Especially today, it is my opinion for all the above-mentioned reasons that we need to hold on the sacred law more than ever. At the same time, we need to remember the Prophetic traditions, *Hadith,* and the practices of our noble master more than ever. Our noble Prophet says: *"You will follow the ways of those who were before you span for span and cubit for cubit until if they went down into the hole of a poisonous reptile you would follow them down."* This brings us back to the saying that in the time when the Prophet was alive, Islam embraced the whole of life, life was penetrated by religion. But shortly after our noble master passed away into the realms of eternal beauty, the religion of Islam experienced remarkable degeneration. One of the bravest souls of the 20th century, Ali Shariati, who died as a martyr, describes the spiritual decay the following way: *"The earliest period of Islam witnessed the most precious and the most appealing of all schools. But in the process of its change led to its degeneration and decline into something horrid and despicable. In other words, the noblest school of thought, the most elevated humanistic mission has become the most decayed, the most negative cause in the world. Ali ibn Abu Talib, may Allah be pleased with him, put this remarkable decline in history into a small sentence using a metaphor from daily life that is simple, precise, beautiful and right to the point: "Islam became like a dress of sheepskin worn inside out"* (the last sentence of *Khutbah* 107).

The Essence of Islamic Worship

The absolute condition for the personal salvation of mankind; unless we become aware of the sacred reality within ourselves, we will not earn any real success, neither in Prayer nor in life nor in the Hereafter.

The five pillars of the sacred law represent Allah's answer for the deepest desire of the human being. The essence of Islamic worship answers the irresistible wish of the human heart and spirit for the Creator. With the sacred worship duties, the believers realize their desire for their Creator. Human beings are created with the essence of fasting, the pilgrimage, almsgiving, the ritual Prayer, as the deep seated quality within them. That is to say, praying, fasting, and almsgiving are part of human nature. Therefore, human beings need the sacred pillars for their spiritual wellbeing. But the sacred worship duties need also man to be completed and shine in the mirror of sincerity and modesty in beauty from the secret regions of the worshipper's hearts. The Qur'an states: *"Then set your face upright for religion in the right state—the nature made by Allah in which He has made men; there is no altering of Allah's creation; that is the right religion, but most people do not know"* (Rum 30:30). Man's desire for worship is the longing for eternity, for immortality, for everlastingness. It is the deepest and most elevated longing of all creatures, the eternal desire for the realm of the spirits. It represents the desire for home-coming, the longing for the lost Paradise. This desire was born with the fall of man from Paradise on earth. Our father Adam was expelled from Paradise into this world. At the birth of the human being, the very moment when the spirit becomes linked with the body, need is born, hunger is born. It is precisely the driving force for man's actions in his life. In that sense, the five sacred pillars return the deep longing, the profound desire of the human spirit.

The nature of the human being is based on religion. He is of sacred origin, endowed with a pure nature. All Divine Names and Attributes are manifested in him. At the time of man's creation, Allah breathed from His Essence the spirit into him. Therefore, the Creator's love for His creatures is directed towards their very nature, that is to say, God's love is due to the sacredness of their existence. Man's very nature is God's pure love for him. Allah's creatures are His supplication. Man's essence is His secret. Therefore, man possesses a great desire for worship due to his very essence. He feels drawn towards the essence of worship because his spiritual potential is equal to the essence of worship. That is to say, the sacredness of man's existence mirrors the internal richness of the Prayer rituals; its inner treasury answers the irresistible wish of the human spirit. Praying to the Supreme Divinity nourishes the spiritual potential of the worshipper and this sacred infiltration will bring man closer to its Creator and at the same time closer to his own sacred potential.

Thus man feels an irresistible attraction towards the Divine; it is the sacred thirst to reach eternity. The only real thing in man is his spirit, and the spirit belongs entirely to God. All spirits want nothing but Him, consciously or unconsciously. All people in this world are in search of the eternal spring, they are in search for the sweet scent of the Paradise, of intimacy with Him. There are the ones who are unaware of the thirst of their spirits. They are enslaved by the world, so they are unaware that their hearts turned into a desert. There are the ones who feel the longing, the burning passion for their Lord because they have shed off the world's weight and with their burning lips look to find the water of life in the dry desert of existence. When Prophet Adam, peace be upon him, fell from Paradise into the desert of worldly existence, he had a fire of search in his breast.

God created man in His character, which means we have an intimate relationship with God. That is to say, the human being is created to love. Thus, worship is an expression for the love of God. Worship is an expression of adoration towards God. Worship is an expression of thankfulness towards God. Worship is an expression of servanthood towards God. To perform the sacred duties to the extent Allah desires from us, we have to enter the sacred areas of intimacy with the One and Only. Intimacy with the One and Only will nourish our hearts with light and give us Divine inspiration and bestow on us the state of speechless wonderment and awe. An often uttered sentence by our prince of the universe: "*O Lord, let me marvel at You!*" It is an absolute secret Divine condition for the worshipping believers *to* enter Prayer in a state of awe, admiration and to have a deep desire for intimate discourses of love with the One and Only. If we are not in love with God's infinite beauty and perfection, we cannot establish the true Prayer.

Our beloved Prophet said: *"The Qur'an and man are twins."* Whatever meaning the Divine verses of the Holy Qur'an convey is found in the human being and whatever meaning is gathered in the human being is found in the Holy Qur'an. The worth of a human being is equal to the worth of the Holy Qur'an. This means that the sacred wisdom of the Qur'anic revelations can be discovered within the storehouse of the human faculties. Man is the brother of the Qur'an. The great Caliph Ali said: *"I am the walking Qur'an."* Aisha, may Allah be pleased with her, described our blessed master as the "living Qur'an." This is what is meant by a caliph, the representative of God on earth. By the fact that the human being is created as a caliph, he becomes a perfect mirror of God on earth. He represents the embodiment of God's answers to humanity.

God states in the Qur'an: *"Read your book! Yourself suffices you this day as a reckoner against you"* (al-Isra 17:14). *"And also in your own selves. Will you then not see (the truth)?"* (adh-Dhariyat 51:21) *"We will show them Our manifest signs (proofs) in the horizons of the universe and within their own selves, until it will become manifest to them that it (the Qur'an) is indeed the truth. Is it not sufficient (as proof) that your Lord is a witness over all things (just as He is witnessed to by all things)?"* (Fussilat 41:53).

Ibn Arabi comments: *"The perfect man (al-insan al-kamil) is the brother of the Qur'an, or the Universal Man (al-insan al-kulli) is the Qur'an. After the death of the Prophet, who was the paradigm of all perfection (uswa al-hasana), his wife Aisha said: 'His nature was the Qur'an.'* Further he remarks: *"It sums up all that creatures should aspire to... He who knows himself knows his Lord, and he also knows all things. If you reflect on yourself, that is enough for you, since there is nothing outside of you."*

The leader of the gnostics, Ali ibn Abu Talib, said: *"Your cure is within you, but you do not know, your illness is from you, but you do not see. You are the 'Clarifying Book' through whose letters becomes manifest the hidden. You suppose that you are a small body but the greatest world unfolds within you. You would not need what is outside yourself if you would reflect upon self, but you do not reflect."*

To conclude, the Islamic worship rituals carry in their essence the potential for the perfection of love. It is worship beyond worship, the way to the realms of eternity, the prostration of the heart, the ascension of the spirit, the circumambulation around the secret essence of the heart, a manifestation of universal mercy, the light of sacred wisdom, the spirit's inspiration; it bears the essence of the glory of the universe's utterance: "*Poverty is my pride.*" Not wholeheartedly turn to one's Creator in active worship, service, and contemplation is actually as grave as denying one's own self. When one distances oneself from religion, one becomes a stranger to one's self because one turns away from one's very essence, one's spiritual potential. To neglect the religious duties means to be deprived of the light of God's wisdom.

The Effectiveness of Supplication

"Say: 'My Lord would not care for you were it not for your Prayer. Now that you have denied (His Message), the inescapable punishment will cleave to you'" (al-Furqan 25:77).

"Pray to Me, (and) I will answer you" (al-Mumin 40:60).

"When (O Messenger) My servants ask you about Me, then surely I am near: I answer the prayer of the suppliant when he prays to Me" (al-Baqarah 2:186).

"He Who answers the helpless one in distress when he prays to Him, and removes the affliction from him" (an-Naml 27:62).

Aisha, may God be pleased with her, said: *"No believer makes dua (supplication) and it is wasted. Either it is granted here in this world or deposited for him in the Hereafter as long as he does not get frustrated."* Prophet Muhammad, peace and blessings be upon him, said: *"Nothing is more honorable to Allah the Most High than dua"* (*Sahih al-Jami*, 5268). *"The most excellent worship is dua."* (*Sahih al-Jami*, 1133). *"The most incapable person is the one who does not make dua, and the most miserly person is the one who does not give salam"* (Sahih al-Jami, 1055). *"Verily your Lord is the One modest and Generous, and when His servant raises his hands to Him in supplication, He is diffident (in some wordings, shy or hesitant) from returning them empty"* (*Abu Dawud* and *At-Tirmidhi*).

True *dua*, supplication, needs the flowing of words. We have to enter the sacred space alone with Him in order to take inspiration from the inexhaustible source, the manifestation of Allah's Attribute *"As-Samad,"* the source. There we can satisfy all of our needs because we arrived at the treasury of intimacy, the place of inner pilgrimage, the secret essence of our heart. It is the Paradise which overpowers all other Paradises. There the veils are lifted, and we can taste the delights of seeing and hearing. There we are freed of all worldly concerns, desires, and goals. It is the land of *"Know well that the friends (saintly servants) of God—they will have no fear (both in this world and the next, for they will always find My help and support with them), nor will they grieve"* (Yunus 10:62). This is the era of the inexhaustible source where the supplication finds its words, the world of Allah's proximity. It is the heart talking and singing the praises of love and the lamentations of sorrow.

True *dua* needs the breathing of words. In order to breathe the Divine words, we need the spiritual oxygen. All existence is breathed by His Divine breath of mercy. When we talk to the One and Only with the tongue of impotence in profound humility and admiration, we will become part of His breath of mercy.

When the human being is in disorder, disharmony, and darkness, his supplications get stagnated into a mechanical routine. The electric energy will decrease, the Divine inspiration will disappear. But in the contrary, when the supplicant feels modesty and humility in front of the sublime Majesty, he receives a heightened voltage of energy and beauty that it becomes physically manifest in the trembling of the body and shedding the tears of awe and wonderment. Only the love for worship and the love for the Worshipped One will transport us to the highest spiritual pleasures. Supplicating to the One and Only needs a sincere heart, a submissive heart, a loving and fearful heart, a heart full of gratitude and humility before His infinite Grandeur and Majesty. It needs a heart full of compassion for the whole of humanity, a heart which beats the universal pulse of love for all humanity, a heart which embraces all people as one body, one family, and one brotherhood.

The servant's supplication is like the cord of an embryo. He is holding on his Lord like the cord of the embryo connected to its mother's womb. Without the cord feeding the embryo with the sustenance of life, the embryo will die. Thus holding onto the cord connecting us with our Lord with utmost intensity and insistency is an absolute necessity. Once leaving the cord we might fall into the danger of a spiritual death.

Sincere supplication can only be done with the charity of the self. Only selflessness can activate God's mercy towards the poor and needy. Only a generous heart can supplicate and reach the Supreme Majesty. Only when one loses oneself supplicating to one's Lord in the sea of tears of sorrow for one's brothers and sisters in the world one can reach the Supreme Majesty. Only when one melts into the river of affection and compassion supplicating to one's Lord for the needy, lonely, and destitute one can reach the Supreme Majesty and become one with the pleading universal pulse of love of all the supplicants streaming throughout the whole universe. When one forgets oneself while making *dua* for others, God promises that He will give the supplicant two times more of what he wished for his brother. True supplication necessitates self-sacrifice. True pleading to one's Lord has to be cleansed of all ulterior motives; it has to be cleansed of one's own desires, wishes, and advantages. The supplicant has to learn the art of living for others, the art of giving; he has to be favored by the Almighty to live the secret of love. In other words, a sincere believer has to arrive in a state in which he will satisfy the needs of others and become indifferent to his own needs. When he supplicates, the heart has to talk so that his tears may give witness of the sincerity of his pleading, longing, and whispering with the Lord of Majesty and Bounty. The worshipping believers should be concerned to heighten their admiration for the One and Only and the noblest of all men, the honor of the universe, Prophet Muhammad, peace and blessings be upon him. He used to pray: "*I cannot count Your blessings,*" and "*O Allah, increase my bewilderment in You.*"

Allah wishes to win our hearts; He wants to take us to His realms of intimacy. Therefore, He arranged a time in the night which is the most precious of the daily 24 hours. It is the hour of dawn. This is the hour of purity, the hour to converse loving whispers with Him, to dwell in intimacy with Him, to inhale the sweet scent of remembrance of Him. Allah the Almighty is pleading with us every night unceasingly. He is repeatedly inviting us and asking to show our servanthood towards Him. His plead is expressed in His wish for us to plead for and with Him. He says: "*Is there no one? Is there no one? Is there no one to ask from Me? Come, come, where are the nobodies so that I might show Myself to them? Come, come so that I might answer Your supplications. Supplicate, that I might forgive Your sins, that I might lift your burden. That I might heal your illness. There is a door of Mine which is never closed. It is the door of your needs towards Me. Come, come, the destitute, the distressed, the lonely, the weak, the sick, the helpless, the sinners, the lost, the poor, the tyrannized, and the nobodies. The door of pleading, longing, desiring for Me never closes.*" This door is the door of all the doors. There is no other door because there is no other refuge. This door is the door of His Mercy. This is the door where we are offered the drink of eternal life. This is the door for the ones begging before His Majesty, begging to receive an audience with the Supreme Divinity, the door of the Divine promise for help, comfort, healing, protection, sustenance, shelter, and care. The Almighty says: "*Those who do not abandon Me, I do not abandon them. The ones who open their hands towards Me, I will fill them. The ones who are sad, sorrowful, and broken-hearted, I will be their friend. The ones who love Me, I will love them. The ones who come with their sins, I will cover and forgive them. The ones who are lost, I will protect them. The ones who are in distress, I will give them relief. The ones who are helpless, I will give them help.*" This is His measure, His Divine promises demonstrating His loving care towards His creatures. His words prove His merciful care and Divine acceptance for our pleading, our tears, our longing, our burning, and our trembling towards Him.

The truth is that all people of this world are invited by His Majesty every moment of their lives. He calls for the pilgrimage; he invites us for intimate love discourses at the hour of dawn. He invites us the realm of His Nearness in every performance of the Prayer. He calls His creatures: "*My servants!*" Ibn Arabi writes about God in his book, *Theophany of Perfection*: "*O My beloved! How many times I have called you without your hearing Me! How many times I have shown Myself without your looking at Me! How many times I have become perfume without your inhaling Me! How many times I have become food without your tasting Me! How is it that you do not smell Me in what you breathe? How do you not see Me, nor hear Me? I am more delicious than anything delicious, more desirable than anything desirable, more perfect than anything perfect. I am Beauty and Grace! Love Me and love nothing else. Desire Me. Let Me be your sole concern to the exclusion of all concerns!*" If God utters a hundred cries of "Labbayk," if the water laments; where is the drinker, if our bread is seeking us, if the stars long for our growing consciousness, if the bounty looks for the beggar, if generosity looks for a guest, if beauty is seeking a mirror, what is our situation? Rumi says: "*What is bounty without a beggar? Generosity without a guest? Be beggar and guest; for beauty is seeking a mirror, water is crying for a thirsty man. They way of Moses (Musa) is all hopelessness and need and it is the only way to God. From when you were infant, when has hopelessness ever failed you? Joseph's path leads into the pit; don't flee across the chessboard of this world, for it is His game and we are checkmate! Checkmate! Hunger makes stale bread more delicious than halvah. Your discomfort is spiritual indigestion; seek hunger and passion and need! A mouse is a nibbler. God gave him mind in proportion to his needs. Without need God gives nothing."*

On the other side, God's most Beloved, the mercy for all the worlds, Prophet Muhammad, peace and blessings be upon him, never ceased pleading his whole life for his community. He called all of humanity unceasingly for the unity of universal brotherhood of love. He called his community to reach true humanity, like a father calling his own children for love and surrender. Did we answer in the past; do we answer now? Unfortunately, we do not respond to the mercy of the whole world pleading with his Lord for nearness to his community. In terms of our Creator calling us, inviting the believers for the pilgrimage, the great majority of believers answering His call and proclaiming: *"Labbayk Allahumma labbayk"*—*"Here am I, O Allah, answering Your call. I am here to do Your bidding."* But where are these pilgrims who offer themselves wholeheartedly to the Lord of all the worlds? Where are these believers who strive sincerely and steadfastly in the way of truth and enter the sacred trade with their Lord? Believers answer: *"Yes, Here I am to do Your bidding!"* But where are the carriers of truthful servanthood, love, and submission? Where are the believers who carry His trust? Yes, they answer His invitation, but for personal gain, for advantages, respectively, they wish to win the ticket to Paradise.

Although it is God's desire to meet with us, although He proclaimed His desire to be known to all humanity, why is it that such a small number of people arrive at the door of His Mercy where the Exalted Majesty is eagerly waiting to receive us? As His creatures do we not feel hungry and thirsty enough? Are our lips not dried enough, does our stomach not hurt enough? Are we not weak and tired and overloaded enough? Are we not deserted and left alone enough? Are we not threatened and suppressed enough? Is it that we are not poor and sick enough, not bankrupted enough, in order to feel urged to turn eagerly towards Him pleading unceasingly? We have to ask ourselves, is living in too much comfort, luxury, success, and wealth the reason that we are not in need of Him? Is being spoiled, living a life in self-sufficiency the reason not to depend on the Almighty or anyone else? Indeed, why should the celebrities of this world want anything from someone they do not even see? Why should the powerful, the successful of this world do something so contrary as to plead when they possess everything? They arrived at the peak of world-ly success and power, why should they need God? Unfortunately, we can observe that only the weak, powerless, the deserted, the suppressed, the helpless and the poor are the ones who feel urged to turn to God and submit. These are the ones who arrived at the peak of destitution, noth-ingness, degradation, poverty, and living a life in total need. This is the crucial point. The end of human strength is where God's power and mercy is acknowledged. It is the most precious borderline, representing the secret connection of the servants to their Lord, of the creatures to their Creator. This borderline represents the arrival of the humbled believers at the Gates of God's eternal Kingdom. This indicates that the collapse of all human strength and will power becomes the point of departure towards Him; the declining of human capacities becomes the rising towards the eter-nal sun of God's good fortune. In other words, the end of worldly digni-ties, wealth, and possessions leads into the opening of the glorious realms of the Hereafter. Thus, the Exalted One responds to human weakness with His strength, to nothingness with richness, to helplessness with help, to loneliness with union, to brokenness with wholeness, to imperfection with perfection, to poverty with wealth, to incapacity, shortcomings, and forgetfulness with salvation, to destitution with elevation. This is the Divine policy of the Almighty. We should realize that offering ourselves in total need towards our beloved Lord is our gain. Only through poverty and loss we will be able to truly love.

Human suffering is given because we forget God. There is never the last call in the religion of Islam. God renews His invitation every moment for the seeing and hearing heart. The Water is looking for the thirsty. The unblemished mirror is looking the beautiful face. The bounty is look-ing for the beggar. The Prophet is looking for his home in the heart of each believing servant. Our Lord created us only to bow down to the Truth day and night. God's ultimate invitation for His servants: "*Enter, then, among My servants (fully content with servanthood to Me)! And enter my Para-dise!* " (al-Fajr 89:29–30). It says in the Holy Qur'an: "*So, flee to (refuge in) God*" (adh-Dhariyat 51:50). There is no refuge from God except in Him. The believers have to be efficient, totally focused, and fast in the execu-tion of their intentions. They have to hurry up with their spiritual real-ization. They have to run towards God in high speed. They have to mount on the heavenly steed Buraq of love and use the wings of intellect of the Archangel Gabriel.

To be effective in supplication, we have to fulfil some Divine rules: First we have to become worthy to supplicate to Him; then ask from Him. To become worthy of asking, we have to surrender and show commitment towards the One we ask from. The secret is to become worthy to receive His help. We have to do what is necessary in order to receive the Almighty's support, protection, and guidance. Rumi says: *"Even if reliance on God is a guide, fulfil preliminaries in a practice of the Prophet who told a Bedouin loudly: First fasten your camel and then rely on God."* Shaqiq of Balkh tells us a story about the famous saint Ibrahim Adham, who was once ruler of Khorasan: *"Sometime after he had forsaken his kingship and became a sultan of the heart, he happened to be going about the city of Basra when the people of that town gathered around him complaining: 'O father of Isaac, although God says in the Qur'an: 'Call upon Me and I will answer your prayers,' we have prayed many times and yet our prayers have not been accepted.' The saint Ibrahim Adham replied with this advice: 'Because of ten things your hearts are dead; if a person has these ten bad qualities in him, how should God accept his prayer?' Then he enumerated one by one of one to the people of Basra and began to count: 'These are your shortcomings:*

1. *You acknowledge Allah, you pretend to acknowledge Him, and yet you do not give His due. God's due is helping the needy.*
2. *You read the Qur'an, yet you do not observe its commands and prohibitions, you do not practice what you read.*
3. *Although you say that Satan is your enemy, you follow him and obey him.*
4. *You call yourselves members of Muhammad's Community, yet you do not follow the example set by the Messenger.*
5. *You claim that you will go to Paradise, yet you do none of the deeds that must be performed to gain access there.*
6. *You wish to achieve salvation from Hell, yet you throw yourselves into it by the bad deeds you do.*
7. *You know that death is the Truth and you say so, yet you make no preparation for it.*
8. *You pay a lot of attention to the faults of your brothers in religion, yet you do not see your own faults.*

9. *You consume the bounty of your Lord without giving thanks to Him.*

10. *You bury your dead without taking warning, as if the same end will not befall you also."*

This most valuable advice shows us how important it is to clean one's heart from hypocrisy, low desires and bad habits in order to become ready and worthy to ask His help. While turning to the Almighty, praying and supplicating to Him, and asking forgiveness from Him, if one does not forgive one's friends or enemies, it is unacceptable. Asking for healing of one's sicknesses and not visiting sick people, is unacceptable. Asking protection from the Almighty and not giving shelter to the poor and homeless is unacceptable. Asking for mercy and in the same time acting aggressive, careless, egotistical towards one's fellow beings, is unacceptable. Asking for His protection and help, but not trying to serve one's fellow beings, who are in desperate need of him, is unacceptable. When we are of those who do not thank people, it is equal as not do thank God Almighty. When we are of those who are not content and show patience with each other in severe examination and misfortune, how can we ask God to release our afflictions and pains?

Although Pharaoh was one of the greatest tyrants human history knows, God granted his supplication over the supplication of His own Prophet, Moses. Once they were competing with each other about God's acceptance over their supplication to let the current of the river Nile swim in the reversed direction. God granted the Pharaoh's wish because he continued his supplication the whole night with burning longing and greatest insistency, whereas Prophet Moses, peace be upon him, was convinced that it is enough to make a single supplication. Rumi recommends in one of his discourses: *"Pleading is tremendously desirable..."*

The Secret Essence of Repetition in Worship, Supplication, and Remembrance

We have to repeatedly knock on the door of need if we wish to attain real success. The believers of Divine unity belong to the religion of: *"Knock on the door of hunger."* This is the heart's door of intimate conversations with the One and Only. It will be opened through the sacred efforts of a believer continuously knocking on the heart's door of hunger, desire, affection, heat, search, need, and longing.

The nature of prayer is repetition. The essence of remembrance is repetition. The essence of supplication is repetition. Through constant repetition within invocation, remembering, supplicating, and prayer, the spiritual self becomes strengthened, confirmed, awakened, and emphasized. The worshippers clean, purify, and wash away the dust and dirt of the mirror of the heart and remember what is forgotten.

Praying to Allah is nothing else than the repetition of need towards Him. We intensify and increase our appetite, our desire, our dependence, and our longing for Him, with Him, towards Him, and through Him. Repetition in prayer is the expression of love towards the One and Only, provided that the invocation is a confirmation of what is in one's heart. Through repetition we prove our submission towards Him, our affection for Him, our contentment within Him, and our yearning for Him. Repetition in prayer causes need, wakefulness, and appetite for the Divine. Spiritual need is expressed through repetition. There is need for repetition in order to increase the need for the Divine. So repetition of prayer arises from the need for the truth, the need for love. Indeed, love is in need of repetition, repetition is in need of love. The desire for repetition is the desire for love. If we do not fill the repetitions with love, the invocation is dry and mechanical. Repetition filled with love is increasing illumination.

Repetition increases the sacred thirst. When a lover is thirsty, he does not look for water, he looks for thirst. When a sincere invoker discovers the secret of repetition within his devotions, he looks to increase his desire, longing for his beloved Lord. The more lovers consume sacred knowledge, the more they are involved in sacred conversations, the more they thank, remember, and send prayers to their Lord, and the more a never-ending insatiable stream of appetite, hunger, thirst, burning, and need does arise in their breast.

Rumi says: *"Our drunkenness is not from grapes; there is no end to our drunkenness."* An encounter of Sahl al-Tustari with the supreme saint Bayazid al-Bistami demonstrates this subject of the infinite sacred thirst and need of the spirit. Sahl al-Tustari sent a message to him saying: *"Here is a man who drank a drink which leaves him forever refreshed."* Bayazid al-Bistami replied: *"Here is a man who drank all existences, but whose mouth is dry and burns with thirst."* The famous Arab poet, Umar ibn al-Farid says: *"We have drunk to the remembrance of the Beloved a wine, where with we were drunk before the wine was created."*

The Qualities of Humility
and Modesty

The Qur'an states: "*Prosperous indeed are the believers. They are in their Prayer humble and fully submissive (being overwhelmed by the awe and majesty of God)*" (al-Mu'minun 23:1–2). "*Call upon your Lord (O humankind) with humility and in the secrecy of your hearts*" (al-A'raf 7:55).

When a tree grows, the branches straighten up. When they bear fruits, the branches lower towards the earth due to their weight. Nobody in this world bore so many fruits like our noble master. Thus his humility reached the deepest grounds. When we inherit his noble character, we will witness the heavy weight of holy responsibilities on our shoulders. That is why Rumi said: "*I am the dust in his footprints.*"

Praying to God means showing efforts, works, struggling, and cleaning in order to bring forth the jewels of human character. The treasury of the human heart consists of the qualities of humility, mercy, modesty, thankfulness, compassion, servanthood, tenderness, and kindness. Love encompasses them all. All worship activities will enhance these noblest virtues of the heart; they are the result of purification through worship. These most worthy jewels of character represent the illumination of the human essence of servanthood. Its perfection culminates in the perfection of the love for God the Majestic. The perfection of servanthood is the beloved Prophet himself, manifested in his noble character. The more a worshipper will adapt his noble character features, the more he will be blessed with the light of the sacred attributes of humbleness, servanthood, and thankfulness. Our blessed Messenger's greatness lies in his poverty, nothingness, servanthood, and servanthood. His nature was such that the more God blessed and favored him, the more he became humble and submissive. Our blessed master was drawn towards Divine love and Divine beauty. His essential reality was such that he was given the inspiration to love. He was an adorer par excellence. He was the most exalted lover. He was the living proof of the grace of intimacy with his beloved Lord. He was made to love things of this world by Divine love. They gave him the vision of Divine beauty. They brought him close in order to witness the eternal beauty of his Lord of all the worlds.

All worship activities are given to regain the capacity to cry tears. It means to water the desert of our souls with our tears of admitted incapacities. It means to soften our hearts with modesty and humility. A Companion asked our noble master: "*What is the secret to receiving the spiritual delight, to take pleasure and joy within the worship practices?*" He answered: "*Humility!*" The highest ethics of in all the religions are demonstrated by those believers who get the greatest pleasure in being obedient towards their Lord, as opposed to those who wish to get drunk, to get lost in the ocean of love, or those who are looking to accelerate their ecstatic experience.

Why is humility so important within all worship activities? Only a heart trifling in humility can perform Prayer. Only such a heart knows its real position before its Creator. It knows the full extent of its worth before Allah's infinite Might, Greatness, Majesty, and Power. Modest worshippers use their helplessness, weakness, modesty, and shame as capital and favor. That heart has its eyes wide open. It sees with the highest intelligence, namely with the knowledge of humility.

Only a kind, compassionate heart is able to receive from the Divine realms. Only a modest heart is in a state of perfect receptivity and can become a receptacle for a holy channel. The worth of man compared to the rest of creation lies in the capacity to listen, to receive, and to open the heart for spiritual influences. With his receptive faculty, he differs from all other creatures. To increase spiritual "hearing" is an absolute necessity for the traveler on his way to the Truth. Receptivity for the Divine is usually degenerated in human beings. Prophet Jesus (Isa), peace be upon him, said to his disciples: "*Let those that have ears to hear, hear.*"

Only a heart which feels the quality of humility is able to feel the responsibility for servanthood. A man without a trace of servanthood is lacking humanity. In order to feel His Lordship, we have to feel our servanthood. Nowhere else than in the religious duties can we get the spiritual taste of servanthood. It is our true nature, our condition. A servant earns Allah because he carries the responsibilities of being human. Servanthood represents the highest stage of annihilation in God. A true servant belongs entirely to Allah. He is without absolute free will. He is like a slave obeying his owner. His servanthood reaches such perfection that he becomes unrecognizable. His appearance blends in with everyone. This is the state of our blessed master; he acted always like a man in a row, never demonstrating his supreme station. Every day our blessed master asked for forgiveness a hundred times and prayed repeatedly to his beloved Lord: *"Glory be to You, we have not been able to know You as Your knowledge requires, O Known One, Glory be to You, we have not been able to worship You as Your worship requires, O Worshipped One!"* Both illuminated and illuminating he cried out: *"O Lord, show us things as they are!"*

Only a heart equipped with the secret essence of spiritual poverty can enter Prayer in a truthful way. Rumi states: *"The miraj to heaven is non-existence."* Our blessed Messenger used to pray in utter humility: *"O Lord, let me live as the poor, let me die as the poor, and resurrect me among the poor,"* and his well-known utterance: *"Poverty is my pride."* The matchless beauty of his heart demonstrates that poverty is the greatest wealth human beings possess.

Only a heart equipped with the human virtue of thankfulness can pray in a truthful way. Our blessed master supplicated: *"O Lord, we have not been able to thank You as thanking requires, O All-Thanked One,"* and *"O God, help me mention You, thank You and worship You in the best way possible."* It is nothing other than profound thankfulness that the praising one gets lost in the Praised. The body movements of the ritual Prayer are precisely movements of thankfulness in their significance. The body shows gratitude in standing, bowing, and especially in prostration. Gratitude and thankfulness are the direct expression of one's humanity. By the simple fact that we are alive, we send prays of thankfulness to our Lord, it means to breathe with gratitude. Devoted servants will wholeheartedly with all the cells of their being melt in love and utter thankfulness before the Lord of Majesty and Bounty. Giving praises and thanks will become their state and penetrate all thoughts, feelings, behaviors, and actions of their lives. We know from the traditions that our blessed master prayed all night long until his feet became swollen, and Aisha wondered: *"Since God has forgiven all your sins that you may have committed and may commit in the future, why do you tire yourself so much by observing long Prayer vigils?"* He answered: *"Shall I not be a servant grateful to my Lord?"* In another tradition, our blessed master said: *"Prophet David*

(Dawud), peace be upon him, *asked God Almighty: 'O Lord, how can I be thankful to You, since thanking You is another favor that requires thankfulness?' The Almighty responded: 'Just now you have done it.'"* Thus our noble Messenger opened up the awareness of the absolute necessity of thankfulness to his community, that is to say, he showed us that living in the full awareness of the duty of thankfulness is an absolute essential for a believer. One educational piece of advice for his community: *"One who is not thankful for little is not thankful for abundance. One who does not thank people does not thank God."* Ingratitude is nothing else than being blind to Allah's favors. To reside in Allah's Presence requires an absolute condition: modesty, *haya*. Modesty is the sacred awareness that comes from the belief and knowledge of Allah. To the degree one inherits this noble feature one will receive closeness to the Almighty proportionally. That is to say, nearness to Allah requires shame, humility, and modesty. In fact, the power of Allah's Majestic Presence will peel off our veils of falseness and the beauty of *haya* will shine in luminous brightness. The Almighty declares: *"O son of Adam! As long as you maintain your modesty and feeling of shame before Me, I make people forget your defects."* To possess the virtues of humility and shame means to possess the knowledge that one's life belongs to Him. One lives in the consciousness of being always in His Company, as the Qur'anic verse states: *"He is with you wherever you may be"* (al-Hadid 57:4). Such consciousness causes automatically true humility because one is immersed in the Divine Mercy; one becomes constantly shameful, lowering one's head in true humility, prostrating oneself in thankfulness and admiration. We can say the degree of one's modesty determines one's true humanity. Our noble Messenger said: *"Be as modest before God Almighty as the necessity of being modest before Him requires. Let him who is blessed with this degree of modesty always control his mind and its contents, as well as his stomach and its contents. Let him always remember that death and decay follow. One who desires the afterlife will renounce the adornments of the world. One who is able to do that can feel as much modesty before God as being modest before Him requires... If you have no modesty, do whatever you wish."*

Rumi says: *"Self-existence brings terrible drunkenness; it removes intellect from the head and modesty from the heart."* With the example of Prophet Adam, peace be upon him, we learn that modesty, *haya*, determines the relationship we have with God. That is to say, the feeling of shame before God determines our true human state. It is nothing else than the feeling of love for God the Majestic. Prophet Adam, peace be upon him, the possessor of true shame and humility, showed us that these features are the highest ethical qualities of a human being. Shame and humility were the first sensations he felt having arrived on earth after he was made to leave Paradise. He possessed perfect consciousness of his imperfections. He felt his own insufficiency in front of the Greatness, Might, and Majesty of his Creator. In other words, he felt shame out of love for God. The first human being created, Prophet Adam, peace be upon him, demonstrated with the purity of his behavior in his life on earth the fear and love for His Supreme Creator. He felt guilty for his sin committed in Paradise and cried for forty years asking forgiveness until his beloved Creator granted his pleading. Adam, the father of mankind, is perfectly opposed to the nature of the devil. He represents the attributes of love, shame, and modesty, but the devil represents the attributes of envy and arrogance. This is the crucial point of the devil's eternal failure which brought him from the supreme heights of angelic existence downwards to the lowest level of the accursed devil. His ignorance and refusal to prostrate and submit to God's commands resembles exactly the modern man who is full of himself, arrogant, calculating, greedy, envious, and therefore spiritually blind. The devil's refusal to see the treasury of the sacred wisdom, the beauty of the Divine light, the infusion of the Divine breath of mercy of Adam can be compared with man's arrogance, heedlessness, and shamelessness in modern societies. It is the absence of humility, shame, and love. Rumi gives us an excellent description: *"Though Iblis had knowledge, he had nothing of religion's love, so he saw naught in Adam but an imprint in clay." "Around the horseman dust has arisen: you imagine the dust to be the man of God. Iblis saw the dust and said: How should this offspring of clay be superior to me with my fiery brow? As long as you see the saints as men, know that you have inherited your vision from Iblis"* (*Masnawi*, I/3958-3962). Iblis uses rational argument in order to justify disobedience against God's command to prostrate. He said according to the Qur'anic verse: *"I am better than he, for You have created me from fire, and him You have created from clay"* (al-Araf 7:12). Reasoning, rational analyses of reality happens through the absence of sacred awareness, the absence of love and the loss of the dimensions of inwardness. Through that misinterpretation of reality, man externalizes his life. It represents the eternal problem of humanity. The root of all sicknesses is the attachment to the world. Man is living on the surface, in the world of appearance. His attachment to the world makes him spiritually blind. Rumi comments: *"Sell your cleverness and buy bewilderment. Cleverness is opinion, and bewilderment is vision. He that is fortunate and confidant of the mysteries knows that cleverness is from Iblis and love is from Adam. Close your Iblis-like eye for a moment. After all, how long will you gaze upon form? How long? How long? Learn from your great-grandfather Adam. When he lost the union, the tears that fell from his face made every valley in Ceylon full of fragrant spices and herbs. And you still say you cannot choose the road? The stubborn angel said that. And he was the one who refused praise to the inner man. When a human being has experienced the ecstasy, he knows. He doesn't say; please lay out your system of proofs for me. From the outer layers of the unconscious, logic; from the inner man, love..."*

God's Essence is love; He says: *"My Mercy has outstripped My Wrath"* (Divine *hadith*). The whole of creation is enveloped in His Love and Mercy. The mystery of His Presence compromises therefore the attribute of modesty, *haya*.

A Prophetic tradition demonstrates the excellence of this feature and demonstrates in the same time the infinite Mercy our beloved Creator feels for humanity: *"God Almighty asks an old man on the Place of Resurrection to account for his acts in the world: Why did you commit such and such sins? The old man denies that he did so. So the All-Compassionate commands the angels: Take him to Paradise. The angels want to know why the Almighty has commanded so, even though He knows that the old man committed those sins. The Almighty answers: I know, but I looked at his white beard as one belonging to the community of Muhammad and I felt ashamed to tell him that I knew that he was lying."* When the Archangel Gabriel told this news to God's Messenger, his eyes filled with tears, and he said regretfully: *"God Almighty feels ashamed to punish those of my community whose beards have turned white, but those of my community with white beards do not feel ashamed to commit sins."* This tradition implies the utter importance and absolute necessity for every single human being to feel continuous shame before God Almighty. Our Creator envelopes each one of His creatures with His Mercy whatever they might do. Although we steel, lie, curse, murder, and gossip, Allah never stops saying: *"My servants!"*

The source of existence is love. The Almighty loved to be known, so He created man. If we become aware of our Creator, we will return His sacred desire to be known. This means, the more one's heart is alive through the belief and knowledge in the Almighty, shame, love, and modesty will arise. In fact, the more one knows Allah, the more one loves Allah. The more one loves Allah, the more one will feel shame in His Majestic Presence. The Merciful spoke to Jesus: "*O Jesus, first advise your own selfhood. If it accepts your advice, then you may advise others, or else you must feel ashamed of yourself before Me!*"

If the incapacity of human beings to take themselves to account, to face themselves, and to control their selves necessitates feeling shame and embarrassment, what does this indicate for us? From the reverse perspective, shamelessness means unawareness of the Divine Presence. Shamelessness means the absence of love. Heedlessness, insensitivity, and ingratitude are all a result of disbelief, which means a dead heart.

Divine Beauty and Perfection

I n a tradition, our master says: *"One who is pleased with God as the Lord and Islam as the religion and Muhammad as the Prophet has tasted the delight of belief."*

The Qur'an states: *"Whoever seeks as Religion other than Islam, (which is the standard Religion conveyed by all the Prophets during history, and is based on complete submission to God,) it will never be accepted from him, and in the Hereafter, he will be among the losers"* (Al Imran 3:85).

Rumi: *"Everything except love of the Most Beautiful is an agony. It is really an agony to move towards death and not drink the water of life!"*

The ultimate goal for the believers of Divine unity: to become an instrument of His Will.

God says in the Holy Qur'an: *"This day I have perfected for you your Religion (with all its rules, commandments and universality), completed My favor upon you and have been pleased to assign for you Islam as religion"* (al-Maedah 5:3). *"... Whereas God refuses but to complete His light, however hateful this may be to the unbelievers"* (at-Tawbah 9:32). *"They found (there) one of Our servants to whom We had granted a mercy as a grace from Us and taught a special knowledge from Our Presence."* (al-Kahf 18:65).

With the seal of the last Prophet, the truth of the religion prevailed and the religion of unity became evident, the glorious *sirat-al-mustaqim*, the straight path, got established. The religion of Truth invites all of humanity for the ultimate fulfillment of spiritual life on earth. When Prophet Muhammad, peace and blessings be upon him, honored the world, Divine perfection has been established, sainthood has been established, true love has been established, the reality of Divine Mercy has been established, and the reality of Divine intimacy has been established.

The world is born of love for perfection. The world is born of love to be known. The religion of Islam is the call for perfection representing the highest school of thoughts and the highest standards of morality. It is belief in the Divine unity. Islam is the call for the perfection of love. Islam is the call to the truthful death in order to be resurrected in the Truth. Islam gives prescription for sainthood. Islam gives method for human resurrection. Islam gives prescription to unveil the 70,000 veils of the soul. In a Divine *hadith* the Almighty says: "*I was a hidden treasure and I wanted to be known, so I created creation.*"

"*I wanted to be known*" represents the call for human perfection; it represents the call for sainthood. The religion of Islam invites the believers to perceive Divine beauty and perfection, the realization of the Attributes and Names of God. Islam invites the believers for the attainment of the highest spiritual realization, the development of the precious strength of the spirit. Islam invites the believers to undergo the spiritual journey to the inner essence of the heart where one will be able to reach the realms of God's proximity. Thus, the followers who belong to the community of Muhammad have the duty to look at creation in the way Allah meant it to be. Believers have the duty to investigate the purpose of their lives on earth. They have the duty to observe the pattern in which God created them. They have to be concerned to regain, restore and elevate human existence to its original worth and meaning. They have to be concerned to regain their verticality. They have to research the complexity of their souls. They have to be concerned to represent God on earth and become an instrument of His Will. They have to be responsible towards the One who is the Blower of the Divine breath of mercy. They have to be responsible towards the One who taught them all His Names and Attributes. They have to fulfill His Desire to be known. They have to actualize their virtual nature as caliph that God has assigned to humanity. They have to realize the Hidden Treasure. They have to be truthful to the promise they made in the realms of "*Alastu bi Rabbikum? Qalu bala*"—"*Am I not your Lord? Yes indeed!*" (al-A'raf, 7: 172).

Everything changed when the noble Prophet honored the world with his holy appearance. He brought a religion of infinite elevation, ascension, purification, and illumination. All differences were eliminated, all limits were lifted. The noble master raised all minds and hearts to the exalted places of God's sacred beauty and perfection. History entered a new phase; human development entered a new era. Immense value was brought to humanity. The best community sprung up from mankind. The Qur'an states: "*We have made you a middle-way community*" (al-Baqarah 2:143)

The light of Divine guidance of God began to shine throughout the whole universe, the star of love began to shine in the desert of worldly existence. The universe was flooded with pure light. A. Yusuf Ali comments: "*The light of Islam is the biggest bounty possible, if we truly understand, we should glory in it.*" The sacredness of existence has been established. Perfect faith got established. The consciousness that all life is Divine was revealed. Divine secrets got revealed. The good news of the ascension of the spirit beyond time and space, the Lote-tree of the Uttermost End, *Sidrat'ul-Muntaha*, has been given to man. The good news of: "*He was well pleased with them, and they are well pleased with Him*" (al-Bayyina 98:8) "*God loves them and they love Him*" *(al-Maedah 5:54)* has been given to man. The marvelous sun of discovery rose to the utmost limits and dispersed all darkness of unconsciousness. Humankind received infinite wealth, the fullness of Allah's Divine gifts, infinite grace, the treasures of Divine generosity, and highest standard of morality. The whole of creation is infused with His merciful Breath, meaning His Mercy, is omnipresent throughout the whole universe, every time, everywhere. God the Exalted declares in the Qur'anic verse: "*God's mercy is indeed near to those devoted to doing good, aware that God is seeing them*" (al-A'raf 7:56). The Almighty made a promise long before the creation of the world: "*My Mercy encompasses by far My Wrath.*"

The noble Prophet brought the perfection of the religion, the union of the internal and external revelations, and the union of worldly and spiritual matters. God proclaims in the Holy Qur'an: "*We will show them Our manifest signs (proofs) in the horizons of the universe and within their own selves*" (Fussilat 41:53). In consequence, the minds as well as the hearts of the honored members of his community get nourished. A perfect balance of inner and outer knowledge was established, which leads to the unity of being. On the one side, humanity received the gift of infinite sacred knowledge, supreme consciousness, endless illumination, the inheritance of the truth of Muhammad, and on the other side, humanity received the highest standard of morality, the sacred attributes of compassion and mercy, the highest features such as humbleness, shame, reference, humility, the inheritance the wisdom of the Prophet's noble character. It means that the believers are blessed with the possibility of human perfection, the highest spiritual realization, the development of the precious strength of the spirit. Thus, the religion of Islam unifies the heart with reason, submission with love, faithfulness with the mind, the intellect with the treasury of mercy, character features with sacred awareness, compassion with heedfulness, self-sacrifice with sound perception, servanthood with sacred awareness, tears with intelligence. A direct relationship of the heart with knowledge is established, that is to say, human passion, need, longing, affection, emotions, desire are connected with vision, intellect, contemplation, mind, wisdom, human consciousness, and sacred awareness. It is the eternal union of knowledge and love, the union of the heavenly steed of love, Buraq, with the sacred intelligence of the Archangel Gabriel. This union brings forth the highest jewels of human character. The highest virtues are all compromised by the noblest character of the beloved Prophet. The owners of such a heart and reason carry within themselves the capacities of leadership pared with submission, intellectual brilliance pared with modesty, authority pared with love, sacred awareness pared with servanthood, and kingship pared with generosity. Such servants are the heroes of submission, self-sacrifice, generosity, and love. True knowledge humiliates, true knowledge trains the ego, and true knowledge illuminates the inner self. The result is an intelligent character, a faithful awareness, an illuminated servanthood. To bring forth the jewels of character necessitates the light of sacred awareness. Only selflessness can bring illumination. Only through selflessness we can accelerate the speed towards the proximity with Allah. Only through selflessness we can become an instrument of His Will. Only through selflessness we are allowed to approach the mystery in the dwelling within the Paradise of intimacy. Only through selflessness we get admittance to the palace of His Divine Mercy and grace.

Islam is not only a belief system. It is the state of being. The believer travels backwards to roots of his existence, his original home, his essence, the home of absolute contentment and peace. That is where the truth of Muhammad is gathered. Like never before we need to wake up into higher awareness and we need to realize and establish the beauty of the noble character of our beloved Prophet, which are the treasury of Islam. This is the teaching for the modern societies. We have to gain our lost treasury of intimacy, the intimacy with our beloved Prophet and intimacy with our most beloved Lord of all the worlds.

Human beings need the essence of Islam in order to survive and find the honor, the elevation, and the worth bestowed on them. Without the truth of the religion, humanity will sink into despair and destruction. True belief necessitates to belief in the Hereafter the same way you belief in the existence in this world. Man did not come into this world to become owner of this world; he came into this world to give witness to the truth. Why did the Companions win the wars they fought with our blessed master? Because they believed with certainty in the Hereafter as they believed in the world. The condition for true belief is to belief like the Companions in the existence of the world and in the existence of the Hereafter. The purity of their hearts could give inner witness to the truth, because they had access to the two worlds. The Companions were pure receptacles of the inner meanings. They carried the full responsibility for their belief on their shoulders and many of them paid the price with their lives.

The highest form of life is belief. The highest form of belief is the faith in the Divine unity. The religion of Islam corrects the misinterpretation of reality. It extinguishes false ideologies. The ultimate discrimination is between truth and falseness. When the believers fight on the way of truth, paired with the light of faith, they become able to distinguish unity, *tawhid*, versus the diabolic forces of polytheism, *shirk*, setting partner to Allah. They become able to distinguish tyranny versus justice, anarchy versus the law, irreligious philosophy versus *tasawwuf*, carnal pleasures versus spiritual elevation, wildness versus civilization, degeneration versus perfection, misguidance versus righteousness, materialism versus spiritualism, and deviation versus the *Sunnah*. The ultimate discrimination is *tawhid*, unity, versus *shirk*, idol-worshipping, which leads into the discrimination of truth versus falsehood.

God brought a universal message to humanity. The noble Prophet was sent by God towards men in their totality, to the entire human race and it is for this reason that the Prophet is spoken of in the Qur'an: "*We have not sent you (O Muhammad) but as an unequalled mercy for all the worlds*" (al-Anbiya 21:107). He was send by God not to a particular nation, but as a mercy to the whole world. He brought Divine guidance for all nations. A bridge between East and West was established. That bridge symbolizes the unification of the whole world. The religion of Islam is not limited to the Middle East. Thus Prophet Muhammad, peace and blessings be upon him, represents a universal guide to humanity; he represents the living truth of religions universality. The Qur'an is a universal call, revealing the universal truth, a universal system of education. The Qur'anic revelations carry the light of universal unity to all humanity; they cover all ages, all nations, all manners, all cultures, and all costumes.

In the religion of Islam, all knowledge is presented on an utterly lively stage, nothing is simply dry history lesson, nothing is just dry information. The believers of Divine unity are able to follow an unbroken chain of Divine tradition of spiritual illumination. In Islam the art of life is identical with the art of love. In the school of religion, one learns the art of life. In the school of saints, one learns the art of love. That school is the school of love where one learns the perfection of love. It means to realize sacred love as an art-form. One learns through sacred beauty, sacred taste, and sacred nourishment. There are some differences to study the religion. One learns the knowledge from books or one learns through realizing one's knowledge in one's life. Such knowledge is only earned through the great struggle, the struggle with our own *nafs*, respectively this knowledge is only earned in the realms of *jihad,* the internal struggle. Rumi describes himself: *"I had followed the way of the Prayer carpet and the mosque with all sincerity and effort. Love came into the mosque and said: 'O great teacher! Rend the shackles of existence! Why are you tied to Prayer carpets? Let not your heart tremble before the blows of My sword! Do you want to travel from knowledge to vision? Then lay down your head!"* *"I was the country's sober ascetic, I used to teach from the pulpit—but destiny made me one of Your hand-clapping lovers."* The scholars teach lessons in the classroom from the pulpit; saints encourage followers to enter the Way. True knowledge does not come from books, lessons, but through the familiarity with God and His beloved Prophet. It comes from the wish to be guided by God and from the wish to be intimate with the beloved of God, Prophet Muhammad, peace and blessings be upon him, and from the desire to resemble him and imitate his noblest behavior and actions. In that sense, submission to what we know is more important than knowledge. Being on the way to God is more important than to reach the goal. To feel longing, need, the heat of search due to the pain of separation, is more important than to unify.

The treasury of love and the principle to follow has been established by the religion of Islam. Islam exists since the creation of the first human being, Prophet Adam, peace be upon him. Only with the coming of Prophet Muhammad, peace and blessings be upon him, into this world, the treasury of love and the light of sacred awareness finds its realization. It is nothing else than to realize the actions of Prophet Muhammad, peace and blessings be upon him, in one's life which leads into the perfection of love. To achieve true belief, we need to follow the followers who followed the followers up to the Companions who followed the noble Prophet. True followership means to be dominated by the wish to be guided, by the need to learn, by the wish to become a learning servant, by the desire to search for the sweet smell of the Divine mysteries, by the wish to seek for the hidden treasure, and by the wish to find the water of life.

The wisdom of the religion of Islam lies in the teaching that the fruits of eternity and Divine harmony are only earned through our habitual actions in daily life. This is why our Prophet became the sultan of the *Sharia*. He was sent to perfect good behavior. Our blessed master represents, therefore, the illumination of our earthly existence. He demonstrated with his noblest character, the perfect example of a teacher, healer, guide, master, father, consultant, warrior, husband, and worker. The earthly plain represents actually a plain for the Hereafter. The earth is a Divine stage where one earns the fruits for eternity and where one realizes the perfection of love. Divine beauty and perfection are perceived here and now. Paradise and Hell grow here and now. The religion bears the highest dynamics of life itself. This Divine Power is, to the utmost degree, a flowing, ever-present. It is an uninterrupted, dynamic education, because it is based on the *Sunnah*. The majority of people take this life for real. Actually we are all actors in a Divine drama, the author and director is our Creator and we are given our parts to play on this worldly stage. Therefore we have to adapt the conscience playing a role on this worldly stage. The sacred awareness enables us to see one's life as a school.

By acknowledging the fact that one is created as a vicegerent of God, he becomes a perfect mirror of Divine Names and Attributes on earth. He represents God on earth. Man has been given knowledge of all things as stated in the Qur'an: *"(Having brought him into existence,) God taught Adam the names, all of them"* (al-Baqarah 2:31). He is living the essence of servanthood. He is an instrument of God's Will. He carries the greatest responsibilities referred as the "Trust" or *amanah*. Rumi says: *"There is one thing in this world which must never be forgotten. If you forget everything else, but not that one thing, then have no fear. But if you perform, remember and do not forget all things, but you forget that, you have done nothing. "We offered the Trust to the heavens, and the earth, and the mountains, but they shrank from bearing it, and were afraid of it (fearful of being unable to fulfill its responsibility), but man has undertaken it; he is indeed prone to doing great wrong and misjudging, and acting out of sheer ignorance"* (al-Ahzab 33:72). *"Assuredly We have honored the children of Adam (with many distinctions)"* (al-Isra 17:70), *God did not say, "We have honored the heavens and the earth." So man is able to perform the task which neither the heavens nor the earth nor the mountains can perform. When he performs that task, he will no longer be "sinful, very foolish"* (Fihi ma Fihi, 14–15/26).

We have to become aware of the Divine drama, playing the role of a deputy in the Divine scenario. This necessitates making the greatest efforts possible in order to convert our way of life into the way of life of the Hereafter, namely to transform the worldly stage into a sacred stage, to exchange the worldly concerns into sacred concerns. If we are able to realize our responsibilities as His representatives on earth, we will receive sublime spiritual pleasure. It is the sacred taste of knowing Him, which overpowers all other satisfactions because we comply with the reason for His creation, His Desire to be known.

The Almighty says: *"I created everything for you, but you I created for myself"* (Divine *hadith*). All and everything is created for man, but man is created for the One and Only. All is given to us, but we are for Him. The All-Merciful says: *"Man is My secret and I am his secret."* The realization of the truth of these words is the realization of the secret of love. Without doubt, the greatest secret within all existence is the secret of the relationship of the human being with the All-Holy. As He says in the Qur'an: *"We are nearer to him than his jugular vein"* (Qaf 50:16). We have the duty to investigate the secret connection with our Creator and implant this wisdom in our lives. He has to be the only One worshipped, He has to be the only One beseeched for help, and He has to be the only One we serve. Only through unconditional love we will discover the secret.

Knowledge of God is a light illuminating all layers of existence. Having reached sacred awareness, we can see reality as it is, we can perceive Divine unity. It is certainty of belief, *haqq al-yaqin*. True existence is existence in God and to be conscious of our true existence means to love God, and loving God means to represent God on earth as a devoted servant. Prophet Moses, peace be upon him, found true faith after he fell unconscious. When he woke up from the darkness of his unconsciousness, he saw that he could not see. That is where true faith begins. It is God's greatest gift to humanity. Arriving in true belief, all discussion will disappear, illusion will disappear, imagination will disappear, reasoning will disappear, heaviness, worries, and concerns will disappear. The result is peace of heart, contentment, trust, freedom, and absolute certainty. When we see with the eye of our hearts, the world becomes a jail and the Hereafter the only desired place to be. Not as a garden of Paradise to dwell therein, but as a place that reveals Divine inspiration, eternal richness, and beauty to our inner being.

God's revelations are the lights of Divine Wisdom. Through the light of belief the servants of God find true existence. They will be resurrected in the Truth. The power of belief adds life within life. Looking from the opposite direction, unawareness of the Divine Presence is equal to shamelessness, heedlessness, insensitivity, baseness, and ignorance. In other words, it is the darkness of unconsciousness. It is the heart that is blind. It is the cloud of our own unconsciousness that veils the sun. The awareness of our own spiritual reality will enable us to see through this cloud. In this transitory world there are gates opening up to the exalted realms of eternity.

Every command from the Holy Qur'an originates from Divine Mercy. Allah is the Lord of all the worlds, and Prophet Muhammad, peace and blessings be upon him, is a mercy to the whole world. It is only through humbleness that we can realize the purpose of creation. It is through adapting the knowledge of humility that we can realize the truth. It is only when we join the school of mothers that we can earn the treasury of moral compassion. It is only through adapting the treasury of pure modesty, the noble character of our beloved master, that we become true believers. It is only through adapting the consciousness of human responsibility and servanthood that we are able to live the essence of our worth, honor and exaltation. It is only through showing submissive joy, tearful longing, following the dust of the footsteps of the honor of the universe, that we become lovers of the lovers of the lovers, up until the most exalted lovers, the Companions of our blessed master, may Allah bless their exalted souls. It is only through drowning and get lost into the ocean of Allah's Mercy and melt in love for the mercy of all the worlds that we become honorable members of the community of Muhammad.

Sacred awareness is far more than knowledge, because it is the wakefulness of the heart. A heart's liveliness depends on its owner's belief and awareness of God. Sacred awareness is a spotless mirror where the Divine reality is reflected and Divine secrets shine at you. When the flame of realization of the believer gets lit, the horizons of understanding, insight and wisdom will open up, and the heights and depths of the spiritual dimensions will stretch out to infinity. Increasing sacred awareness is equal as waking up from the darkness of unconsciousness. The truth of the Divine revelations will take the believer from the darkness of unconsciousness into the light of faith. The secret treasures of faith will illuminate his innermost self. There is nothing more valuable for a believer than to wake up towards higher consciousness, which is the eternal realm of His nearness. God says: "*So give the good news to My servants who listen to the word (of Allah), then follow the beauty in it. Such are they whom Allah has guided. And such are the men of understanding*" (az-Zumar 39:17–18). Rumi teaches the following supreme wisdom: "*The inhabitants of Hell are happier in Hell than they were in this world, since they are aware of God, but in the world they were not. And nothing is sweeter than the awareness of God. So the reason they wish to return to the world is to perform works in order to become aware of the locus of manifestation for God's Gentleness. It is not that the world is a happier place than Hell.*"

The religion of Islam does not refer often to spiritual perfection, heavenly exalted stations, and angelic beings. In the contrary, the way of perfection ends in confronting oneself with oneself in the first place. There is nothing closer to one's self than one's own self. The greatest knowledge is the knowledge of oneself. The noble Prophet said: "*Begin with your self.*" One must confront oneself with one's family, friends, fellow beings, colleagues, neighbors, and citizens. Further, one has to turn one's whole attention to the whole humanity. This necessitates finding peace in oneself and having reached harmony, trust, tranquility, and peace within oneself will affect one's environment, and if God wills, spread throughout the whole world. This is what is meant by being a caliph, a true representative on earth. This is love in the true sense.

The Wealth of the Inner Dimensions of Islamic Worship Rituals

Without submission to God's commands, there is no spiritual growth. God says: "*They remember and mention God (with their tongues and hearts), standing and sitting and lying down on their sides (whether during the*

Prayer or not)" (Al Imran 3:191). *"I have not created the jinn and human-kind but to (know and) worship Me (exclusively)"* (adh-Dhariyat 51:56).

The *Sharia* symbolizes the highest ethics of the religion of Islam. It signifies the spiritual journey to the Ka'ba of the heart. It represents the greatest Divine design ever given to humanity. The worship activities of fasting, pilgrimage, charity, ritual Prayers represent an exercise to strengthen the truth in ourselves. Through the performance of the religious duties the falseness of the self will gradually be peeled off and the truth will start to appear. It is the light of our spirit which will shine in full splendor. Only when we find the secret essence buried within our hearts, we will be able to be truthful in life and in worship.

The religion of Islam is built upon the five fundamental pillars, the sacred law. The first pillar represents the profession of faith, *Al-Kalimah al-Shahadah*. One bears witness that there is no deity but Allah and one bears witness that Muhammad is His servant and Messenger. The *Sha-hadah* represents the door to the house; one pronounces the testimony of faith and enters the religion as a believer. The other four pillars represent the wall of the house. If we submit wholeheartedly to the sacred law with the light of faith, we will illuminate the inside of the house as well as the outside through the windows of the heart. To connect the walls with each other, we need an active contribution on our part with the works of good deeds, noble behavior, and loving servanthood. The light of faith will bring the required quality to the worship practices of fasting, charity, pilgrimage, Prayers and those qualities will become apparent in our hearts and will transcend into our lives. If one pillar of the law is omitted, the light of the inside of the house will slowly fade away and turn into darkness. If we omit all of them, the good attributes of our hearts will disappear and will be replaced by the low desires of greed, laziness, envy, stubbornness, pride, heedlessness, perfidy, stinginess, and blasphemy. Rumi gives us a vital image: *"The house without a window is like Hell. The foundation of religion, O servant of God, is to make windows."*

The ritual worship duties are pure love, because they nourish our human spirit. These practices have a direct effect on our whole being; they protect us, support us, illuminate us, and strengthen us. They are designed to touch the deepest interior of our hearts. They revive our lost treasury of intimacy with our Lord and the noble Prophet. Whatever human beings are empowered spiritually in terms of faith, sincerity, and love, whatever they lack inwardly, will be given through the practice of the sacred law. The five pillars give measures, clean, nourish, strengthen, purify, harmonize, and tranquilize our inner selves. In that sense, the Prayer rituals increase our sensitivity of hearing, perceiving, and receiving, which are man's excellent attributes. Through the worship activities we clean the storehouse of the breast in order to make room to become pure receptacles of the sweet taste of inner meanings. Praying to God means entering the Divine Mercy. Therefore, praying to God clears away the dirt, dust, and trash of the heart.

The law in the religion of Islam is sacred. It is far more than just a religious necessity, a mechanical obligation compared to the necessities like eating and drinking and sleeping. These sacred rituals represent and contain the secret prescription for sainthood and are exclusively given by our pride of humanity, the beloved of the beloved, the noblest of all men, our blessed master. The laws of the previous Prophets were not raised to the level of absolute perfection. Only with the religion of Islam, the revelations of God got completed and the religion of the absolute truth got established. It is the *sirat al-mustaqim*, the straight path, the path of absolute perfection.

The merits of the five pillars are immeasurable. The perfection of the sacred law is as evident as the existence of the sun. It is for the worshipping believers to see, comprehend, understand and live its perfection. As a result sacred beauty will be revealed. Perfection generates beauty. Showing obedience to Allah's commands is showing utmost respect to the Divine decrees. Only this way the belief in the Unseen will lead to the degree of certainty. This way the quality of the performance of the sacred law will establish the link to the eternal. The One and Only is present in the *qibla* of every one of us. The worship activities have to be directed towards the Lord of all the worlds, His beauty and perfection. Therefore the direction for worship is towards eternity, which is perceived everywhere and all times.

The five pillars are given to humanity from our Creator to experience His beauty and perfection. The Divine commands represent elevation, illumination, and ascension for the worshipping believers of the community of Muhammad, because they are nurtured with His Light. They are brought to humanity by the chief of the Prophets, the master of the praiseworthy station, the beloved of Allah the Almighty. No one else than our blessed master expressed the love for the sacred law and the beauty of servanthood so perfectly. Without his supreme example, his beautiful conduct, and his noble character, the law of the religion would just be a mechanical routine. He fulfilled the sacred with pure love for his desired community. His infinite beauty and goodness radiated into the hearts of his true followers. The pure light of his Prayers, charities, sacred teachings, supplications nourish the spirit of every true believer who is ready to receive his inexhaustible blessings. We have to know that all the Prophets and saints did nothing else than nurturing the rites of the sacred law with their pure intentions. During their acts of worship, they constantly felt spiritual pleasure, highest affection, pure joy, awe, wonderment, and admiration.

The law of the religion all doctrine and method are given to reach spiritual maturity provided that one includes the sayings from the beloved Prophet, and his *Sunnah*, way of life, conducts, actions, and behaviors. When our noblest of all men honored this world with his holy appearance, pure love descended and the world got enlightened. The noble Prophet said: "*I came to perfect good behavior.*" He brought the law of religion and completed it with the example of his life, namely the example of his noble character, conduct, practices, and sayings. Ibn Arabi says: "*Sainthood is earned through works of the sacred law, not those of thinking.*"

We have to follow the path of truth in accordance with the religious law. The true followers of this path are seekers. They feel the need for the truth and the heat of their search draws them to implant the religious practices into their daily lives. The seekers follows an inner example, by which they let themselves be guided up to the point of submitting all of their free will to the Great Will, that is to say, the heat of their search, the thirst for the truth makes them dissolve in their desired object. So they become the truth they seek. The seekers and the Sought become one; the lovers and the Beloved become one. The true seekers only know one goal to follow: our blessed master. For all the believers of Divine unity, he is the sole subject, hope, salvation, and happiness. Once they annihilate themselves in the Messenger, *fana fir'Rasul*, they become inheritors of his blessed spirituality. This has to be the sacred goal for all believers. For only through following the beloved Prophet with utmost sincerity, we can reach the Lord of Exaltation. God says in the Qur'an: "*Say (to them, O Messenger): 'If you indeed love God, then follow me, so that God will love you and forgive you your sins.' God is All-Forgiving, All-Compassionate"* (Al Imran 3:31). When servants show the highest degree of struggle to obtain the excellence of our master's noble character, the greatest Divine reward will be given from our Lord, namely the Exalted Majesty will love us. In the religion of Islam, believers have not accomplished the level of perfect faith if they do not love Prophet Muhammad, peace and blessings be upon him. More than anything in this world, even their own selves. The noble Prophet is reported to have said: *"None of you will have faith till he loves me more than his father, his children and all mankind."* To arrive at the heights of belief can only be achieved when we love the Prophet more than ourselves. The Qur'anic verse states: *"The Prophet has a higher claim on the believers than they have on their own selves"* (al-Ahzab 33:6).

The nourishment for the sacred thirst and need is given in total abundance within the sacred law. The spirit can find infinite satisfaction. For this reason, the pillars of *Hajj, Zakah, Salah,* and *Sawm* are exactly what man misses most in his life, knowingly or unknowingly. Man's soul cannot survive without the sacred worship rituals. Being deprived of this holy nourishment, man lives in his own tyranny, oppression and cruelty. Deprived of the sacred worship duties, his spiritual heart will decay and degenerate. Thus the sacred law represents a treasury of sacred healing.

God endowed His creatures with the faculties of speech, sight, and hearing. He taught us His wisdom, His Holy Qualities, His Names and Attributes. Nowhere else than through the performance of the Divine law we will become aware of His Holy Attributes. The duty of the sincere worshippers is to seek, gradually establish, and make grow the most beautiful manifestations of the Divine Attributes and Names within themselves. In this way, they will be able to exercise the opening of their awareness of Him, the deepening of communion with Him, the increasing of their joy of obedience towards Him, the deepening their knowledge and love of Him, the heightening of contentment within Him, and the increasing of intense yearning for Him. God's Attributes and Names will have a multiplying effect on the worshipper's spirit, generating the light of His beauty and grace.

It is impossible to reach perfection without the sacred law. When we see it as a means to reach the awareness of fasting, the pilgrimage, almsgiving, and ritual Prayer, we can reach the ultimate goal. Therefore we must look for the worship beyond worship. We have to reach the spirit of fasting; the spirit of pilgrimage, of charity, of the ritual Prayer, then we will recognize that all five pillars are one made out of the same substance. Sacred conversation between the worshipper and the Worshipped constitutes the very spirit of the ritual Prayer. Dying before death constitutes the very spirit of the pilgrimage. Self-sacrifice, the art of living for others, the art of giving constitutes the very spirit of charity. Isolating oneself from everything worldly in seclusion with Allah and become aware of our Creator's infinite favors and bounties constitutes the very spirit of fasting.

The sacred law is nothing else than to exercise the sensitivity for the Divine Presence, that is to say, to gain sacred awareness. It gives instruction and helps to approach the indestructible Divine secret, our spirit. In other words, the sacred duties help us to find and understand the rank of our spirit. Sacred awareness is the awareness of our inner nature, our sacred origin, our roots, the spirit breathed into man with the breath of the All-Merciful. This means that we have to try to incorporate the following wisdom in our lives; to go internally on *Hajj* outside of *Hajj*, to fast internally with our senses, eyes, mouth, ears, thoughts, feelings, heart outside of the month of Ramadan, to pray, remember, supplicate internally all times in all places outside of the prescribed time of the ritual Prayers, to give alms all times, being continuously concerned nourishing the need of the human beings outside of giving *Zakah*. We have to renew, restore, and revitalize our intentions, our belief, our contemplation, our remembrance every day, every hour, every moment. This is the dynamics of the *Sunnah*. The highest, most powerful, noblest of all actions and behavior in a believer's life is to try to resemble our blessed master in all his behaviors and actions. Thus, the *Sharia* is given in order to leave the level of simple practices and to arrive at the level of its realization within one's life, that is to say, a fasting life, a life of Prayer, a life of pilgrimage, and a life of almsgiving.

With the performance of the sacred worship duties, the believers exercise the part of the whole existence. The worshipper is exercising the coming from Him and the return to Him. Man has to adapt the consciousness that he lives in exile, because he lives a separated existence from his original home. One who becomes aware of this separation and experiences its pain becomes dominated by the wish to go home, to return to his origin, the state of innocence and purity. The practices of the sacred law are precisely given to rehearse the return to the One and Only, to reemerge in order to attain the roots of one's being. In that sense, the worship duties offer the opportunity to remember one's sacred source.

The five pillars are designed in such a way that they ask the whole of man. God wishes all that we have and all that we are: mind, body, senses, heart, emotions, soul, and spirit. While praying to the Almighty, the worshippers must offer themselves wholeheartedly, psychologically, physically, mentally, and spiritually. This way, they exercise their capacity for love and sincerity. For, if we fast and take pleasure in backbiting and looking at unlawful things, if we go on pilgrimage and act as if we are at home, behaving in an ignorant and selfish way, if we give alms and live a careless life in pomp and luxury and think low of the poor and needy, if we perform the ritual Prayer and have not left the world in order to reside in the Divine Presence, we will violate the law of the religion.

With the practice of the pillars we exercise the internalization of our human state, the transition from the outer, physical, transitory, and temporal realm to the inner, spiritual, and eternal realm. It is the work of the purification of matter towards the light, from heaviness towards lightness, from material towards spiritual, and from baseness towards elevation. During the Prayers, our bodies, our organs, the inner faculties get educated, their chemistry get transformed, the cells get renewed, and the blood and the skin get changed. The substance of the Prayer rituals is like a sacred infusion into the body. The blood circulation penetrates the human organs and they get washed clean. We train our eyes, tongues, ears, hands, speech, stomach, mind, concentration, and will power. The ultimate goal of a believer is to become a holy channel, an instrument of His Will, a receptacle of Divine grace, where God will become the eyes with which we see and the ears with which we hear.

We need to conform ourselves to the Divine order of the cosmos. All existence, the universe, our planet, our body is made out of the same substance matter, the four elements, earth, water, fire, air. They are all in constant movement making millions of changes every moment. With the Prayer, we oppose these heavy transactions and therefore cut off the material attachments to the material realms of the body, the world, and the universe. For this reason, the body is most involved in the worship rituals and the performance on the exact time is highly requested. For example giving alms to the poor is an excellent method to cut off the attachments to personal possessions, status, fame, and wealth. The fast of Ramadan is an exquisite training to reduce the activities like eating, drinking, as well as trying to fast with our senses, like with our eyes, ears, and tongues. In later stages, one tries to fast with one's mind and heart. The pilgrimage represents the most profound physical struggle, turning one's back to the world and becoming aware of the Hereafter. The human being is a highly sensitive creature, with a very delicate balance. He is sliding between clay and light, between his physical and spiritual nature. To establish the inner balance is not easy. The regulations of the body's chemistry are of highest complexity. Millions of changes happen every moment simultaneously. In one second there are 30,000 new cells created. It is for this reason that our Creator gave the believers a miraculous prescription to attain control over the inner organs and senses, the five pillars. In that sense, the Prayer rituals are the medicine to regulate all bodily functions day and night, cleaning the senses and the inner organs, regulating all of the bodily functions, bringing tranquility and peace of our psyche, thoughts, and mind and bringing spiritual joy to the heart and spirit.

If we do not give due respect to the inner wealth contained in the ritual Prayers, if we do not dive in the infinite sea of its meanings, if we do not travel upwards towards the light of Divine beauty, if we do not realize its inner treasury, we cannot please or reach our Lord of Majesty and Bounty. Worship will be dry, empty, meaningless, and lifeless. The material self directs itself to the material *qibla,* the direction for Prayer, belonging to the world. There the self finds its expected advantages, the satisfaction of a full table for the desires of his belly and senses. The spiritual self directs itself to the eternal direction of the Lord of all the worlds. There the self finds eternal bliss and enters in the land of *"God is well-pleased with them, and they are well-pleased with Him"* (al-Bayyinah 98:8). There are two sorts of believers, the ones seeing the religious duties as something forced upon them and the ones seeing the religious duties as something pleasurable, something to enjoy. The former lacks the sacred goal in his life. He will cause heresies in his life, because he lives purely in order to satisfy his own carnal soul. The latter is full of longing and love for Allah and Prophet Muhammad, peace and blessings be upon him. He experiences utter joy within the performance of his worship duties; he feels happiness in giving and feeding the needs of his fellow beings.

In order to reach such perfection of love, we have to leave the level of simple execution of worship-routine, the level of simple obedience. For the lovers, the obligational worship duties are not even a concern because the religious ordinances have mingled with their flesh and blood; they became a part of their life like sleeping and eating. But in the contrary, they spend all their time and effort for the practices of the beloved Prophet. For these lovers, it is an absolute necessity, an unavoidable fact, and an urgency, to live the practices of the Messenger. In fact, their only concern is trying to resemble their beloved master, trying to please him, shedding tears of sorrow with him, tremble, sweat, and strive with him. The voluntary actions from their heart reach such a climax, that their will ceases to exist up to the point of self-effacement and self-extinction. Living in such closeness to the honor of the universe, they arrive at the level of the perfection of faith. Love is the condition to reach perfect belief. In the religion of Islam, believers have not accomplished the level of perfect faith if they do not love Prophet Muhammad, peace and blessings be upon him, more than anything in this world, even their own selves. The love for the noble Prophet is like the blood in the veins of the body; the blood flows through the arteries into the heart and keeps the body alive. To perform the *Sunnah* is nothing else than realizing the love one feels for him. This love comes from Allah. It is His love for His beloved Prophet. So if you love what Allah loves, how can you have thoughts of your own, how can we have a will on our own, how can we have goals on our own, how can we act on our own? To become truthful followers of the noble Prophet, we have to become lovers of the first grade. Thus, we have to establish the conditions which allow us to imitate his noblest character. Primarily we have to replace our worldly concerns with the sacred ones. Throughout the entire life of our blessed master, there was never one moment, one wish, one intention, one supplication, one goal, one deed, and one action that he made for himself. His life on earth was centered on his sole concern; his community. If we wish to resemble the beloved of God, we have to try to answer his never-ending call for his community. We have to try to be ever-present to his call, his infinite pouring of mercy, blessings, goodness, and compassion. For if we comply with our blessed master's longing, it will brings us to the level to be able to comply with our Lord's desire for His beloved.

In a famous Divine *hadith*, Allah addresses to His believers: *"O my servant, when you were in the world I was every moment with you, and you, who were you with?"* When our blessed master told this tradition to his Companions, it had such a penetrating effect on their pure hearts that they fainted. We have to ask ourselves, when we listen to the recitation of the Divine revelations of the Qur'an, when we listen to the speech of the saints, when we listen to the sermons at Friday Prayers, when we listen to the call of Prayer, when we listen to hymns, what happens? Do we get affected, does it leave any marks, does it change something, does it make us cry, or do we tremble? In today's world, without doubt, the believers lost to a great degree the spiritual sensitivity, the ability to be able to listen, to comprehend, to be receptive, and to be able to feel. We can observe that the greater part of our modern societies lost the connection to the Divine realms of the Hereafter. This happened due to the fact that the capacity of the hearts are to the highest degree degenerated in today's lives, because the sublime sensitivities of the Divine realms are in total contrast to the activities of the modern world. Being busy with the world like superficial occupations, gossip, sensual pleasures, excessive sleep, bad habits, laziness and so on, keep us away from sacred realms. We are covered with thick layers of heedlessness and ignorance, walking around like corpses. Therefore the necessity for the sacred pillars is crucial more than ever. These religious practices will revitalize the sensitivity for the sublime realities we lost. The ritual Prayer, fasting, charity, service to the needy, the pilgrimage are all designed to exercise our sensitivity of the unseen worlds, the eternal values, the realms of the Hereafter. What we miss is the sensitivity of feeling supervised by our Lord. We are not being overwhelmed, overpowered by God's Majestic Presence. We are not attracted by the All-Glorious Truth. The Companions possessed such purity that they became perfect receptacles for the sweet taste of inner meanings. That is why they fainted. They actually saw their Lord talking to them with the secret eyes of their hearts. When they heard the Lord say, *"I was with you, who were you with?"*, they felt such shame in His Presence, that they fainted. Today we are not in a state of awe, wonderment, and admiration anymore, which means believers lost the love and fear for the Almighty Creator. Instead, they love and fear the world Spiritual blindness, numbness, and deafness is the result. We live in a state of spiritual paralysis.

There is pleasure in religion, there is joy in faith, considered that one feels pleased and content with God. Whatever happens in one's life, good or bad, tragic or pleasurable, enlightened or darkened, must be welcomed, because one knows that it comes from God. All events have to be received with moderation and endured with patience, especially the happy ones. The more we receive gifts from God, the more we might distance ourselves from Him. Like Rumi says: *"Health and wealth are the biggest obstacles between man and God."* Only the Almighty knows what is beneficial for us or what is harmful for us. God says in the Qur'an: *"It may well be that you dislike a thing but it is good for you, and it may well be that you like a thing but it is bad for you. God knows, and you do not know"* (al-Baqarah 2:216). Today the majority of believers does not receive spiritual pleasure in obedience, submission, and worship anymore. They are deprived of the sacred taste, the inspirational joy; their eyes are blind, their ears are deaf, and their hearts are sealed. The main problem humanity is facing in this world is due to their lack of knowledge and their deep involvement into world, living a life of matter devoid of spirituality. This was the greatest worry of the noble Prophet. He was not so much worried that people are setting partners to Allah, *shirk,* which is a direct offense against the Divine unity, but he was deeply concerned that they lose themselves and become attached to the world. Our blessed master was asked: *"What is worldliness?"* He answered: *"Everything that makes you heedless and causes you to forget your Lord."* In another occasion he commented: *"Whoever prefers this world over the Hereafter will be afflicted with three things: a burden that is never eased, a poverty that is never turned into wealth, and a hunger that can never be satisfied."* The world is not the appearance of what we see; the mortal aspect of the world is unawareness of the Divine. The world is the absence of eternity, the absence of immortality, and the absence of the Hereafter. Not knowing God is tyranny to oneself. A heart devoid of God is sick. Rumi makes an important and profound statement about people living in this world with the absence of the need for the truth and the search for the truth: *"Everything except love of the Most Beautiful is really agony. It is really an agony to move towards death and not drink the water of life."* This vision represents one of the essential body in Rumi's teachings. He uses a harsh language: *"They are killing with their own hands their eternal life."* *"To follow one's own desires it to flee from God and to spill the blood of spiri-*

tuality in the presence of His justice." He suggests: "*Abandon desire and so He will reveal His Mercy. You have learned by experience the sacrifice He requires. Since you can't escape, be His servant and go from His prison into His rose garden*" (*Masnawi*, VI/377–384). With these verses, Rumi presents a radical vision to the world which tears apart the misunderstanding of human existence on the planet earth. Ibn Arabi uses exactly the same demanding and strict formulations; he exclaims that the absence of a spiritual master curing one's spiritual sicknesses can cause one's spiritual death, meaning, it is as grave as committing a spiritual suicide.

We do not always need a mosque in order to pray. We do not always need to circumambulate the Ka'ba in order to fully surrender. We do not always need to fast in order to fully abstain from the satisfaction of our egos. We do not always need to give alms in order to become generous. When the heart is woken up to perfect consciousness, true worship, true peace, true generosity, true thankfulness, and true fasting will arise from the core of our being. It is the hidden treasure within ourselves. In a pure heart, nothing can be falsified, nothing can be veiled, and nothing can be demolished. But in order to soften the heart, to give it its required sensitivity, to make it receptive for the Divine, to awaken it from the sleep of ignorance, we need the practices of the sacred law.

The sacred religious duties must be combined with the sacred rules of human behavior, moral conduct and vice versa, otherwise the practice of the religious duties is invaluable and inacceptable in the sight of God. The worship modes and the behavior modes, the rules of Prayers and the rules of moral conduct must nourish each other. To perfect our behavior within our daily lives, Ali, may Allah be pleased with him, gives us examples of educational advice: "*May Allah shower His Beneficence upon the one who knows his worth, who knows to stay within his bounds, who watches his tongue, who does not spend his life in idleness. Your words depend upon you until you utter them, but once you have uttered it, you will depend upon them.*" Umar, may Allah be pleased with him, encountered a group of people sitting around lazy and doing nothing. They said that they put their affairs in the hands of God and trust in Him. Umar responded: "*Indeed you do not. You are nothing but freeloaders, parasites upon people's efforts. For someone who truly trusts in God first plants the seed in the belly of this earth, then hopes and puts his affairs in the hands of God the Sustainer.*" The great saint Abdul Qadir al-Jilani comments: "*Spiritual culture, Sufism, is not acquired through long conversations, but through going hungry and giving up things that are familiar and pleasant."*

Every human being needs a balance, one wing is worship and the other is good behavior and action. Good behavior and good deeds will generate good prayers and truthful and sincere prayers generate good action and behavior. A believer has to nourish his conduct with his worship and vice versa. The way we live our lives is the way we pray and the way we pray is the way we live. Our worldly lives have to reach out for the Hereafter and our spirituality has to be translated into the world. The body has to reach our spirit and the spirit has to be translated into the body. When we succeed to establish a balance between the earthly and the sacred realities, we will be able to reach contentment, peace, and union in our lives. In this way, the life of this world will turn into the way of a life of the Hereafter. Rumi comments about the quality and aspiration for true belief and worship: *"Whatever it is you wish to marry, go absorb yourself in that beloved, assume its shape and qualities. If you wish for the light, prepare yourself to receive it; if you wish to be far from God, nourish your egoism and drive yourself away. If you wish to find a way out of this ruined prison, don't turn your head away from the Beloved, but bow in worship and draw near."*

Our intention, our desires, our focus will determine the quality of our worship and the level of our faith. We have to try to contemplate the meanings of the religious practices of the formal rituals to the same degree that we carry them out. We have to pay as much attention to the inner realities as we concentrate on the external aspects. In all our religious activities, we have to try to combine our earthly struggle, our physical and psychological nature with our sacred roots, our spiritual nature. It means we have to try to combine the realities of the east and the west, heaven and the earth, spirit and body, inner and outer, spiritual and material, the unseen and seen, and the sacred and profane. The *Sharia* is given to work for the internalization of one's being. Whereas the majority of religious practitioners have the opinion that only *Tariqa* is responsible for the educational methods and aims of the inner spiritual realities. But without form, there is no content, without the work of submission to prescribed rituals, there is not spiritual growth. Without a jug, the water cannot be contained, and without water there is no need for a jug, without meaning the word cannot exist. Without heaven, the planet earth has no reason to exist. Without the spirit what is the use of a body? The ultimate truth lies in the tradition: *"I was a hidden treasure and I loved to be known so I created the creation"* (Divine *hadith*). Without our Merciful Lord there is no reason for human life on earth. This is the wisdom of the religion of Islam, the inner needs the outer as much as the outer needs the inner. The work for each believer of Divine unity is precisely the unifying the exterior and internal realities and arrive at the supreme station of the consciousness that all life is sacred.

Thus, the gift of the religion of Islam is that one worships what one knows, that is to say, knowledge intensifies worship and consequently worship intensifies knowledge. More precisely, the practices of praying, fasting, almsgiving, and pilgrimage intensify knowledge, increase sacred awareness. The level of awareness of the worshipper will define and increase the value of the performance of the sacred rituals and this perpetual nourishment will go on ad infinitum. In other words, what brings success and quality to the prescribed Prayer rituals is sacred awareness, because it will heighten and nourish the performance with the light of faith and open up the channels to comprehend and experience the wealth of its inner dimension. Only through expanding our breast and widening the horizons of spiritual knowledge, we can find inner peace. The noble Prophet said: *"A moment's reflection is worth more than a year worship, and further seventy years worship and further a thousand years of worship."* We can learn with these most valuable utterances of our blessed master that Divine gratifications and favors are only given to the degree of one's capacity to reflect, respectively the value of one's reflection. Abdul Qadir al-Jilani gives the following interpretation: *"Whoever contemplates an affair receives the value of one year's worship and whoever contemplates his devotions receives the value of seventy years worship and whoever contemplates the sacred wisdom receives the equal of a thousand years of worship."*

Allah designed the five pillars in such perfection that they complement each other and nourish each other. Everyone is in need of the other. Only giving due respect to each of them brings the real success to all of them. They are designed in such perfection that when one pillar is omitted, the other Divine commands will lose the wealth of its inner dimension, diminish their treasury, lose their spiritual significance, and lose their heights and depths. Contemplation without obedience towards the commandments is unacceptable before Allah. Knowledge without service and love is unacceptable. Charity without worship is unacceptable. Prayer without sacred awareness is unacceptable. Almsgiving without love is unacceptable. Fasting without charity is unacceptable. Recitation of the Holy Qur'an without contemplation is unacceptable. Love without religious practice is unacceptable. Remembrance without good conduct is unacceptable. Worship without fasting is unacceptable. Self-sacrifice, almsgiving, service without sacred awareness, without love, without submission, will turn into an empty and meaningless gesture.

One day the Lord asked Gabriel: *"O Gabriel, had I made you a human being, how would you have worshipped Me?"* *"O Lord,"* cried the angel, *"all secrets are open to You!"* *"Yes indeed,"* said the Lord, *"But let My servants be aware that they do not know what I know."* Gabriel then went on to say: *"I would worship Your Divine Essence in three ways: First by helping those in poverty, second by covering up the guilt of sinners, third by quenching the thirst of the thirsty."* The Exalted One said: *"It is because I knew this about you, that made you My trusted agent for the transmission of My revelations."* If one worships God without compassion towards humanity, how can we stand in His Presence? If one does not enter Prayer with compassion, how can he reach the All-Compassionate? There is a story of the saint Dhu'l-Nun al-Misri who went once on pilgrimage. In the desert, he saw a dog whose thirst was making him lick the ground. As he had no water with him, he caught up with his caravan calling: *"O Pilgrims, this is my seventieth pilgrimage. I offer the reward of all my seventy pilgrimages to anyone who gives water to this dog."* If one gesture of giving water to an animal is equal of the worth of seventy pilgrimages or even more, don't we have to reflect and go through the registers of our own good deeds? Furthermore, there are believers who love worship and do not pay much attention to contemplation. There are the ones who run from *sohbet* to *sohbet* (conversations), practically devouring the books, but do not devote much attention to the ritual Prayers. There are those who love and to do constant self-sacrifice, but they cannot find true awareness, they do not acquire knowledge of God. There are the ones who love to fast and are constantly occupied with their own diet, but are far removed from showing compassion, service towards their fellow beings. Furthermore, with the example of fasting; we can see that charity, the pilgrimage, and the ritual Prayer are carrying the elements of fasting. The pilgrimage, *Salah,* and charity represent in the same time a true fast, namely fasting from the world, isolating oneself from everything worldly in order to be in seclusion alone with the Almighty. This is the very spirit of fasting. Each one of the pillars carries the other within. When we fast sincerely, we experience the spirit of almsgiving, the spirit of the ritual Prayer, and the spirit of the pilgrimage. In other words, the true fasting happens when it compromises the other ritual obligations. *Hajj* and *Salah* are sisters to each other, they complement each other. The pilgrimage and ritual Prayer are nothing else than a rehearsal for the Hereafter. *Salah* and *Hajj* are rituals, where God blesses the worshipper with His Presence. Therefore *Salah* in its symbolic meaning is the true pilgrimage. That is to say, the ascension of the believer during the performance of *Salah* signifies an inward pilgrimage. So the pilgrimage is in its essence the ascension; it is the pilgrimage of the spirit to his original home, the essence of the heart. If pilgrimage is ascension, *Salah* is a pilgrimage. In the same way, *Zakah* and *Sawm* are sisters to each other. *Zakah* and *Sawm* represent a method of education, exercising self-restrain, replace selfish behavior with selflessness. They represent a means to reach material and spiritual cleanliness of body, mind, heart, and spirit. They reduce the life of the material self, the heaviness of the body and increase the life of the spiritual self. *Zakah* and *Sawm* are given to clean one's inner being, a dirt which is gathered one year. Moreover, fasting and almsgiving increase the sensitivity for the performance of the ritual Prayer and the performance of the pilgrimage and vice versa. *Zakah* and *Sawm* are hidden actions, hidden worship, invisible, whereas *Hajj* and *Salah* are visible worship rituals. For the worship duties of fasting and the pilgrimage, there are two sacred months which signify the most precious time during the Islamic year. The believers celebrate the treasury of the religion of Islam. *Hajj* and Ramadan represent God's greatest gift to the community of Muhammad. In no other time, such immense spiritual blessings are generated during 30 days. Throughout the month of fasting, the believers celebrate the beauty and perfection of the religion and in the month of the pilgrimage, the believers celebrate the religion of unity. On *Hajj*, the Ka'ba represents the answer from God for the longing of the pilgrims for their Lord. Ramadan represents the answer from the fasting believers for the longing of beloved Prophet for his community. On *Hajj*, the pilgrims are living the joy of giving the answer to God's invitation with the *talbiyah*:

"Here I am to your bedding—Labbayk Allahumma labbayk." In Ramadan, the believers are living the joy of responding to our master's exclamation: *"My community, my community!"* On *Hajj* the pilgrims immigrate to the sacred land of Mecca undergoing the experience of the spiritual journey. In contrast, the sacred treasury of Ramadan enters into the life of the fasting believers. The soul of Ramadan inhabits the community of Muhammad, that is to say, Ramadan makes the believers experience its value and meaning covering all levels of life with its Divine essence. Ramadan; keep the stomach empty in order for the light of *Marifa* to prevail. *Hajj*; enter the sacred trade of the Hereafter, cut the jugular vein of the carnal soul in order to win the eternal life. Ramadan; fast in the world from the world in order to increase the love and sacred awareness for the Lord. *Hajj*; experience the selflessness in order to earn the gratification of rebirth. Ramadan; become the king of one's heart and win the treasury of love and sacred awareness. *Hajj*; earn the Divine light through self-sacrifice, become an orphan, slave, servant, refugee in front of God.

The ultimate wisdom is that love has to be linked with knowledge and knowledge has to become love. We have to nurture our minds with supreme consciousness and in the same time we have to nurture our hearts with the most valuable and highest standards of morality. Knowledge and love have to unite. Rumi comments: *"There is self-sacrifice and there is knowledge. Some people have generosity and munificence, but not knowledge. Others have knowledge but no self-sacrifice. But if a person should have both he will be mightily successful."* We can never mention enough the great woman saint Rabia al-Adawiyya expressing in her famous prayer: *"O God, if I worship You for fear of Hell, and if I worship You in hope of Paradise, forbid it to me. But if I worship You for You, do not hold back from me the Everlasting Beauty."*

The Prayer rituals ordained by God carry the greatest power of healing potential especially for man's mental and spiritual sicknesses. These are thousand times more difficult to cure than our physical sicknesses. The human being is a drop of water with thousands of anxieties. The majority of believers gathers and stores one year of dirt, dust, dump, rubbish, illnesses, and moral distortion before they begin to clean. It is the time from the month of Ramadan to the following year of the fasting month. Within these 11 months their heart takes the shape of a garbage dump and God forbid, turns into the state of a grave with stinking fumes,

Divine Beauty and Perfection | 53

darkness, and rotten flesh. The human heart is the most precious sacred existence where the jewels of the human character are stored. It is man's inmost consciousness, his inward spiritual reality. The heart is directly connected with God; it is the place of His manifestations. God says in a Divine *hadith*: "*Neither My Earth nor My Heavens can contain Me, but the heart of a believing servant.*" God fashioned the heart as His most exalted creation. Bayazid al-Bistami describes the greatness of the heart: "*If all that exists in and around the Throne of God, that vastest of all of God's creation, were to be placed in a corner of the perfect man's heart, he would not even feel the weight of it.*" Ahmad Samani: "*When one looks at the human essence, it is tainted and distracted. It is muddiness, some dark water, a clay. Hence, all those attributes appeared within it. But, the site of love is in the heart, and the heart is pure gold, the pearls of the breast's ocean, the ruby of the inmost mystery's mine. The hand of no one else has touched it, and the eye of no one who is not a confidant has fallen upon it. The witnessing of God's Majesty has polished it, and the burnisher of the Unseen has placed its seal upon it, making it bright and limpid. Since the heart's work has all of this, the Presence of Exaltation has a love for it. He held the beauty of that love before the hearts of the great ones, and the traces of the lights of unqualified love's beauty appeared in the mirror of their hearts. So, our love abides through His love, not His love through our love.*" Rumi comments: "*Opposites manifest through opposites: In the black core of the heart, God created the eternal light of love*" (*Masnawi*, I/3865). As much as man is turning away from God, to that degree his heart darkens, decays. As much man is remembering God, praising God, to that degree God will become the heart's Guest. That is to say, the heart turns either into a place of fire or a rose-garden, either into Hell or into Paradise. It is a tragedy that God's most precious sacred existence turns into decay due to our carelessness, heedlessness, sleep of ignorance, and laziness. Some believers gather their dirt and sicknesses in their hearts from pilgrimage to pilgrimage, which can be 10 or 30 years or even their whole life before they start to work on their inner selves. Some even worse, they never refrain from accumulating their sins during their whole lives and only when they die, they will be given the opportunity to wake up from ignorance and heedlessness and will eventually be confronted with the truth and see things face to face. But in contrast, there are such believers; they do not miss any opportunity to bring themselves in order. They face their own selves and make account of their doings, their behavior every moment. They clean and purify the state of their hearts continuously. These are the ones who yearn for the sacred hour of *Jumu'a*, in the Friday Prayer, every week where they get a chance to celebrate their belief in the One and Only. Some believers adapt this state of alertness from one ritual Prayer to the following one. Whatever failures, false behavior, bad habits, heedlessness, sinning occur from one to the next Prayer, they immediately correct themselves. Whatever weaknesses and imperfections they discover, they feel regret and repent immediately. These are the ones who are alert and wakeful at all times and in all places. Such sincere devotees are called "the sons of the moment." They take themselves to account before they get taken to account, they die before dying, and they faces themselves before they get taken to the Divine Court. They attained the secret of truthful worship, inhaling within every breath His Name *Hayy*, the All-Living, and exhaling within every breath His Name *Hu* (He).

Sincere believers through the heat of their search feel urged to run from experience to experience. They are like restless travelers. They never rest as they are continuously concerned to serve their Lord. So they find themselves automatically, without a conscious decision, on their part between worship and service, contemplation and self-sacrifice, Prayer and fasting, pilgrimage and *Zakah*, seclusion and charity. They are so engaged in their spiritual work, they forget themselves, because they are drawn by the love they feel for the Lord of all the worlds, and they are drawn by the love they feel for the prince of the universe, the beloved Prophet of God. Running from experience to experience means being able to align oneself with the needs of one's time, being utmost alert to the demands of one's time. A lover of Allah feels that he has no choice than to give himself to the tasks and duties the Almighty spreads in front of him. So he finds himself in the situation that others need him that the world runs after him. Rumi gives an interesting interpretation: "*If a man runs, when he runs for religion he is sitting. If he is sitting, when he is sitting for this world he is running. The Prophet said: 'Whoso makes all his cares a single care, God will spare him all his cares.' If a man has ten concerns, let him be concerned with religion. God will see to the other nine without his having to see to them. The Prophets were not concerned with fame or bread. Their only concern was to seek God's satisfaction, and they acquired both fame and bread. Whoever seeks God' satisfaction will be with the Prophets in this world and the next; he will be an intimate of 'Those whom God has favored—the Prophets, and the truthful ones, and the witnesses, and the righteous ones.'* (an-Nisa 4:69). *What place is this? He will be rather sitting with God, who said: 'I sit next to him who remembers Me'* (Divine *hadith*). *If God were not sitting with him, there would be no desire for God in his heart. Without a rose, there is no rose-scent; without musk, there is no aroma of musk"* (*Fihi ma Fihi*, 49).

The worshipping congregation of Muhammad's community must perform the Prayer rituals at the requested specific times in order to receive the heavenly bounties, the light, and the grace. Prophet Muhammad, peace and blessings be upon him, was asked what is the most beautiful action in the life of a Muslim and he responded: *"To pray the ritual Prayer at the requested time."* The saints of Islam proclaim: *"Time is a sword, if you do not cut it, it cuts you."* At the day of Resurrection when mankind will be assembled, the faces of some will be bright like stars. The angels will ask them: *"What good conduct has brought you to this degree?"* They will say: *"As soon as we heard the call to Prayer in the lower world, we would rush to make ablution in order to enter the Presence of Allah."* There will be others whose faces radiate such light as the moon and they will answer that they were already in a state of ritual ablution when they heard the call to Prayer. There will be others whose faces are bright like the sun and they will answer that all the things they earned was by lawful means and all they consumed was lawful. They will answer that they used to give part of their income to the poor and needy, and they would go to the mosque even before the time for Prayer and hear the call from inside the mosque. So we see that the degree of the spiritual reward for *Salah* is given in proportion to the readiness and the desire we show to enter its performance. In other words, believers have to spend their time with greatest respect, give utmost care to its value. This means to concentrate with one's mind and heart towards living in the moment, that is to say, showing efforts in trying to increase the sensitivity for the sacredness of the moment. The Qur'an states: *"Every (moment of every) day, He is in a new manifestation (with all His Attributes and Names as the Divine Being)"* (ar-Rahman 55:29). The ones who manage to live wholeheartedly in the present time, they will live in ongoing grace and blessings because they serve, live and worship for His sake. They are the ones who understand the treasury of the *Sharia* and they are the ones who live the beauty and perfection of the *Tariqa*. This is what it means to fulfill human destiny. It is never-ending servanthood. It means to offer love within every breath. Our blessed master has advised his believers: *"Part of the excellence of a man, is paying no attention to that which does not concern him."* Correct behavior means spending our time with meaningful and beneficial actions. Therefore, the faults of other people should be of no concern to us and that our imperfections should be the only concern to us.

The greater part of the work is outside of the practice of the religious duties. All is preparation, to get ready for true worship. In order to get into a state where we perform the ritual Prayer in the way pleasing to God, it requires greatest preparation and a heightened state of alertness and most of all a great longing to meet with one's Beloved. There was a Companion, when he was close to enter *Salah* he almost fainted, his face flushed red and he cried out: *"How can I stand in front of the Lord in my wretched condition!"* The way we spend our day we will go to sleep. The way we sleep we will wake up. The way we wake up we will spend the day. The way we spend the day we will go to sleep. So the way we prepare ourselves for the audience with one's Lord for the ritual Prayer, will define the degree of truthful conversation with one's Lord. Similarly, with the pilgrimage, the emptier we go, the more we discharge ourselves from the heaviness of the world, the more we will be able to receive spiritual richness and blessings, the more we will become ready for self-sacrifice, the more we will be able to fulfill the ultimate condition for the true pilgrimage, namely dying before death. The works of preparation in order to enter the Divine Presence, will determine the success we have for the ritual Prayer and the pilgrimage. But the work after returning to the world from *Hajj* and returning to daily life routine after the ritual Prayer is even greater. Not to lose the infinite spiritual merits of *Hajj* and *Salah* requires an enormous struggle. Not to lose the Divine gifts one earned is utterly difficult. Not to get sullied by the world's dirt requires a great deal of work and attention.

The solution for all difficulties during one's worship duties is always the same: love. The ones who truly regret that *Salah* and the pilgrimage is over and are waiting with great longing for the next invitation again, are saved from the danger to get involved with the world. Such hearts are filled with longing for the next rendezvous with their Beloved. When they give the salutation to the right and left marking the end of the ritual

Prayer, they do not leave inwardly the Presence of God. It means a sincere believer does not leave the Presence of his Lord when he finishes his Prayer; he glides without interruption from one Divine Presence into another Divine Presence. This means that a sincere worshipper is continuously in God's Presence before *Salah*, during *Salah,* and after *Salah*. The same principle we can observe with the pilgrimage, a sincere believer never turns back home from his pilgrimage, because his heart stays forever on the plain of Arafat in supplication, his heart is always in prostration, and his feet are always walking in circular, doing *Tawaf* around the Ka'ba. When the worshipper performs the ritual Prayer, he is actually in front of the House of Allah with the secret essence of his heart. It is the admittance of one's insignificance, one's incapacity, one's insufficiency and the admittance of God's Greatness, Might, Glory, respectively one's nothingness and God's Totality, which can render one's lifelessness, dry, mechanical worship of imitation into a worship with sincerity, truthfulness, and illumination. If during their worship duties the devotees do not feel heightened excitement, admiration, love and longing, they will not be able to revitalize, refresh, renew, and rebuild their human condition. Abdul Qadir al-Jilani comments about the inner worship: *"The time for inner worship is timeless and endless, for the whole life here and in the Hereafter. The mosque for this Prayer is the heart. The congregation is the inner faculties, which remember and recite the Names of the unity of Allah in the language of the inner world. The leader of this Prayer is the irresistible wish. The direction of Prayer is toward the oneness of Allah, which is everywhere, His eternal nature and His beauty. The true heart is the one which can perform such a Prayer. A heart like this neither sleeps nor dies. A heart and soul like this are in continuous worship, and such a heart is in constant service. The inner worship of the heart is his whole life. There is no longer the sound of recitation, no standing, bowing, prostrating or sitting. His guide, the leader of his Prayer, is the Prophet himself. He speaks with Allah. Saying: "Thee do we serve and Thee we beseech for help" These Divine words are interpreted as a sign of the state of the perfect man, who passes from being nothing, being lost to material things, into a state of oneness."*

Worship subdues the ego, surpasses mundane passions. If our worship does not leave rational thinking, calculation, ulterior motives, personal gain, we cannot become intoxicated with something otherworldly, we cannot get a sacred taste, we cannot penetrate into the realms of the unseen, and we cannot perceive images of the eternal realms of beauty. If our worship does not leave the desire for position, possession, rank, status, family, children, friends, we cannot enter the ocean of Allah's Mercy. We cannot look at the sacred mirror of generosity. We cannot get lost in the infinite ocean of Allah's oneness. We cannot see the beauty and perfection with the eyes of our hearts. If the worshipper is not in love and admiration with Allah's Beauty and Majesty, he cannot perform the true Prayer.

The secret for true worship is to feel attracted by God Himself. It is a Divine gift. For only the Divine Reality, the Sole Power of God can draw people away from themselves. God bestows the highest gift of His irresistible sacred attraction to His chosen servants as stated in a Divine *hadith*: "*A single instance of the All-Merciful's attraction equals to the nearness to God acquired through the good actions of both humanity and jinn.*" He honors His friends, lovers, saints with the beauty of His Presence. They earn this Divine favor in proportion to their admiration, need, surrender and love for Him. The greater their yearning, longing, need, and admiration for God, the greater the pull of the sacred attraction. They have reached a general state of human vulnerability, a state of humility, of admitted incapacity and insufficiency; their hearts are softened and filled with love and mercy. Thus, for the majority of believers, there are absolute conditions one must fulfill in order to feel attracted by the Divine Presence. Firstly they have to knock on the door with true need; it is the door of hunger, the door of sacred thirst, the door of longing. It is the desired state of every true believer is to leave this plain of existence, to break out of these earthly limitations, knowingly or unknowingly. Knocking on the door of hunger will enable sincere servants to break out of the jail of corporality. Once having broken out they will not be able to return because God's power of attraction becomes irresistible and overwhelming. The ones having tasted His Divine attraction will be favored to quench their thirst from the eternal source as stated in the Qur'anic verse: "*their Lord will favor them with the service of a pure drink*" (al-Insan 76:21). Moreover, it needs a pure heart, a heart which is totally submitted like a loving slave to his owner, in order to feel drawn by His sacred Power. Once a believer feels drawn by the beauty of the light of His Majesty, it will joyfully accept all of the Almighty's invitations.

There are some wonderful poems by saintly men expressing this elevated state: "*There is a kind of madness called attraction, which is a true triumph. By means of it madness reaches mysteries lofty and great. I am by nature so attracted to the roaring rise of the sea, that I feel as if engulfed in the bounteous gifts of God.*" Bediüzzaman Said Nursi says: "*Everything is intoxicated with the wine of love of God, the attraction of this love. Celestial objects and angels are intoxicated; the heavens and earth are intoxicated, elements and plants are intoxicated, animals and human beings and all other beings are intoxicated.*" One of the purest saints, Uways al-Qarani, is regarded as being chosen for the highest degrees of Divine attraction. His love for the noble Prophet was of such overwhelming power, elevation, and purity, that he was raised to the highest degree of all his lovers. Although he never saw his most beloved Messenger in his life, he lost his own existence in him, intoxicated by the excessive joy of the love for him. Rumi says: "*Wherever a man travels the Way, he displays God's attraction.*" The secret for true belief, God has to become the object of desire. The whole mystery of human existence; we have to be in love, in love with God. When we love, we are attracted to the Whole. When we desire, we are drawn towards the Desired. When we seek, we are attached to the Sought. When we love, we become a learning servant, a humble student, a tearful admirer, and a sincere searcher. When we love, we follow the Beloved. When we love, we live by love and we die for love. That love will give birth to the love for the need of the truth, for submission, for obedience, and for followership. That love will give birth to the love for the one who was sent as a mercy to the whole universe. That love will give birth to the love for the *Ahl al-Bayt* and the venerable Companions. That love will give birth to the love for all the lovers who became enslaved to the beauty arising from the luminous brightness of servanthood of the honor of the universe. To conclude, the gift of the irresistible Divine attraction is given in proportion of the devotee's admiration and love towards his Beloved.

There is an essential wisdom particular to the religion of Islam: The highest degree of awe, wonderment, and love is experienced within the limits of the sacred law. Islam is the way of moderation, perfect measures, and balance. It is within the absolute submission to God's Will that we find the highest spiritual satisfaction, the greatest bliss for the heart. In fact, the more we enter into the precise discipline of the religious law, the more we will earn the heights of illumination and the more the All-Merciful illuminates the face of our spirit. That is to say, the more we operate with sincere faith, the deeper the submission, the more spiritual pleasure will be experienced and the greater the Divine reward will be given to our hearts. More precisely, the more we show the highest precision in the execution of the Prayer rituals, the more we will be able to leave the corporal existence and transcend time and space. In other words, the higher the degree of educational practice, the greater will be the witnessing of Divine manifestation. The verse of the Qur'an states: *"Is he (who derives lessons from God's acts in the universe, and so) whose breast God has expanded to Islam, so that he follows a light from his Lord (is such a one to be likened to one whose heart is closed up to any remembrance of God and, therefore, to Islam)?"* (az-Zumar 39:22). In fact, the feelings of delight, joy, awe, intoxication, and all types of ecstasy are only given to the quality of the performance of the rituals. The highest ritual discipline our Creator gave to humanity is the ritual Prayer and therefore the Divine reward is equally excellent, namely the believer's ascension beyond the corporal existence where time and space get suspended, the spiritual ascension. It explains why not in his daily life but during the performance of the ritual Prayer, our blessed master experienced the highest delight, of which he commented: *"The Prayer is the light of my eyes."* This explains the event of Ali, who needed a small operation due to an arrow stuck in his leg in the battle field. He advised his friends to remove the arrow during *Salah*. The spiritual delight during his performance was of such heights and depth that he did not feel the slightest pain during its removal. The following *hadith* proves again that the feelings of delight and spiritual satisfaction are given to the degree of the believer's submission. When believers show total obedience with the submission of a slave, the fruits of eternity and sacred harmony will be earned. When servants show the highest degree of struggle to obtain the excellence of our master's noble character, the Exalted Majesty will love us. A friend of the Almighty said: *"Whoever overflows with the desire to meet with God, despite his inability to fulfill the requirements of the way leading to his goal, God Himself comes to him."* All is fulfilled when we show sincerity in our belief: *"We are nearer to him than his jugular vein."* (Qaf 50:16); *"He is with you, wherever you may be"* (al-Hadid 57:4); *"Neither My Earth nor My Heavens can contain Me, but the heart of a believing servant"* (Divine *hadith*). This is the state of excellence, *ihsan*, namely to feel, without interruption, supervised by the Almighty, to feel continuously His Gaze. Thus, the highest ethics of Islam are not attained in experiencing spiritual ecstasy and get lost in the ocean of love, but it is earned by those believers who get the greatest pleasure in being obedient towards their Lord. This attitude, this submissive joy, distinguishes a saint from a common man. There is nothing more pleasing to God than the obedience of a true slave to its owner, most perfectly expressed in the beauty of servanthood.

Believers of Divine unity are the ones who carry the burden of His Trust. His Trust is our honor. Believing in Divine unity means to fulfill a secret condition: to pass beyond one's own self by loving God. When lovers supplicate to their Lord, they are in a state of self-forgetfulness. When they perform the prostration, they annihilate themselves and lose their own existence in the Almighty. When they go on pilgrimage, they die before dying. When they perform *Salah*, they orient themselves towards the eternal direction of God's beauty and perfection where time and space get suspended and reach the Lote-tree of the Uttermost End, *Sidrat'ul-Muntaha*, surpassing the material realms. When they give charity, they reach the boundless, inexhaustible beauty of generosity. When they fast, they fast with their hearts and mind and they will break the fast only when they die. Believing in Divine unity means arriving in a state of poverty and nothingness, consequently wishlessness. Such a state of a perfect lover is Prophet Abraham, peace be upon him. When he was thrown into the fire, Archangel Gabriel came and asked him if he wished something from the Almighty and he answered that he did not wish for anything, it is enough that his Lord knows his situation. The great saint Abu Bayazid al-Bistami with his all-comprehensive exclamation is showing the highest level of faith: "*I was only conscious three times in my life. Once I saw the world. Once I was conscious of the Hereafter. Then one night I saw my Lord who asked me what I wished, and said He would give it to me. I told Him that I wished for nothing, for He is the Only One.*"

A friend of Allah commented about some selected devotees: "*They are so highly attached to the sacred pillars that they proclaim: "I cannot live without praying, I cannot live without fasting, I cannot bear to be without the pilgrimage, I cannot bear to live without charitable acts!*" Further the friend of Allah exclaimed: "*This is what love is!*" Love demands to rub each other's shoulders during *qiyam* (standing position) of *Salah* like that of the Prophet's Companions to such an extent that one's shirt gets torn apart. Love is executing servanthood every moment. Love is joy and pleasure for submission, obedience, worship, and faith. Love is entering the sacred trade with God on the pilgrimage. Love is when your heart turns into a fire-place of yearning, pleading, burning longing, intense searching, and high aspiration. Love is to possess heroic generosity like that of the Companions. Love is inhaling the fragrance of the perfume of existence at the Ka'ba in Mecca and the resting place of our noble master in Medina. Love is reaping the fruit of awareness of love during fasting. Love is to taste the purity of belief. Love is inhaling the breath of Divine Mercy during *Salah*. Love is acknowledging one's shortcomings, baseness, inadequacy, insufficiency, limits, failures, and imperfections. Love is the inheritance of the Prophet's state of orphanhood, unletteredness, poverty, and universality. It is reported that the blessed master said: "*If I have to die, I would prefer to stay in this world exclusively for the love of three things: the prostration, the performance of the fasting month in the hot summer season, and the 'muhabbat' between people.*"

The Holy Qur'an as a Pure
Form of Worship

F or each believer of the community of Muhammad, it has to be said that next to the four obligatory worship duties an absolute necessity arises; it is the recitation, the listening and the interpretation of the Holy Qur'an to such an extent that the Divine revelations become part of his life. Muhyiddin ibn Arabi makes a significant comment: *"It is not man who inhabits the Qur'an; it is the Qur'an that dwells within man; the Divine word takes possession of the "arif billah" in such a way that the Qur'an becomes his nature."* No worship mode is more exalted, valuable, nourishing, than to occupy oneself with one's mind, heart, and spirit with the Holy Qur'an. If we wish to find God, the Divine revelations of the Qur'an are the most precious source. Thus, to comprehend, understand the truth of the Holy Qur'an means to become to know God and achieve nearness to Him.

Approaching the Qur'an means to approach the book of light containing the all-compassing Truth. It means to penetrate into the meaning of the seven oft repeated verses, *sab al-masani*. God reveals the verse: *"We have neglected nothing in the Book"* (al-An'am 6:38) and *"If all the trees on the earth were pens, and all the sea (were ink), with seven more seas added thereto, the words of God (His decrees, the acts of all His Names and Attributes manifested as His commandments, and the events and creatures He creates) would not be exhausted in the writing"* (Luqman 31:27).

The meaning of the revelations are exclusively delivered to the submissive, sincere, and receptive believers and servants, that is to say, the Qur'an opens up to those who are obedient, to those who follow the sacred law, those who follow the beloved of God, Muhammad Mustafa, peace and blessings be upon him. First we have to get the sensation of yearning for God, and then approach the Qur'an. Read with a clean heart, read with sacred longing, with true love, with the sensation of the sacred thirst, and with the eye of need. Only a clean heart can enter into the ocean of Divine Mercy and be illuminated by the light of the holy verses in order to receive the sweet taste of inner meanings. The more one increases the sensitivity for the Divine, the more one is pulled by an irresistible power of attraction towards the eternal realms of eternal beauty. Every Word of God carries the scent of healing and radiant light. True believers are able to receive the sweet taste of inner meanings and participate in the eternal flow of Divine grace and will be illuminated by the light of the holy verses. They inhale the sweet taste of the Hereafter; they breathe the Divine breath of mercy.

We have to know that the Qur'an does not only deliver information of guidelines for human life. The Qur'an does not only teach what is commanded and what is forbidden, what is right and wrong, what is *haram* and what is *halal*. The Qur'an does not only give information how to be saved from Hell and reach Paradise. The Qur'an is inspiration, Divine light, Divine Mercy, and intimate talk with God. The Qur'an is inspiring people for the ultimate fulfillment of spiritual life of "*no fear and no worry*" as opposed to fearing death and loving for this mortal world. The Qur'an is an inspiration to enhance to need for the truth, the search for knowledge, the desire for servanthood, followership, and true love. The Qur'an was revealed to inspire people for love, to invite for the realization of the truth, to invite for the perfection of love, for the sacred awareness of the truth, to invite for the *miraj*, to invite for the Paradise of intimacy. The Qur'an is healing as opposed to spiritual illnesses. The Qur'an is spiritual awakening as opposed to heedlessness. The Qur'an is resurrection as opposed to blindly following orders. The Qur'an is inviting the believers to enter the sacred trade with their Creator as opposed of looking for advantages, earning good deeds, trying to get the ticket to Paradise. To conclude, the Qur'an is the book of Divine Mercy where we may achieve the awareness of love. The crucial point is; in order to approach and to comprehend the truth of the Qur'an, we are obliged to live its truth. Once we manage to live the truth of the Holy Qur'an, we will be able to enlighten the Qur'an with our existence. We will be able to serve the Qur'an. We will be able to open the window of the heart and read the revelations with the light of our belief. We will become the server of the Fatiha, like Mahdi, the rightly guided one. Then the Qur'an will illuminate our souls. In other words, the Qur'an will show itself to the believer provided he is concerned with the struggle to travel upwards. The sacred condition we have to fulfill in order to approach the Qur'an truthfully: We have to offer all what we are, cleaning ourselves of all ulterior motives. Rumi gives an excellent vision how to approach the Qur'an truthfully: *"Many people have gone astray with the Qur'an; with that saving rope, one group fell into the well. The rope has no sin, O quarrelsome man! But you are unconcerned with travelling upward!"*

We have to learn how to advance on the way of truth in our daily lives as opposed to reading and studying the pages of the Qur'an. We have to learn how to integrate the knowledge we gained from the Divine revelations into the daily 24 hour-routine. We have to learn how to hunt the truth. We have to learn how to take refuge in God Almighty. To be able to take refuge in the One and Only is equal as living the truth of the holy verses of the Qur'an. The truth is not given for nothing. Today we mention God very cheaply. We have to realize that for the slightest advancement on the path of truth, we have to pay a price. This necessitates that we have to learn how to pay this price. In order to reach nearness to God, in order to reach the Paradise of intimacy with God, we have to pass beyond ourselves with love of Him. We have to divorce the temporary aspects of this world and cut the attachments and enter the sacred trade of the Hereafter. Human existence in this world is in need of self-sacrifice. We have to offer ourselves to the Lord of all the worlds and in return He will give us eternal life, the gratification of the water of life. There is no death without resurrection, no self-sacrifice with new life, no poverty without eternal richness, no annihilation without rebirth. In the words of Rumi: *"To experience the day of Resurrection, you have to die first, for "Resurrection" means making the dead come back to life. The whole world has taken a wrong way, for they fear non-existence, while it is their refuge."* The lesson we can draw is that by giving up our existence, we will gain real existence. It needs a firm deep-rooted intention of the believers to cut the attachment to the mortal world in order to enter the plain of the Hereafter. We have to work in the trade of true love. The more we will give from our substance, the higher price we pay, the higher will be the honor of catching some sweet scent of the Paradise of intimacy with our Lord of Majesty and Bounty and His beloved Messenger, and the venerable Companions.

The Qur'an speaks the language of the heart for the heart. The language of the heart is understood without letters and sound. It is the silence of the heart's speech. In a Divine *hadith*, God the Majestic declares: *"Neither My Earth nor My Heavens can contain Me, but the heart of a believing servant."* How can we not find the Qur'an in the heart when the One Who sends it is residing there? Muhyiddin ibn Arabi comments about descend of the revelations into the heart of man: *"The commentator report that the Qur'an in its entirety descended as far as the heavens of this world, all at once, and that from there it descended in a shower of stars upon Muhammad's heart. That voyage will never cease as long as the Qur'an is recited, in secret and aloud. From the servant's point of view the lasting laylatu'l-qadr (the night of power) is his own soul when it is purified. This purification by which the being is ummi. 'Ummi' usually translated as unlettered, is defined in the Qur'anic verse, 'He who is as when his mother gave birth to him' (al-Maedah 5:116). When the Qur'an which is a result of a Divine Attribute—and the attribute is inseparable from that which it qualifies—descends upon the heart, it is then He Whose Word the Qur'an is that descends with it. God said that the heart of his believing servant contains Him; it is of this descent of the Qur'an upon the heart of the believer that the sacred descent in the heart consists.*

> *When the Words of the Divine revelation reach the heart, ever new sciences spring forth like sparks from a flint when it is struck. The theophanies are born from this encounter with the Word of God.*

> *God has answered the request that has been addressed to him with the words "My Lord, increase me in knowledge!"* (Ta-Ha 20:114).

He whose understanding is identical in the two successive recitations is losing. He whose understanding is new in each recitation is winning. As for him who recites without understanding anything, may God have mercy on him.

Furthermore, the manner to approach the Qur'an truthfully can only be done in adapting the state of unletteredness of our blessed master. In order to reach true belief, we are obliged to inherit the states of being *ummi* and orphan, "immigration," "poverty," and "universality" of our blessed master. These conditions the Prophet found himself at his birthplace in the desert of Saudi Arabia are of immense significance for the followers of his community. Inheritance of his character necessitates not only his supreme features like humbleness, generosity, servanthood, poverty, but comprehend and adapt the state of an orphan, an immigrant, and an unlettered. The same responsibility for the follower of his communities is incumbent in terms of the first revelation *Iqra*—"*Read*" (al-Alaq 96:1). The mistake we make that we separate the Prophet from his community. It is God's Will that whatever happened to His Messenger in his life becomes the treasury of inheritance for his community. The crucial point: *Iqra* is for us. God says, read your own book, read yourself, read human existence, read the signs within and without you, and reflect on yourself, the world and the cosmos. This is the true vision. Man can perceive his own interior kingdom. The greatest knowledge is the knowledge of ourselves. Self-knowledge will enable us to reach our original state of purity, our true humanity. Thus, we will be able to perceive the Divine Presence reflecting from the mirror of the heart. Our blessed master could not read nor write, he was unlettered, or *ummi*, but he became the most perfect receptacle for the completion of the Divine revelations of the Holy Qur'an. He was an orphan but God raised him to be the intercessor of the Day of Judgment. He was unlettered and he became the mercy for all the worlds. He was poor and God raised him to become the honor of the universe, the chief of all imams. Ibn Arabi comments about the concept of *ummi*: "*One can be "ummi" without being illiterate from the moment that the intellect is capable of suspending its operations. For us, ummiyya consists in renouncing the use of rational speculation and judgment in order to give rise to meanings and secrets. As did the Prophet, the virginal receptacle of Revelation, a being should open himself entirely to the lights of grace.*" "*To hear Him man must thus return to the state of infancy—an expression that might after all be the most exact translation of ummiyya. This state of infancy is what the Qur'an describes in the following terms: "God brought you forth from the wombs of your mothers when you knew nothing*" (an-Nahl 16:78). *Among the possible meanings of a word, or verse, there is no choice at the end of a mental process; the true meaning—that which is true at that very moment for that very being—is that which wells up, in the nakedness of the spirit, from the very letter of Divine speech. It is to this letter and to it alone that he whose heart is ready to welcome that "shower of the stars," which will cease only on the day that the Qur'an is no longer recited "in secret or aloud," will listen.*"

Rumi comments about the concept of *ummi*: "*Does anyone write something on a place that has already been written over, or plant a sapling where one already grows? No, he seeks a blank piece of paper and sows the seed where none has yet been sown. Sister, be bare earth; be clean piece of paper untouched by writing, that you may be ennobled by "the pen of revelation", so that the Gracious One may sow seed within you" (Masnawi, V/1961–1964). "The Sufi polishes their breasts with invocation and meditation so that the heart's mirror may receive virgin images" (The Unseen World, I/3154).*

In our modern societies we can observe that the majority of people can only perceive the outward, the apparent reality. They are not in the state of receptivity for the Divine light of guidance in order to understand the deeper layers of meaning of the revelations, nor are they capable to realize the knowledge of the Qur'an in their lives. On the ones who are not fortunate to comprehend the revelations in its entire meanings, Ibn Arabi comments: *"Just as God has put a seal on their hearts and their ears and a veil on their eyes (al-Baqarah 2:7) such that they are unable to perceive the smell of the breath of essential truths or to distinguish at all the difference between angelic visits or satanic visits in their hearts. The noble Prophet said: There are reciters who read the Qur'an without it going any farther than their throats. That is the Qur'an that descends upon tongues and not upon hearts. God said the contrary about him who tastes (this descent): "The Trustworthy Spirit brings it (the Qur'an) down" (ash-Shu'ara 26:193). Such a man is he in whom this descent causes an immeasurable sweetness that surpasses all joy. When he experiences it, he is (truly) the person upon whom the ever new Qur'an has descended. The difference between these two kinds of descent is that if the Qur'an descends upon the heart, it brings comprehension with it."*

The majority of people need help to understand and realize the truth. Such help is only effective when it is of sacred nature. Divine guidance, support, education, healing, and nourishment can only come from the chosen and honored men of God. These are the Prophets and saints. Thus, it is through their abundant servanthood, their martyrdom for the sake of humanity, that we are able to take the light of Divine guidance from the verses of the Qur'an. They gave their lives in order for the following generations to learn, see, comprehend, experience, and live the truth of the Divine verses. There is no other way than to learn from pure beings, illuminated examples, and the noble presence of the saints. The truth is; these supreme saintly examples enlighten our darkness of unconsciousness due to their self-sacrifice for the religion. They became martyrs, they were tortured, and they lost everything. I believe that we owe God for striving in His cause and for humanity's good. Believers of Divine unity owe God the consciousness of becoming a representative of the truth. We owe God to accomplish the features of sincerity and truthfulness.

To conclude, the Divine revelations of the Qur'an must be organically linked with the inner self of man. The fact is that one's moral condition, one's character perceives the treasury of the noble character of Prophet Muhammad, peace and blessings be upon him, while approaching the Divine revelations of the Qur'an. The essence of man meets the essential Truth of God. This is the perfect relationship with the Qur'an. Believers belonging to the community of Muhammad should realize that loving the noble master requires loving the Holy Qur'an and vice versa. As much as we love the noble Prophet as much we are obliged to love the Qur'an. If only we could love the Prophet by following him! If only we could follow the Prophet by loving him! If only we could love the Prophet by adapting his *Sunnah*!

Salah (The Ritual Prayer)

S alawat, invocation of peace and blessings upon the noble Prophet, from in the collection "Signs of the Treasures" compiled by Muhammad al-Jazuli, may his secret be sanctified, Shadhili Tariqa:

"O Allah, please shower Your blessings upon our master Muhammad,
the Ocean of Your Lights,
the Mine of Your Secrets,
the Tongue of Your Proof,
the Bridegroom of Your Sovereignty,
the Imam of Your Presence,
the Embroidery of Your Empire,
the Treasury of Your Mercy,
the Way of Your Sharia, who delights in Your Unity,
the Pupil of the Eye of Being,
the Reason for Everything Brought into Being,
Essence of all Essences of Creation, dispatched from the Light of
Your Brilliance,
Shower Your blessings upon him as long as Your Eternity lasts,
As long as Your Subsistence subsists,
Never ceasing without Your knowledge,
As pleases You and him and as You will be pleased on our behalf, O
Lord of the worlds."

Another *Salawat*:

"O Allah, shower your grace upon the subtle Unity of the
Muhammadan Essence,
The Sun in the Heavens of Secrets,
And Locus of manifestation of Lights,
The Center of the Orbit of Majesty,
And the Pole of the Spheres of Beauty,
O Allah by his secret that is in Your Presence
And by his journeying toward You,

Safeguard me from my fear and eradicate my offense,
And take away my sadness and my avarice.
Exist for me, and take me to You from myself
And sustain me with passing away (fana) from myself
And do not let me be captivated by my carnal soul (nafs)
Nor veiled by my feelings (or senses)
And reveal to me every preserved secret,
O All-Living! O Self-Manifesting and Timeless One!"

Prophet Muhammad, peace and blessings be upon him, declared: *"Even I could not be saved (from Hellfire or God's punishment through my own actions), if God did not embrace me in His mercy."*

He is for everything and everything is for him. His home is in the heart of his lovers. He occupies the greatest place in our hearts, because he occupies the greatest place before Allah. The All-Merciful raised him to the highest station of all human beings, he became His beloved. When Allah mentions His most desired Prophet that exalted night of the heavenly ascension, He says with admiration: *"My Paradise will be adorned with the dust of My beloved's feet."* When the Exalted One converses with him, He says: *"O My beloved, great indeed is the honor in which I hold you. Were there a hundred Thrones, the dust your foot has trodden, would be dearer to Me than them all."* He was an orphan and Allah raised him to become the honor of the universe and he became the mercy for all the worlds. Allah raised him to become the noblest of all men. Allah raised him to be the chief of all imams. He was unlettered and he became the intercessor of the Day of Judgment. He gained this station of exaltation, closeness, honor and nobility due to his humility, poverty, modesty, and servanthood. His noble character is the best of Allah's creation, compromising the best of all the virtues a human being possesses, carrying the treasury of pure modesty. Due to his noblest virtues, he received the honor of the ascension, the *miraj*; he was raised to the highest levels in proximity to his beloved Lord.

Infinite fruits of sacred wisdom are displayed when we observe the conduct and practices of his daily life. He never demonstrated his supreme sainthood, his highest illumination, but secretly deprived himself of sleep and prayed the whole night expressing his contentment, gratitude, although he received the worst curses, treatment from his enemies. He was the treasure house of goodness and generosity, but he hides himself behind ordinary behavior and stayed awake for countless nights of his life shedding tears and asking for forgiveness and mercy for all humanity. Such is our beloved of Allah, he resided in continuous admiration, thankfulness, contentment with his beloved Lord whatever threats, hostilities from his enemies and unbelievers might have befallen him. He expressed his overwhelming love praying in tears most of the hours of his nights. He cried in such intensity, that his tears reached Aisha's bed and the sheets got wet waking her up from her sleep.

If our blessed master's behavior is not an expression of total servanthood, what else? If his behavior is not an expression of total gratitude, what else? Staying in the eternal lights of His Merciful Lord for all the hours of the night not an expression of celebration, is it not an expression of his abundant thankfulness? This indicates for the believers of his community that the value of one's spiritual life does not show in the numbers of Prayers or fasting days or good deeds, nor in the knowledge one possesses, but in the ability of how much one is able to be content with one's Creator whatever He has given and how much one is able to show continuous thankfulness to Him, although one might live in poverty, sickness, oppression, or cruelty. In other words, the ultimate wisdom is feeling profound gratitude with one's Beloved under all circumstances. Only then one has attained sacred wisdom, *marifa*, *irfan*, or *gnosis.*

Let us know that mercy is a result of purification of character. Only after polishing the mirror of the heart, mercy can arise. Only after adapting the most worthy feature of modesty, mercy can arise. Only after being content with Allah under all circumstances sacred wisdom, *marifa*, can arise. Only after showing efforts, works, struggling on the way of truth, mercy can arise. Only after sickness, poverty, oppression, loss, and misery, mercy can arise. That is to say, mercy is a result of loving surrender to one's Lord of all the worlds.

Our Prophet's wisdom of praying all night is symbolized by the *Tahajjud* Prayer, the voluntary Prayer in the night before the hours of dawn. *Tahajjud* represents the station of the *Maqam al-Mahmud*, the sublime station of the Prophet himself. The *Tahajjud* Prayers symbolize the Day of Resurrection. *Tahajjud* is resurrected consciousness. *Tahajjud* is the projection of the eternal life. *Tahajjud* symbolizes the resurrection after death, the rising of the servant from the darkest moment of the night in the Divine light of eternal conversation with the Lord of all the worlds.

The servant's heart is resurrected in the truth where he meets with the One Who is closer to him than he is to himself. *Tahajjud* is living the secret of seclusion, exchanging loving whispers in highest privacy, the top rendez-vous of top secrecy. *Tahajjud* is breathing the eternal life. *Tahajjud* is the conscience of the immortality of one's spirit. *Tahajjud* is to win the eternal strength of one's spirit. *Tahajjud* is to breathe the Divine secrets of the Ever-Living, Self-Subsisting. *Tahajjud* is to experience that one is forever alive, that one is immortal. *Tahajjud* is to shut down the functions of eating, sleeping, drinking, and talking, and being satisfied with the Divine light. Through the experience of *Tahajjud* we become able to experience *Tasawwuf.* The substance of *Tasawwuf* and *Tahajjud* are one. The essence of the religion of Islam is symbolized by the spirit of *Tahajjud.* The most tragic loss of our time is *Tahajjud.* When we lose the spirit of *Tahajjud,* we lose the treasury of submission, the treasury of the prostration, the treasury of the Surah Al-Fatiha, and the treasury of the most beautiful Names and Attributes. What is lost is the noble character of Muhammad, peace and blessings be upon him. What is lost is the treasury of the unity, *tawhid.* What is lost is all and everything what Allah values and loves in the human being: contentment, generosity, kindness, sincerity, modesty, courage, bravery, self-sacrifice... What is lost are the noble virtues of the four caliphs: truthfulness, justice, modesty, and knowledge. What is lost is the connection to the noblest *Ahl al-Bayt,* the Prophet's family, and the most venerable Companions.

Abu Bakr, may Allah be pleased with him, the possessor of the highest station of loyalty, made the following supplication to his Lord: "*What will become of my state, I approach You but I have no good deeds to offer to You!*" Ibrahim Adham cried the whole day and prayed the whole night as a way of life. He left everything, his wealth, status and honor and still says, that he cannot find the sleep because of his sins he committed. The saint is distinguished from the average man in the way he looks at his own sins and how he looks at his wealth and how he looks at his status in society. He is unable to acknowledge something belonging to himself; he is unable to see himself in any position, status, authority, ruler, superiority except perceiving his poverty and nothingness in front of the Perfection and Greatness of the Almighty. The only things he can see in terms of himself are his sins, insufficiencies, and imperfection. In terms of Allah the Greatest, the only thing which he can see is His Mercy. When he prays, he enters the Divine Mercy; when he contemplates, he perceives Allah's Mercy; when he works, he is surrounded by Allah's mercy. In his social life he is embedded in the Divine Mercy. The conscience of a saint is that he is admitting his sins and incapacities in front of His Creator, that means he is admitting his need and dependence for the One and Only. The beloved of God, the possessor of the highest illumination, pleads with his Lord: "*O Lord, do not leave me for one moment, for the blink of an eye, with my own soul alone.*" What does this indicate for his community?

The Night of the Ascension and Servanthood

Nowhere else than through the event of the ascension we can observe the mystery and most exalted station of servanthood. "*All-Glorified is He Who took His servant for a journey by night from the Sacred Mosque to the Farthest Mosque the environs of which We have blessed, so that We might show him some of Our signs (of the truths concerning Our Divinity and Lordship). Surely He is the One Who hears and sees*" (al-Isra 17:1). Allah called our noble master as a servant to the heavenly ascension: He did not refer to him as His Prophet. Due to his servanthood, he was taken to the highest station. Due to his servanthood, he became the beloved of Allah, he became the chosen, the most honored of all Prophets, he became the mercy for all the worlds. Due to the treasury of his humbleness, Allah raised His Beloved to become the honor of the universe. Our blessed master did not ascend by himself, he was taken, he was transported by his Lord. The Qur'an states: "*All-Glorified is He Who took His servant for a journey by night.*" He was made to see all the levels of Paradise and Hell and he was finally brought by his Lord to absolute proximity. He was taken to the furthest point of the creation and beyond because of his abundant love and service for his community. At this moment, God declares in the Qur'an when they conversed eternal secrets: "*He revealed to His servant what He revealed*" (an-Najm 53.10), referring to him as His servant. This is the nature of the noble Prophet; he was made to love the things of this world by Divine love. He says: "*I was made to love women, perfume, and the Prayer in this world.*" This shows his station of absolute servanthood. On the ascension, when he witnessed the realities beyond this world of appearance, he knew well that he was made to see by the grace and mercy from his beloved Lord. Servanthood is the essence of Islamic sainthood. God describes with the seal of His Prophets, the pride of humanity, in the creed of Islamic faith: "*There is no deity but God, and Muhammad is His servant and Messenger.*" Therefore, true inheritors of the noble Prophet never proclaim sainthood but give their whole lives with the intention to be useful to God's creatures. All their actions are done in secrecy with the only wish to please their Lord. These are the intimate friends of God. They preserve God's truth, so Allah preserves them. Their secret wealth is hidden through their undistinguished appearance, their state of poverty, their nothingness. The utterance of Rabia al-Adawiyya, the great woman saint, showed her unconditional servanthood to our Majestic Lord. She made a very significant and educational statement: "*O Lord, I swear by the beauty of nearness to You that I have not worshipped You either for fear of Hell or out of the desire for Paradise. I have worshipped You because of You.*" Rumi defines the stages towards the perfection of servanthood: "*Human being has three spiritual states. First, a person pays no attention whatsoever to God and worships anything—sex, money, rank—but God. When he starts to learn something deeper, then he will serve no one and nothing but God. And when he progresses, he grows silent; he doesn't claim; I don't serve God,*" nor does he boast "*I serve God;*" *he has gone beyond these two positions. From such beings, no sound comes into the world.*"

Another proof of our blessed master's perfect servanthood is that he separated from his most beloved Lord, he left the highest Paradise, and the Paradise of God's Essence and returned to the world as a humble servant to the poor sinners, giving his life to his community. His return to the world represents the greatest act of love. The great saint Bayazid al-Bistami, dwelling in unity with his beloved Lord, took only one step back towards creation and fainted. He could not bear the separation. But God, the Ever-Living, the Self-Existing, addressed him: "*Go out to My creation in My form, so when they see you, they see Me.*" There is a wisdom for the follower of the noble Messenger's community; having attained unity with Him, and descending to creation in order to serve, teach and guide, is a higher level than staying in unity with Him. The most pleasing action for Allah is returning to the world of works and responsibility. It is an act of true generosity and compassion towards all existence. There is a significant statement made by Sheikh Abu Madyan: "*To flee from created being is one of the signs of a novice's sincerity. To reach God is a sign of the sin-*

cerity of his flight from created being. To return to created being is a sign of the sincerity of his having reached God."

Here we should mention the Prophet Joseph (Yusuf), peace be upon him, because his servanthood was without measure. Although he was saved from the well, although he was saved from the imprisonment, although he became the king of Egypt, although he reunited with his father Jacob (Jaqub) after being separated for 40 years, he did not choose to enjoy the overflow of Divine blessings and favors his Lord bestowed on him in this world. Instead, Joseph kept on praying every night for forgiveness for many years for his brothers. Rumi gives us a visionary description Joseph's devotional sacrifice: *"I have heard that for 10 years Joseph never slept at night. That prince kept on praying to God for the sake of his brothers: "O God if you forgive them, so be it. But if not, then I will fill the worlds with mourning. Punish them not, O Lord, for they are full of regret for the sin that suddenly overtook them!" Joseph's feet became blistered from his night vigils, his eyes full of pain from weeping and wailing. The lamentation spread to the celestial spheres and the angels, and the Sea of Gentleness bubbled up and then broke the bonds. Fourteen robes of honor arrived; all fourteen of you are Prophets, emissaries, and chiefs among My servants." Such is the effort of the sheikhs night and day, in order to deliver the creatures from torment and corruption"* (*Diwan*, 9788–9794). This verse reveals one of Rumi's most fundamental descriptions of the role of Prophets, saints and servants. It gives deep insight about their function within human society. A true servant is someone when the duty is fulfilled, he prefers the Hereafter. When the Angel of Death (Azrail) came to the Prophet Elijah (Ilyas), peace be upon him, he was weeping and he said: *"My death will be the end of my servanthood. I shall not anymore be able to serve Him. This is the reason why I am weeping not because you came to take my life."* Does not Rumi's famous utterance, *"I am the dust on the pathway of Muhammad and I am the slave of the Qur'an,"* express the noble features of abundant humility and servanthood? In a poem he gives expression: *"I have become a servant, become a servant, become a servant; I have bowed and doubled myself up with serving You. Servants or slaves rejoice when they are emancipated; whereas I rejoice when I become Your servant."*

When we look at the night of the heavenly ascension, we can see that this event is a result of the noble character of Muhammad. Our noble master was dearer to God than all the other Prophets due to his noble character. Although he was always in deep concern and sadness about unbelievers, he never asked his Lord to lift the cruelties done to him. Although he was threatened, tortured, mistreated, he showed complete patience, surrender, love, and mercy; he stayed in deepest thankfulness, never wishing, pleading, and seeking anything from his Lord. His sole concern was the salvation of his community. This is the noble character of our blessed master as it is described in the Holy Qur'an: *"There has come to you (O people) a Messenger from among yourselves; extremely grievous to him is your suffering; full of concern for you is he, and for the believers, full of pity and compassion"* (at-Tawbah 9:128). *"Lower your wings (of compassion and protection) for the believers"* (al-Hijr 15:88). *"The Prophet has a higher claim on the believers than they have on their own selves"* (al-Ahzab 33:6).

So that night, the night of the heavenly ascension, the greatest Divine favor ever given to a human being by God, was not given due to any supplication or request on his part. That night Allah comforted His beloved without his asking, invited His beloved without his pleading, favored His beloved without his wishing. It is through his abundant servanthood for his community, his sacrifice, his love, his infinite compassion, that he received the honor of the heavenly ascension and was raised to the greatest honor to become Allah's beloved.

We are able to understand the worth of the night of the heavenly ascension, when we observe when and why it was given. It happened in the most difficult phase of our blessed master's life, he just returned from the village of Taif, where he experienced the greatest hostilities in his life. The children of the village threw stones at the honor of the universe till he bled everywhere. His own relatives told him the most condescending words like: *"In your own city Mecca, they just threw you out. Do you want this sickness now to let infect us?"* He was never threatened by his enemies to such utmost degree; he was never attacked by the unbelievers to such unbearable depths. When our blessed master stayed in prostration during the ritual Prayer, his enemies used to strangle his neck or Abu Jahl threw even some camel's stomach over his blessed head. In this desperate time, our noble master lost his most beloved wife, Khadija, as well as his uncle Abu Talib, and his little son Ibrahim. At the peak of injustice and cruelty done to our blessed master, where our blessed master arrived in a state where he could hardly breathe, in this very moment, God conferred the greatest favor on His beloved, pleasing him with union that night, although not the slightest complaint came from his lips. God took him to Himself in order to comfort him, to show His abundant love and affection and to profoundly please him. This was the night of the heavenly ascension. The wisdom of this most exalted night shows the essence of the religion of Islam. Paradise is given by the All-Merciful to anyone of His creatures to the degree of showing love and servanthood towards Him. The more believing servants show self-sacrifice, the more Allah rewards us with the honor of His Paradise of intimacy. The more we endure sufferance with patience, the higher the Divine reward. The greater the effort, the greater the Divine grace. The more we show beautiful behavior, the more God will reward us with the beauty of His Presence. The more we show heartfelt thankfulness in severe losses and disasters, the more we will receive eternal strength and happiness. That is to say, to the degree one is able to adapt the noble character features of the beloved Prophet, one will be able to rise to the absolute heights of belief. This indicates for believers when they lose everything in this world, they will win God. Wherever the doors of the world close, the doors of heaven open. All Prophets showed us this wisdom with their own lives, namely that loss becomes our gain, that nothingness becomes our capital, that poverty is our pride. At the moments of the highest degree of hardship they had to experience, God Almighty rewarded them with the greatest Divine favors. He offered His help, His protection in proportion to the degree of patience, endurance they showed. Prophet Joseph, peace be upon him, was saved from the darkness of the well and made into the king of Egypt. Prophet Abraham, peace be upon him, was saved from the tyrant Nimrod's fire. Prophet Yunus, peace be upon him, was saved from the big fish. Prophet Ismail, peace be upon him, was saved from being sacrificed through the knife. Prophet Noah, peace be upon him, was saved from the flood and landed on earth with his ship. This means that the value and treasury of the event of the heavenly ascension, is equal to his degree of sadness, degradation, and sufferance. The worth of his servanthood and his sacrifice is equal to the worth of the heavenly reward of intimate conversation with his beloved Lord. No human beings in this world suffered so much as our blessed master. He felt every small pain and worry of every single member of his community. The extent of his sufferance due to his concern for his community is unimaginable. As the heavenly ascension is a direct mirror and response to his servanthood and endurance, its heights and depths are incomprehensible as well. So the ritual Prayer surpasses by far human imagination because the most exalted experience of the heavenly ascension is equal to the noble character of the Prophet, that is to say, it is himself who represents the treasury of the heavenly voyage.

The Daily Prayers

Allah the Almighty ordained *Salah* as an obligation five times a day for Prophet Muhammad's community. It was given to our blessed master on the night of the heavenly ascension where he was transported through all the levels of heaven by his Lord and arrived in the realm of God's Essence and entered the Divine Presence. That night, the eternal rendez-vous got fulfilled, lover and Beloved were united. In this moment, the unity of Divine Essence was shown to him. In deepest intimacy, they conversed about the secrets of Divine knowledge. This highest privilege to look at the All-Holy, to converse with Allah Himself, was never given to any other creature. Only our Prophet could endure the Sight and the Might of Allah Himself.

In this exalted night, the ritual Prayer was given to our blessed master and for his community. The Prayer represents the greatest Divine favor from the Almighty given to His beloved Prophet and the followers of his community, as it comprehends the meaning and value of that night, the spiritual ascension of the believer. After the most exalted experience of the heavenly ascension, our blessed master returned to his household in Mecca and whenever he was longing for his beloved Lord, he performed the ritual Prayer and as in the night of the heavenly ascension he was able to experience the ascension towards the realms of Allah's Nearness.

It was on account of the Prophet's supplication to his beloved Lord at the night of ascension that the ritual Prayer was given to the believers of his community. During his whole life, our noble master never asked anything for himself, giving up his life entirely for his community. Thus as he was taken to utmost proximity to the Almighty, he immediately plead-ed to give to his community the exalted experience of the ascension as well. To grant His most beloved's wish, Allah said: "*In that case, they shall perform the ritual Prayer.*" That is why the ritual Prayer signifies the ascension of the believer. In the words of the noble Prophet: "*My heart ardently desires these forms of worship. On account of this longing of mine, my Lord gathered together the various acts of worship performed by the inhabitants of the seven heavens to form the Prayer, which He made a religious obligation for my community in honor of me. Any member of my community, who properly performs these five set of Prayers, will accomplish the worship of all inhabitants of the heavens."*

So the ritual Prayer is given to his community as a result of his longing. Do we not owe our Prophet to comply wholeheartedly with his longing, his desires, his pleasure, and his love? It is on account of his wish that all of us who have the honor to belong to his community received the honor to experience the spiritual ascension within the performance of *Salah.* It means to re-experience the journey of the heavenly ascension of the noble Prophet and his arrival at the Divine Presence in the inner world with one's spirit. If we comply with our blessed master's longing, it will bring us to the level to be able to comply with our Lord's desire for His beloved. When we perform *Salah,* we are given the possibility to participate in the greatest gift of the heavenly ascension and eventually participate in the intense pleasure our blessed master felt which he described as: *"The light of my eyes."*

Our beloved Messenger commented concerning the ritual Prayer: *"Everything has a symbol, and the symbol of faith is the ritual Prayer."* The ritual Prayer is the pillar of the religion. The ritual Prayer is the basis of faith. The ritual Prayer is the light of wisdom. No worship act is dearer to Allah than the ritual Prayer performed at the requested time. The word "Prayer" (*Salah*) is mentioned in the Holy Qur'an 83 times. It is the highest precedence of the beloved Prophet. The ritual Prayer fills the whole universe: The countless angels pray till the end of time, covering all the layers of the heavens. The Prayer insures the safe crossing of the Sirat bridge. It is the light in the grave, it is the intercessor at the Resurrection. The Prayer is what the devil hates most next to Prophet Muhammad, peace and blessings be upon him. *Salah* bears the essence of universality. *Salah* compromises the whole universe and what it contains. *Salah* addresses the Lord of all the worlds. A believer's heart expands to universal dimensions with the Qur'anic verse of the Fatiha: *"Praise to Allah, Lord of all the worlds"* opening up to the universe and beyond, opening up the universal truth, opening to infinity, reaching out to the eternal direction of Allah's beauty and perfection. *Salah* represents the transfer from *ayn al-yaqin*, the Eye of Certainty towards *haqq al-yaqin*, the Truth of Certainty. *Salah* is the shortest way to the highest contemplation, the eternal servanthood. *Salah* is the most excellent platform, the supreme Divine stage for all the believers of the religion of Divine unity. Its substance is eternal without boundaries of time and space, because it signifies the ascension of the spirit towards the beauty and grace of the Divine Presence. *Salah* has a double meaning, to pray and to bless. When we pray, God reveals Himself and dispenses His Mercy towards us. God blesses the worshipper with His Presence. It signifies the contemplation of the adorer towards the Adored, the praiser towards the Praised. *Salah* represents the highest form of remembrance, designed to penetrate through the earthly limitations and ascend with one's spirit through all the levels of the heavens in order to arrive in God's Divine realms of infinity, where time and space get suspended. The goal of *Salah* is the ascension. The goal of the ascension is to witness the Divine Presence. We know from the venerable Imam Ali, a famous utterance about the ritual Prayer: "*Do I worship One whom I have not seen?*" The goal of *Salah* is the direct contemplation with Allah. The caliph owned this station which is called *maqam al-mushahada*, the final stage of the ascension. This is the true Prayer, to experience the reality of the conversation with the Everlasting One, *Al-Baqi*, where one witnesses the Divine Beauty of one's beloved Lord.

Allah's first created act is the blessed light of Muhammad, and the Supreme Majesty was in love with the beauty of Muhammad's light. Since pre-existence, the time of the creation of Muhammad's light, the Prophet was the object of Allah's Gaze. The sacred wonder, the love, the admiration of the Ever-Living towards the source of light represents the seat for the good news of the eternal rendezvous for the night of the heavenly ascension. If God did not wonder at Muhammad's light, the sacred bountifulness would not reach and be displayed on earth. That moment, the source of sacred love from Muhammad towards the Divine Essence as well as from the Divine Essence towards Muhammad was born. This represents the eternal dialogue between Allah and Muhammad since the beginning of time. This dialogue finds its absolute fulfillment with the heavenly ascension where lover and Beloved are united. With the event of that night, the eternal dialogue finds its realization on earth. The heavenly ascension, symbolized by the ritual Prayer, is a result of the perfection of the Divine light, Divine favor, and noble character of Muhammad. In other words, *Salah* is such a supreme ritual, the light from Allah is shining towards the light of His beloved Prophet, and the light of God's Majesty is received in utmost awe and wonderment by the light of Muhammad, seen in the mirror of modesty. It is the beauty of Allah's light to the beauty of Muhammad's light. It is Light upon light. This supreme conversation started with the first act of Allah's creation, the light of Muhammad, and is travelled through time until the nights of all nights, where the perfection of the lights got fulfilled, the night of the ascension. This eternal dialogue between the believing servants and the Lord of all the worlds will never end and last until the end of times for the practitioners of the sacred law who perform the ritual Prayer.

As the ritual Prayer represents the highest spiritual ascension of a believer, during its performance the Divine scent of mercy can be reached. God's act of creation is by blowing His Divine Breath into man. This means, human beings are given life through the Breath of Mercy. The Divine breath of mercy emanates from the source. At the source, purity reveals a sweet fragrance; it is the perfume of sacred existence. The first connection of the human bodies with the Divine is through the merciful Breath. The fragrance of the All-Merciful signifies closeness to the Divine Existence. Therefore the human being, since his coming into existence, has a desire for the holy fragrance, has demanded it. Thus, when the human being is able to surpass his own human scent, he will be able to reach the holy fragrance of mercy. The unique ground of this encounter is *Salah*. Therefore the ritual Prayer is the most exclusive, most unifying, most elevated, most mysterious, and most unique of all prayers.

The heavenly ascension is the treasury of "*My Mercy has outstripped My Wrath*" (Divine *hadith*) and "*Assuredly, He will increasingly grant you his favors one after another, and you will be contented*" (ad-Duha 93:5). Uncountable bounties have been prepared for the community of believing servants who say with sincere conviction: "*I testify that there is no deity but Allah and I testify that Muhammad is the Messenger of Allah.*" The moment before our blessed master entered the Divine Presence of his Lord, the Pen said: "*Muhammad is mine.*" The Tablet said: "*He is mine.*" The Throne, the Seat, and Paradise each said: "*Muhammad is mine.*" Then the Exalted One said: "*My beloved, I have given you the Pen, the Tablet, the Throne, the Seat, and Paradise.*" The blessed Prophet said: "*My Lord, I do not wish for these. What I ask of You is my Community.*" Then the Lord of all the worlds said: "*I have given you your community.*"

When our master finally reached the mysterious proximity of the Two Bow-lengths, the Exalted Lord exchanged with His beloved the noble greeting ceremony of *At-tahiyyatu*: The noble Prophet greeted Allah by saying "*All types of worship we do with our physical body and everything we spend from our wealth is only for You to please You. I come to you to declare my covenant and my fidelity toward you and I greet you with those words.*" The Almighty would address ninety thousand words to His beloved. Concerning his community, a very significant conversation took place, our master said: "*My Lord! You gave Paradise to the venerable Adam.*" The All-Glorious One said: "*I did give Paradise to Adam, and then I expelled him from it. I shall give Paradise to your community, but I shall never make them leave it.*" Our master kept on asking his Lord about all the favors He gave to the previous Prophets and His answer was always a thousand-fold increase of favors for his community.

Concerning the Holy Scriptures, our noble master said: "*You gave the Gospel to the venerable Jesus.*" God Almighty replied: "*To you I have given the Surah Al-Ikhlas.*" The noble Prophet said: "*You gave the Torah to the venerable Moses.*" The Exalted exclaimed: "*My beloved, I have given you the Throne Verse, Ayat al-Kursi. I have revealed to you a glorious Surah which is not to be found in the Torah or in the Gospel, not in the Psalms or in any of the hundred Scrolls. That chapter is Surah Al-Fatiha. Such is that glorious Surah of Mine that Hell is forbidden to touch the body of anyone who recites it. Though his parents were unbelievers, I will abate their torment. In honor of that Surah, I have created no servant nobler than you, or greater than you, or finer than you. To read Surah Al-Anam is like reading the essence of the Psalms. To read Surah Al-Ikhlas is like reading the essential truth of the Gospel. To read the Throne Verse is like reading the essential truth of the Torah.*"

The Lord of Majesty also said: "*My beloved, you are dearer to Me than all the Prophets. Because your community is also dearer to Me than all other communities, I have combined the acts of worship of all the inhabitants of Heaven and called them ritual Prayer. I have made the Prayer a religious obligation for your community. Any member of your community who performs this obligation to please Me will have worshipped Me with all acts of worship!*"

Further the blessed Messenger asked his Lord: "*What action is dearest to You?* God Almighty replied: "*O Ahmad, the most meritorious of all actions and the one dearest in my sight is that of entrusting everything to me. O Ahmad, no action is higher than being content with what I have given. I love those who are content with Me, I love those who love one another for My sake and I love those who bring people to Me.*"

Salah and the Saints of Islam

In order to know the value, meaning, and goal of the ritual Prayer, namely to understand its comprehensive significance, we are able to receive its entire wisdom undoubtedly from the noble Prophet. It is our blessed master, who demonstrated throughout his life with all his actions, his behavior, his daily conduct, his thoughts, his advice, what rank the ritual Prayer should occupy in our lives. The noble Prophet demonstrated to his followers that *Salah* must become the central focus point, the top priority in their lives. In other words, he showed his community, how much value is given for this most excellent Prayer by Allah the Exalted. Our Creator loves nothing more than to see His servants binding themselves to His commandments, to see them expressing their commitments in pleasure and thankfulness to Him, expressed in the Divine *hadith*, where the All-Merciful says: "*My servant does not approach Me by something I love more than by those acts which I have prescribed.*" The ritual Prayer, *Salah*, is given by the Exalted One to His believers to reach proximity towards Him, to reach contentment within Him, to reach intimacy with Him, and earn the true success of the Paradise of intimacy.

The noble Messenger said concerning the ritual Prayer: "*Even when you give me 100 camels, the performance of the two-unit sunnah of the Morning Prayer is more blessed, valuable.*"

"*Wrongdoing believers who merit Hell will have their whole bodies burnt by the fire. Only those organs that make prostration to God will be unaffected. Therefore, perform the Prayer with your whole heart.*"

"*If a person does not perform the Prayer, it is as if he has not adopted any religion.*"

"*If Salah does not prevent you from the bad, it will only increase the distance to Allah.*"

"Just as no dirt remains on a person who bathes five times a day in a stream flowing in front of his gate, no sins remains in one who enters the presence of the Almighty five times a day, for he enters the Divine Mercy is granted forgiveness."

At the time when the first revelation descended on a Monday, right away on Tuesday, *Salah* was revealed to our master by Archangel Gabriel, and it was made into an obligation for his followers.

At the interrogation after passing away, the first of all questions in the grave will be about the performance of *Salah* in our earthly lives.

Prophet Muhammad, peace and blessings be upon him, was asked what is the most beautiful action in the life of a Muslim and he responded: *"To pray the ritual Prayer at the requested time."*

The noble Messenger had to endure the greatest threats from the unbelievers at the terrifying event in the village of Taif. Although he was exposed by the most condescending remarks of his own relatives and stones were thrown at him from the children of the village, he asked the Almighty to forgive its inhabitants. In contrast to this most sad and tragic event in his life, there is another encounter where our blessed master had to fight (Battle of the Trench or Ghazwa al-Khandaq). At the time of the Prayers, they could not stop fighting because the spears kept flying at them continuously from the enemy. So the army of the noble Prophet could not pray *Salah* at the requested time. For this reason the Prophet made a supplication, which he kept repeating every morning for a month.

We know from the traditions that our Prophet's feet got swollen from staying in *qiyam* in long night Prayers. He stayed for such long times in *sujud* (prostration) that his household thought he might have passed away.

Junayd al-Bagdadi, one of the greatest saints ever lived, was on his death bed gravely ill and very near to pass away to his beloved Lord, the realms of eternal beauty. At this point of departure, he did not accept anyone to see him. But a young disciple of him was utterly insistent that he forced himself into his presence. When he entered his room, he saw Junayd al-Bagdadi at the Prayer carpet performing *Salah*. The young student was very astonished to see him able to perform the Prayer because everybody told him that his sickness was too severe for anyone to see him. When the saint finished, the student immediately asked him why in his condition he was trying to perform *Salah* and Junayd al-Bagdadi answered: *"In my whole life during the performance of Salah, I could find everything what I was searching for. Should I not desire in the last moments of my life to taste this ultimate fulfillment of my soul?"*

One of the Prophet's Companions in performing his ablution to prepare for the ritual Prayer, he fainted. When asked what caused him to lose consciousness, he replied: *"How can I stand in the presence of my Lord in my condition!"*

The same abundant love for *Salah* was shown by the four caliphs. Ali's last desire lying on his death bed as a martyr was to be able to perform two units. Before entering the Prayer, Ali would sometimes blush red and other times turn pale. The members of his household were astonished and asked him: *"Why is it that when you prepare yourself for Prayers, we see that your face gets sometimes red or pale?"* He replayed: *"I am going up into the Presence of Allah. Is it easy?"* Umar was lying unconscious on the battlefield and the Companions did not know if he already passed away. So they were reciting the call to Prayer in his ear because they knew even in the last breaths of his life, it would be the only thing he might be able to perceive and bring him back to consciousness. So they recited the call to Prayer in his ear in order to revitalize him. His heart possessed such a wakefulness, such utter desire for *Salah*, that the call to Prayer brought him back to consciousness and he asked, *"Is the Prayer already over?"*, fearing to have missed it even in his condition. His body miraculously erected and he was able to stand for some moments on his feet before collapsing on the floor again.

Rumi prayed outside in a cold winter all night long. He remained in the prostration for such a long period of time, crying, pleading with his Lord, until his tears running down his cheek into his beard started to freeze and formed a piece of ice sticking into the ground.

Is it not enough to know for us believers that the highest saints find complete satisfaction, contentment, the highest bliss of body, heart and spirit with *Salah*? Is it not enough that our beloved master told us that *Salah* is the light of his eyes? Is it not enough to know that his Companions could hear a brimming sound coming from his noble breast caused by the immense impact of the Majestic Presence during the performance of *Salah*? Is it not enough to know that the Prophet's family and all the Companions were enslaved to the performance of *Salah*?

Whatever length our blessed master prayed and supplicated during all the days and nights of his life, his intense pleasure never decreased, the light of his eyes never ceased. What is the light? What is this sacred delight, the spiritual joy, the freshness, the coolness of his eyes? What nature was his love for *Salah*? When he said the comfort of my eye is given to me during *Salah*, he meant the intense pleasure he felt to witness the Truth with the secret eye of his heart. He saw & heard his Lord while praying. He had witnessed endless Divine manifestations. So it was not his human eye, but the truth saw nothing else but the Truth, the first light, and the source of light saw the beauty of the Divine Light of Essence. It is Light upon light. This is the reality of the ascension, its real meaning. That is to say, the most pure and truthful heart in this world was witnessing the manifestation of Divine Truth.

The Ritual Prayer: A Sacred Communication

The treasury of *Salah* represents a sacred conversation between the self-lessness of the one who has been sent as a mercy for all the worlds and the All-Merciful Lord of all the worlds. *Thus, there arises wisdom in this most exclusive of all prayers. Compared to other worship rituals, the prescribed ritual Prayer is actually a true conversation, a sacred communication from the servant to the Lord and from the Lord to the servant, from the creature to the Creator and from the Creator to the created. Allah the Almighty says, "I divided Salah between Myself and My servant. Half of the worship belongs to Me and half to My servant. And My servant will certainly receive that which he asks of Me." The Lord ordered us to worship Him, to praise Him, but He also praises the one who praises Him. This is the essence of Salah, dynamic mutuality of the worshipper to the Worshipped, and vice versa. It represents the fulfillment of the Qur'anic verse: "God loves them and they love Him" (al-Maedah 5:54) and the Divine hadith: "As we remember Him, He remembers us." Thus, the response of God Most High is a Divine rule in Prayer, as it is a Divine rule to be merciful to His sincere servants.* This mutuality is the deepest truth that *Salah* bears. *God says through the voice of the imam as the believers are standing erect before going into prostration: "Sami'allahu liman hamidah—Allah hears those who praise and thank Him." In other words, God listens to His servant who praises Him, which means that it is God Himself Who pronounces the words through the mouth of the servant. "God prays on us,"* a reference to the Qur'anic verse,

"*He it is Who (in return for your remembrance of Him) bestows His special blessings upon you*" (al-Ahzab 33:43). A comment from Ibn Arabi: "*Prayer thus comes simultaneously from us and from Him.*" *Thus Salah is the only rite where God prays over us.* The angels respond: "*Rabbana lakal hamd— Our Lord, all praise and thanks are due to You.*"

Because of this profound interconnection, the ritual Prayer is over-filled with secrets. Divine love is mutual. If we are completely present to our Lord of all the worlds within the ritual Prayer, He will immediately reveal Himself, the Divine reply is guaranteed. Through the mutuality of the Prayer, a creative, deep communion between God and man is activated. The believer is given the grace to experience the fullness of the relationship with his Lord.

Surah Al-Fatiha

One of the greatest treasures where sacred communication from the Lord to His servant and the servants to their Lord is activated to its fullest extent is the recitation of the Surah Al-Fatiha during *qiyam*, the standing position. The Surah Al-Fatiha represents the opening verse of the Qur'an, and its recitation in the same time represents the opening of *Salah*. Thus we see a clear proof of the mutual dynamic between the worshipper and the Worshipped. The Majestic has divided the Fatiha in two parts, the first four verses are God's part and the last three verses are man's part. This double nature of the first Surah is explained by the Divine *hadith*, in which the Almighty says: "*I have divided the Prayer (here identified with the Fatiha, which is an essential element of Prayer) into two parts, between My servant and Myself.*" Ibn Arabi comments: "*It is 'the One that opens', the brilliant theophanies. It is 'the Doubled One', for it contains the meanings of Lordship and servanthood at the same time. It is 'the One that suffices', for it includes both trial and security. It is the 'Seven Doubled Ones,' for it includes the seven Attributes of the Essence. It is the 'Immense Sum', for it envelopes the contingent and the eternal. It is the 'Mother of the Book', for in it is found felicity and punishment. One of its sides is suspended in Divine Realities and the other is attached to human realities, while its middle proceeds from the ones and the others.*"

In every cycle of the ritual Prayer, it is an obligation to recite the opening verse of the Holy Qur'an, the Surah Al-Fatiha. The Prayer without the recitation of the Surah Al-Fatiha is not valid. Our blessed master comments: *"The essence of the religion is the ritual Prayer and the essence of the ritual Prayer is the Fatiha."* This means, if the ritual Prayer signifies the ascension of the believer, thus the spiritual ascension can only be reached through the recitation of the Surah Al-Fatiha.

The full sum of all words, *jawami al-kalim*, is only spoken by Prophet Muhammad, peace be and blessings be upon him. He speaks on all levels and in all places of worship. He is the leader of all Prayer rituals. He is the chief of all imams. He is the head of all the universes. By revealing the Divine verses of the Fatiha, the opening chapter of the Qur'an, God expressed the full sum of all words. This means that the Surah Al-Fatiha contains the essence of the Holy Qur'an.

The Qur'an contains all previous revelations; therefore the noble master represents the seal of Prophethood. Like this noblest chapter, our noble Prophet contains the whole wisdom of the Qur'an, that is to say, his essence, his wisdom, his life, his existence, his heart, and his description is symbolized by the opening Surah of the Holy Qur'an, reflecting its truth. This means that the treasury of the Surah Al-Fatiha represents the sacred perfection of the noble character of our master. Fatiha is a blessed code, a key that opens all Divine secrets materially and spiritually; its meanings are infinite and inexhaustible. The noble Ali is reported having said: *"To explain and interpret the meaning of the Fatiha, even if we load 70 camels with books, it still would not be sufficient."*

When a worshipper recites the Fatiha during the ritual Prayer in the awareness of reciting the entire wisdom of the Qur'an, the worlds of the Unseen will reveal. When the Divine verses are recited with one's heart, one exercises the art of approaching the All-Holy so that the veils covering the soul will be removed one after another. Man can find his secret in the meaning of the Fatiha and in man's secret essence the treasury of the Fatiha can be discovered. In other words, man can look through the window of his heart and discover the miracles of creation of the whole universe and within himself. Every letter of the Fatiha is bursting with Divine knowledge, because the seven verses contain the essence of the Qur'an.

The Surah Al-Fatiha is translated as the "opening chapter," with the true meaning of the word; "the one that opens." In that sense, the Surah represents the door, the opening to the Divine Truth. The first Surah is also called the *Conqueror* of the Qur'an. Furthermore, the Fatiha is also defined as the Mother of the Qur'an, which means the essence of the

Qur'an, or the Mother of the book, *Umm al-kitab.* In the Surah Al-Hijr, Fatiha is referred to as *sab al-masani* (7 oft repeated verses): *"And certainly We have given you seven of the oft-repeated (verses)"* (al-Hijr 15:87). Dr. Haluk Nurbaki offers the following interpretation: *"We have given you seven cyphers each of which has manifold meanings that are each double-layered. And more precisely, it means; 'We have given that which is reinforced within the thousand and one layers of seven. We have given you the unrivalled, unprecedented seven: the powerful, the vital seven with the secrets of universes reposed in its bosom.'"* A *hadith* tells us that Al-Fatiha is given its name because it represents the Preserved Tablet, *Lawh al-Mahfuz.*

The Surah Al-Fatiha is the pearl of all sayings. There is no saying pronounced by man which is more valuable than the Fatiha. There are no words and verses which carry more meaning than the Fatiha. There is no sacred communication with Allah more elevated and more powerful than the Fatiha. The seven verses of this noble chapter are summing up all. They teach us all what we have to know. They give us Divine guidance in all circumstances of our lives. They open our sacred awareness for the world and the infinite realms of the Hereafter. They give us the capability to distinguish the truth from falsehood. The endless ocean of meanings of the noble Surah is carrying the flow of heightened Divine love which is not bound to time or space. This love energy deriving from the wisdom of the Divine verses of the Fatiha circulate in the sublime heart of a true believer.

For the meanings of the Fatiha to be revealed and for the love energy to flow, it needs the mutual contribution of the worshipper. It needs his love, his submission and thankfulness for the Lord of all the worlds who revealed these glorious seven verses to mankind and it needs his love and admiration for the Messenger who brought this glorious chapter to mankind and it needs the love for the beauty and perfection for the Fatiha itself. It is actually the treasury of the Fatiha helping one increasing the love for the *Ahl al-Bayt*, the family of the Prophet, and the venerable Companions, because it reveals the treasury of the noble character of the beloved Prophet himself. For only through a mutual trade of love, the endless, uninterrupted, and eternal circulation will run from heart to heart.

Our noble Prophet represents the greatest supplicant humanity ever possessed and the greatest thanks giver to his Lord humanity ever knew and the greatest servant humanity ever possessed. The supreme character features find expression in the first verse of the Fatiha: *"Praise to be to Allah, Lord of all the worlds."* The treasured meanings of the beginning verse represent the door and the means to reach the Divine realms of eternity of our Majesty and Bounty. Is there a greater proof of love than to say, *"Praise be to Allah, Lord of all the worlds"*? To pronounce this sacred phrase carries the spirit of celebration for believing hearts. It is the answer of the sincere servants to their beloved Lord, to His Divine proclamation: *"I was a hidden treasure and I wished to be known, so I created creation"* (Divine *hadith*), saying: *"Yes! We are celebrating the praises of knowing You, the Lord of all the worlds, the most Powerful, the Omnipotent."* The most exalted worshipper in this universe, our blessed master, comprehends in himself the secret of sacred communication from the creature to its Creator, from the servant to its Lord, from the worshipper to the Worshipped. That is to say, its essence bears the secret union of Allah and Muhammad. This secret represents the reality of the Fatiha. Thus it depends on the degree of the worshipper's love for the noble Prophet to determine the proportion of taking an eventual share in the secret treasury of the Fatiha. This indicates that the capacity of the worshipping believers to revitalize the Fatiha with heightened love during its recitation will bring a heightened flow of energy to their inner selves. How much one is able to comprehend the meanings of the chapter with the heat of one's search and love, will determine the degree of knowledge and value one can discover in oneself. How much one burns with sacred longing, desire, and search during its recitation, to the same degree Divine secrets of the Fatiha will be revealed. In other words, the secret of the Fatiha can only spread into the believer's heart and open up the channels for the spiritual circulation of infinite meanings when unconditional love and submission is shown and exercised by the worshipper.

In this sense, the Surah Al-Fatiha represents an absolute measurement of one's own spiritual state. The Divine verses mirror the degree of submission one shows for the Almighty, the degree of sacred efforts and struggling one shows to reach the Almighty, the state of one's heart, one's faith, one's character features. They mirror the degree of one's worship qualities, one's inner cleanliness and purity, and the level of one's sacred wisdom and awareness. That is to say, the Surah Al-Fatiha manifests nothing else than the degree of closeness one possesses to one's Supreme Creator and the closeness to our blessed master, peace and blessings be upon him. It is through the Fatiha that the Almighty gives birth to the art of knowing and reaching His Divinity more deeply and closely. These reflections point to the fact that, knowingly or unknowingly, for all living creatures there is an absolute need for the secret treasury of the Fatiha for their spiritual survival as there is an absolute need for the Divine truth of the Holy Qur'an.

With the fourth verse of the Fatiha, "*You alone do we worship and You alone do we serve,*" the consciousness of servanthood gets heightened and transmitted. It is the essential state for whom the universe was created, in honor of whom the noble Surah Al-Fatiha was revealed. The fourth verse represents the wisdom of yearning for absolute servanthood and true praise symbolized by the noble character of Muhammad. Respectively, the verse represents the blessed character features which reveal the essence of true servanthood, namely, not praying to anyone and not asking for help from anyone except Allah the Majestic One. If the worshipper wishes to become part of the secret meaning and attain its consciousness, he has to align himself behind the noble Prophet. More precisely, he has to annihilate himself in the pronunciation of our blessed master: "*You alone do we worship and You alone do we ask for help.*" In this sense, the fourth verse of the Fatiha represents our Messenger's art to achieve nothingness, of the total surrender of personal will to the Divine Will, described by the *hadith*: "*Poverty is my pride.*" Only selflessness can perform a true Prayer. The power of the Divine guidance for the *sirat al-mustaqim*, the straight path, the fifth verse of the Fatiha, cannot be felt if the ego is not extinguished. The submission of his self must reach sacred ecstasy, thus on the screen of his heart, the Divine Presence can start to appear. Only by inheriting the mystery of the state of the honor of the universe: "*Only You do we worship and only You do we ask for help,*" believers of Divine unity will turn into lovers of first grade.

To conclude, unless a believer gains an intimate knowledge of the essential truth of the backbones of the noble master's attributes, he cannot benefit from the secret of Fatiha in the ritual Prayer. Thus the highest human secret is the wisdom of the noble character of Muhammad, manifested in the *sirat al-mustaqim*.

The Postures of *Salah*

The ritual Prayer consists of the four principle positions. Each one corresponds to a letter of the Arabic alphabet, which writes the Name of Allah. The *alif*, for standing, *qiyam*, is an image of the human state (coming from God). The *lam*, for bowing, *ruku*, an image of the animal state (turning towards God). The *ha*, for prostration, *sujud*, an image of the plant state (experiencing in God). The breathing of the *ha*, for sitting position, *julus*, an image of the mineral state (for God). Consequently, as the body goes through these postures, completing one cycle of Prayer, the worshipper flows formally through the Name of Allah. The ritual postures of *Salah* are of such harmonious perfect order, that each of them leads into the other, each of them prepares for the experience of next one. Before annihilation of oneself in *sujud,* we cannot experience subsistence, eternity, *julus.* We cannot arrive in *ruku,* bowing, without having been in *qiyam.* We cannot arrive in *sujud*, the prostration, without straightening up to the human state of *qiyam.* Completing one *rakah,* one Prayer cycle, the worshipper will arrive at the beginning where he started. On his travel through the postures of one *rakah,* he experiences the flow of eternal blessings. Thus one cycle carries the dimensions of infinity, because its closure leads into its opening, its end leads into its beginning. The perpetual eternal flow is established. This means that the worshipper can flow through the Name of Allah during one set of Prayer. The Fatiha itself, like one cycle of the ritual Prayer, bears the same principle. The meaning of the last (7th) verse: "*The Path of those whom You have favored, not of those who have incurred (Your) wrath (punishment and condemnation), nor of those who are astray*" leads into the meaning of the beginning verse: "*In the Name of God, the All-Merciful, the All-Compassionate; All praise and gratitude (whoever gives these to whomever for whatever reason and in whatever way from the first day of creation until eternity) are for God, the Lord of the worlds.*" The Surah Al-Fatiha is completed through that by which it was started. The same principle is observed with the seven circumambulations, the *tawaf,* around the Ka'ba, the Sacred House of Allah. The seventh circumambulation leads into the first one. Thus, through performing one cycle of *Salah,* the eternal flow of sacred communication with one's beloved Lord is established. The truth of the recited revelations can flow uninterrupted from the Worshipped to the worshipper and from the worshipper to the Worshipped, like the flow and ebb of the waves of the ocean. One cycle of *Salah* generates a never ending eternal flow of the Divine breath. One cycle offers to dive into the ocean of Oneness. One cycle invites us to breathe the sweet scent of the Hereafter.

One cycle carries the glorious gift of the ascension. That is to say, one cycle of the Prayer ritual carries the treasury of the religion of Islam.

We know from a conversation that took place at the night of the ascension, that each level of the Heavens is filled with uncountable angels praying with the worshipping believers, in sharing the *qiyam, ruku, sujud,* and *julus.* Praying behind the devotees, they represent a congregation. Thus during the performance of *Salah,* the worshippers are surrounded by the most sublime symphony orchestra of infinite number of angels praying the hymns of glorification and praises with them.

We learn about the immeasurable blessings of the cycle of *Salah* from the Archangel Gabriel. According to a tradition, at the time when Allah created the Archangel Gabriel in the most beautiful manner, a conversation took place between them. Archangel Gabriel performed two cycles of Prayers, each cycle taking 1000 years, in gratitude towards his Lord who created him in such beauty. Allah the Almighty said: "*No one has worshipped Me like you, but at the end of time a noble Prophet of Mine, My dearly beloved will come. Although his community will be feeble, sinful and not very devout, two cycles of Prayer performed by them for all their absent-mindedness, mistakes and forgetfulness, will be dearer to Me than this Prayer you have performed for the sake of My Honor and Majesty. Their pre-eminence is due to their being the community of My beloved.*" Gabriel asked again: "*O my Lord, what favor will you grant for the Prayer they perform?*" The Exalted One replied: "*I shall give My Paradise.*" Gabriel then replied: "*O Lord, would You give me permission to look around this resort of Paradise You are going to give the community of Muhammad?*" After Gabriel had flown around for three thousand years and again for thirty thousand years, he grew weary and alighted in the shade of one of the trees of Paradise. Prostrating himself to Allah, he begged to know what distance he had covered: "*O my Lord, my strength deserted me. Tell me, how much of this Paradise, which You will the community of Muhammad, have I traversed? Is it half, a third, a quarter?*" The Almighty told him: "*Even if you flew on for another thirty thousand years at ten times this speed you would not cover one tenth of the bounty I have conferred upon the community of Muhammad. Such, O Gabriel, is the bounty I reward a Prayer of two cycles.*"

What is the most important part of *Salah*? The noble Prophet says, *qiyam,* the standing position, vertical position, representing the human state. If we reflect on the whole sequences of *Salah,* most believers would give the prostration as an answer due to the symbolic meaning of loving union with one's Lord it carries, or the sitting position after the prostration, due to the finalization of the ascension of the believer arriving in the holy Presence of the All-Merciful where the worshipper re-experiences and recites the greeting ceremony of our blessed master to his beloved Lord at the night of the ascension. The Prophet's answer has undoubtedly to do with the recitation of the Surah Al-Fatiha and the following recitation of the chapters of the Qur'an. Both *qiyam* and the Surah Al-Fatiha represent the beginning of *Salah*. Thus with the posture of the *qiyam* and the recitation of the Surah Al-Fatiha, the worshippers enter the most excellent palace of our glorious Majesty, His Supreme Divine Presence facing toward the *qibla*, pronouncing the *takbir, Allahu Akbar,* God is the Greatest. The *qibla* is the physical orientation towards the Ka'ba. Ibn Arabi comments: "*Tell your heaven (soul, spirit) not to veil you by its subtlety, and your earth (your body) not to veil you by its density.*" "*Be a circular face... so that the orientation (of your body) toward the Ka'ba will not be a screen for the orientation in the direction of the Divine Presence in the heart.*" Further Ibn Arabi refers to the *takbir*: "*The takbir is a radical refusal to idolize that which is not the Essence itself; it is greater than all that is great, it transcends all transcendence... And this name says: I am God. And it speaks the truth. But it is mandatory that you reply: Allahu Akbar! Know with absolute certainty, that the Divine Essence never shows Himself to you as Himself, but only under the form of one of His eminent Attributes; and know that you will never know the absolute meaning of the Name Allah.*"

Qiyam represents the human state, the vertical movement standing up, the state of dignity, elevation, and honor. The worshippers standing in row reveal the profound meaning of unification in front of God Almighty: Standing in His Presence, equalized as one body of brotherhood, leaving the world behind represent an allegory of the day of the Resurrection. This also explains our blessed master's answer that the posture of *qiyam* is crucial as it gives the worshiping believers the opportunity to train themselves to get ready to face the Last Hour, to face Allah's tribunal. Rumi comments: "*The spirit of all knowledge is only this; to know who you will be at the day of Resurrection.*" In that sense, *qiyam* represents one of the most active help for believers on their hard voyage towards the truth. Standing in the Divine Presence of the Lord, the worshippers train themselves to reach the state of readiness to face the Day of Resurrection, namely to face *Day of Qiyam* with *qiyam*. The true *qiyam* means coming back to live after death, symbolizing the resurrection in the truth, illuminated with the Divine light. The noble Prophet said concerning the posture of *qiyam*: "*Straighten up, so that Allah may have mercy upon you*", referring to the uprightness of character, sincerity, determination, devotion, and honesty. In order to be resurrected in the truth, the believer's selfhood has to be crushed, has to be negated. Like in the first pillar of Islam, the *Shahadah*, half is denial of the truth and half is affirmation of the truth. Ibn Arabi comments about the blessing the worshippers receive standing in the Divine Presence in the posture of the *qiyam*: "*The Most High has called you for intimate talk with you. The most Munificent has called you to pour out His gifts upon you. Be then humble and poor. Raise your hands in recitation of the takbir each time that you lower yourself or that you stand up again and throw behind yourself what has been given to you in each theophany... Place in your purse what you have received and claim another gift and a greater light still, for it does not cease to shine. Divine effusion perpetually emanates from the spring of His generosity. Welcome it in that indefeasible indigence of being that remains attached to you when you contemplate Him. He does not cease to give, nor you to amass. He does not stop elevating Himself, nor you lowering yourself.*" Ibn Arabi gives a further interpretation of *qiyam*: "*Those who begin the Prayer by putting on the mantle of Grandeur, and then taking it partially off.*" In a Divine hadith Allah says: "*Grandeur is My mantle and magnificence is My loincloth.*" Furthermore, in the vertical position of *qiyam*, the worshipper symbolically assumes the function of a vicegerent. Ibn Arabi explains further: "*The mantle is the perfect servant (al-abd al-kamil) created in the character (of God), who unites in his person contingent realities and Divine realities.*" Michel Chodkiewicz interprets Ibn Arabi's thought: "*The perfect man (al-insan al-kamil) is the perfect servant, he whose function of place holding (khilafa) is legitimate and who effectively assumes the grandeur of God in his qiyam, whereas with most men, this position is a mere appearance. He is the 'mantle of God' for God is hidden in him, covered by him as by a mantle, but he never loses sight of his servanthood. If God is as 'annihilated in him,' he is himself obliterated in God. The 'mantle of grandeur,' which is thus borrowed, must ultimately be given back so that the memory of his ontological indigence is not lost. This is the reason for the bow, 'ruku,' in which the human stature is diminished by half.*"

Another important reason for the profound meaning of *qiyam* might be the obligatory recitation of the verses of the Holy Qur'an after the Surah Al-Fatiha. In the month of Ramadan, during the *Tarawih* Prayers, our blessed master used to recite several pages of the Qur'an after each of the recitation of the Fatiha. The value and significance of *qiyam* is infinite. First and most of all it is the expression of one's servanthood to one's Lord of all the worlds. Showing utmost concentration, complete submission, joyful obedience, comprehensive thankfulness, loving fearfulness, utter humility during the posture of *qiyam*, the worshipper will earn true success.

The horizontal posture, bowing, *ruku*, signifies the expression of the noble feature of *taqwa*, complete sincerity. It means leaning towards Allah the Almighty to the exclusion of everything else. All what is not for the sake of God must be erased in one's heart. Bowing the head towards the Almighty signifies loving surrender, an expression of utter humility and the recognition of His Supreme Lordship. Chodkiewicz analyzes Ibn Arabi's thought: *"The upper part of the body, which is cloaked in the mantle, is effaced as it becomes horizontal. The bow, ruku, signifies the intermediate state, the renunciation of all sovereignty, of all claim of autonomy. Bowing where only the upper part of the body is bent, is a barzakh, an intermediate spot between heaven and earth. It shows the double nature of man where the superior realities and the inferior realities are joined."*

After *ruku*, the worshipper will rise up to the human state of uprightness again reciting: *"Sami'allahu liman hamidah—Allah hears those who praise and thank Him."* According to a Divine *hadith*, it is God who pronounces the words through the mouth of the servant, that is to say, the worshipper speaks in the Name of God. The angels respond: *"Rabbana lakal hamd—Our Lord, all praise and thanks are due to you."* This vertical posture prepares the worshipper perfectly for the third movement, the glorious posture of the *sujud*, the prostration, signifying the desired union of a servant with his Lord of Majesty and Bounty. From the vertical, elevated human state, the worshipper lowers himself to *"the lowest of the low"* (at-Tin 95:5). It is like a fall to the earth of the slave in the hands of its Owner, it is the worshipper's vow of absolute servanthood. As for *qiyam*, the value and significance of the *sujud*, prostration, is infinite because it represents self-annihilation of the worshipper into the Worshipped, his complete deliverance unto Him. The ritual posture of the prostration carries the quality of loving submission and intimacy of a slave with his Owner. This is precisely the nature of Prophet Muhammad, peace and blessings be upon him. For this reason, the blessed master was made to love Prayer after perfume and women. When he delivered himself towards his beloved Lord in prostration after pronouncing three times the glory to his Lord, he used sometimes to make the following supplication: *"Put a light in my heart, a light in my ear, a light in my eye, a light on my right, a light on my left, a light before me, a light behind me, a light above me, a light under me, give me a light and make me light."* All worshipping rituals are a sign of submission to the All-Merciful. Complete submission is symbolized through the prostration, the whole self, body, mind, heart and spirit is delivered into the hands of the Beloved. During the prostration, *sujud,* one puts one's head on the ground; it is as if one is swallowed by the earth, disappearing into its womb, where the human free will is extinguished in Divine Will. About the prostration Ibn Arabi comments: *"The face (of the one who prays) does not persist in its prostration, but rather raises itself up again, for neither does the qibla before which it prostates itself persist... but the heart never raises itself in this manner, for its qibla is its Lord and its Lord remains forever."* A Divine *hadith*: *"He who comes closer to me by a hands length, I come closer to him by a forearm's length."* The Holy Qur'an states: *"prostrate and draw near (to God)"* (al-Alaq 96:19). Ibn Arabi refers to the Qur'anic verse: *"It is His name, Al-Qarib, 'He Who is close', which has called you to proximity. You are the lover and not the beloved, which is why He says: prostrate yourself and come closer. Know that in your prostration you are preserved (ma'sum) from Satan, for your prostration subjugates him and he has no power over you. When he observes you in this state, he thinks only of himself and his own refusal to prostrate himself before Adam as God had commanded; consumed by the fire in the citadel of his punishment, seeing you obedient and contemplating the fate that awaits him the day when the Hour of Judgment comes... May God grant that we be, you and I, among those who have prostrated themselves and who have found."*

In another passage concerning the prostration Ibn Arabi says: *"The body prostrates itself toward the earth from which it is made, the spirit before the universal Spirit from which it proceeds, the secret before its Lord." "The second thing that the person says in the prostration (after the pronunciation of ritual phrase; glory to my Lord) is; make me light, that is, make me You. Take me away from myself, and Be my being, then will my eye see everything through You."*

After this sublime experience of self-deliverance, annihilation in God, the believer comes to a sitting position, *julus,* on his knees, which is again charged with highest symbolic meanings. The worshipper is reestablished in eternity, settling himself into God, *baqabillah.* He will be able to experience subsistence within subsistence. *Julus* symbolizes the complete separation from the world, the sacred state of "die before dying." *Julus* is perfect servanthood, the pure presence in God with no trace of duality. Ibn Arabi comments: *"You have reached the degree of 'istiwa'—the state of perfect equilibrium—and you have freed yourself from the power of heaven and earth."* The Qur'an states: *"Everything is perishable (and so perishing) except His 'Face' (His eternal Self, and what is done in seeking His good pleasure). His alone is judgment and authority, and to Him you are being brought back"* (al-Qasas 28:88); *"In whatever direction you turn, there is the 'Face' of God."* (al-Baqarah 2:115). What the worshipper recites in this precious moment is the greeting ceremony of our blessed master to his beloved Lord on the night of the ascension after having travelled through Allah's Kingdom. It is the final stage of Prayer, where the worshipper reaches his climax, his absolute spiritual fulfillment because the worshipper celebrates his arrival in Allah's holy Presence as our blessed master at the night of the ascension pronouncing the affirmation of Divine Oneness and the testimony of faith with all the angels. Ibn Arabi comments: *"Then greet, with a salutation which comes from God, yourself and all the beings of your species, for salam (the greeting, but also Peace, one of the Divine Names) is your Lord and the degree of the name As-Salam is the place of your theophany (at this specific moment). Finally, affirm the unicity of the One and deny that there are equals to him (an allusion to the words of the Shahadah at the end of tashahhud). And then you will need to disappear, for it is in this disappearance that you will obtain what you desired."* After this sacred conversation with the Exalted One, the worshipper sends salutations to Prophet Abraham and Prophet Muhammad, peace and blessings be upon them, which fills his heart with love.

After *julus, Salah* ends. The worshipper turns his head toward the right and to the left where he gives on both sides the greeting of peace: *as-salamu alaykum.* Ibn Arabi comments on the higher and lower meaning: *"In Prayer, there are two categories of Muslims and thus two ways of performing Prayer. Those who unite the one with the other are joining the spiritual realities that correspond to each. The higher of these categories is that of the worshipper who says salam because he has passed (at the moment he comes out of Prayer) from the authority of one name to the authority of another. He is thus greeting the one he is leaving and the one to which he is arriving... The lesser category is that of the worshipper who greets the All-Merciful because he is leaving Him, and the creatures because he is returning toward them... As for those who belong to neither of these two categories, their salam is worthless. They were not near God, and their greeting is thus not the greeting of one who is departing. They never left the creatures, and thus their greeting is not the greeting of one newly arrived."*

Ali ibn Abu Talib reported that our blessed master used to utter the following supplications during the ritual postures: "*And when he assumed the ruku, he would say; 'O my Lord, for You I have bowed down and in You I have placed my faith, and to You I have committed myself. My ears, my eyes, my bones have humbled themselves before You.' When he raised his head from ruku position he would say; 'May Allah listen to those who praise Him. Our Lord, may Your praises fill the heavens, and fill the earth, and fill everything between them, and fill whatever else remains to be filled after that.' When he assumed the sajdah position he would say; 'Our Lord, for You I have made sajdah, and in You I have placed my faith, and to You I have committed myself. My face lies prostrated before the One Who created it, and fashioned it, and opened within it its sense of hearing and its sight. Blessed be Allah, the Best of Creators.'*"

To conclude, this most exalted Prayer ritual, *Salah*, offers the worshippers the pleasure of tasting and experiencing the Divine realities within themselves. With the performance of *qiyam*, the devotees train themselves to get prepared for the *Qiyam*, the day of Resurrection, the Day of Judgment. With *ruku*, they train themselves to get ready for *taqwa*, namely, to lean towards Allah with the exclusion of everything else. With *sajdah*, the prostration, they train themselves to get ready for self-annihilation, self-extinction, and self-sacrifice. With the sitting posture *julus*, they train themselves to get ready to communicate with Allah, in proximity with Allah. With the Fatiha, they prepare themselves for the opening of the sacred awareness. With the *salawat*, salutations and benedictions on the Prophet, they soften their hearts in order to get ready to receive Divine beauty and love. With the *Shahadah* they train themselves to get ready for the strengthening of their faith; they get ready to arrive at certainty of belief.

Reflections on the Ritual Prayer

Nowhere else than in the ritual Prayer, performing in congregation is highly recommended. The believers are able to experience five times a day the equality of race, status, color, and wealth. Praying believers share true brotherhood. Standing in row in *qiyam* reveals the profound meaning of unification in front of God Almighty. Our blessed master gives us the following advice: "*The religion of Islam needs its members to congregate and gather together as a source of strength. The need for congregation on the part of Islam is even greater than the need for it on the part of the believers for the sake of spiritual reward. The reward for Prayer performed in congregation is 25 degrees greater than the merit of Prayer performed on one's own.*"

A very important fact we are obliged to reflect on is the *dua* after *Salah*. The Holy Qur'an states: "*When you are free (from one task), resume (another task), and seek and strive to please your Lord*" (al-Inshirah 94:7–8). Abdul Qadir al-Jilani interprets: "*As soon as you have finished performing the ritual act of worship, you must set to work on Prayer of supplication, dua. You must wish that for which Allah has at His disposal, and beseech Him to grant it.*" The noble Prophet says: "*As soon as the Prayer leader, 'imam' is standing at his niche and the ranks of the congregation are properly aligned, the merciful blessing of Allah will descend upon the assembled worshippers. An angel will then call out: 'So and so has gained a benefit, and so and so has suffered a loss!' The beneficiary will be anyone who lifts up his hands in offering the supplication to Allah, as soon he has finished performing his prescribed ritual Prayer. The looser will be anyone who leaves the mosque without having offered a supplication. If someone does leave without having offered a Prayer of supplication, the angels will say: 'O So and so, how can you manage without Allah? Do you have no need of anything that Allah has at His disposal?'*"

Muhyiddin ibn Arabi gives us the following suggestions for *Salah*: "*After you perform your Morning Prayer, stay with your Lord until sunrise, and after your Afternoon Prayer stay in His Presence until sunset. These are two periods of time when spiritual powers and enlightenment flow in abundance. There is great virtue and merit in performing extra worship of twenty cycles of Prayer between the Afternoon and Evening Prayers and between the Evening and Night Prayers.*" He goes on in his precious discourses as: "*Do not sleep until you are unable to stay awake. Do not eat until you are hungry. Dress only to cover your body and to protect it from cold and from heat.*"

Having completed the ritual Prayer, the channels to the All-Merciful will open and pure love will seize from Him to the servant. The supplication, *dua*, represents the precious moment in the audition with one's Creator as His creatures, because that moment is the perfect opportunity to converse in tearful regret, burning longing, fearful sincerity, and utter humility. Offering oneself with sincerity within *dua*, the Lord of Majesty and Bounty will give the permission to enter into the circle of His irresistible power of attraction. The Almighty is waiting for His servants to plead with Him and He will respond in loving friendship and embracing. The *dua* after *Salah* represents therefore a sort of climax of the ritual Prayer. At the same time, supplicating to one's Lord gives the opportunity to straighten out, complete, balance out, compensate, correct, and equalize the human insufficiencies, mistakes, heedlessness, forgetfulness, sinning, lowness, and imperfections. Especially heedlessness and absentmindedness can be straightened out by one's supplication to one's beloved Lord. It is absolutely crucial for the worshipping believers to turn wholeheartedly to Him, ask only from Him, plead only with Him and most important, ask for forgiveness from Him. God willing, the guilt for one's mistakes, failures and sins will help to compensate our insufficiencies, human irresponsibility, and our lack of service. In doing so, believers will take refuge in Him with all their worries, fears, longings, and needs, and will realize the center verse of the Fatiha, representing a state of abandonment of free will, a complete recognition of one's servanthood to one's Lord: "*Iyyaka nabudu wa iyyaka nastain—We only seek You, serve You and we ask all we need from You.*" As our noble master says that he who prays enters the Divine Mercy and is granted forgiveness, so will the ones who supplicate unceasingly most likely receive forgiveness and Divine blessings. In short, *dua* gives the opportunity to straighten out and strengthen our relationship with our Creator of Majesty and Bounty.

If we wish to increase the capacity and perfect ourselves in the performance of the ritual Prayer, we are given the opportunity with the month of Ramadan. The *Tarawih* Prayer combined with the *Tahajjud* Prayer in

the last ten days of the fasting month, will increase our sacred awareness, deepen our love, and heighten our illumination for this most holy
ritual. Every day, the fasting believers are praying *Salah* for five to six
hours standing in the Presence of the Almighty. To undergo these profound spiritual experiences during 30 days of the fasting month of Ramadan, will make a complete difference for the Muslims community. These
long night Prayers bring the believer closer together. The countless cycles
of the ritual Prayer turn millions of believers in one body of unified brotherhood and sisterhood. Additionally, in every night, after the performance
of the *Tahajjud* Prayer, there is a communal supplication made during
the last 10 days of Ramadan. This indescribable experience represents the
peak of fulfillment for the fasting believers. All this millions of souls melt
together in total want and longing. Naked, stripped off of the worldly,
and torn down the veils from the profound experiences of fasting, the souls
become pure, pleading for their Lord. After each supplication of the imam,
thousands of voices share together the chorus of *amin.* This is the experience of the fact, *"The believers are a single soul."* This is the experience
being together with the Supreme Creator in the realms of the souls, *Qalu
bala[1].* With these long-lasting supplications, the believers share their
longing and their need for the truth. They share the thirst of their souls
for the One and Only. They share the longing for the unique beauty of
the most beloved of Allah, Muhammad Mustafa, peace and blessings be
upon him. They share the greatest pain, the pain of separation from their
beloved Lord. Where in the world can we witness such a picture where
thousands of people shedding streams of tears, people of maturity crying like little infants in the same time?

Every essential spiritual event in one year of the Islamic calendar,
every celebration, festivity, birth, death, the night of power, the night of
absolution, the night of the heavenly ascension, the night of the Prophet's birth, is connected with the ritual Prayer. The rituals throughout one
Islamic year are sanctified by the prescribed Prayer. *Salah* is always the
central event of all worship rituals, such as the congregational Friday
Prayer, the *Eid* Prayers, the Funeral Prayer, the *Tarawih* Prayer, the
Tahajjud Prayer, the *Tasbih* Prayer, the Prayer after the circumambula-

---

[1] *Qalu bala* (They said, "Yes"); the primordial covenant; the event (mentioned in the
Qur'an, 33:172) describing the human profession of God's Lordship in spirit or
conscience, or in a dimension of existence unknown to us with its exact nature.

tion of the Ka'ba, and all the voluntary Prayers in the special nights of Islamic celebrations. Furthermore, in all situations in a Muslim life, the performance of two units of Prayer are highly recommended; when one is angry, when one is thankful, when one experiences profound sadness, when one is absentminded, when one is highly pleased, when one took the ritual ablution, when one is heedless, when one enters a room as guest, one visits a mosque, or when one is visiting a grave. In other words, one sanctifies and blesses the different situations of one's life and in various religious events with two units of Prayer. This demonstrates an important fact in the religion of Islam, when believers celebrate Islamic festivals, when they bury the dead, when they complete the month of Ramadan, when believers celebrate a festival, they do not dance, play music, clap their hands, or eat and drink a lot. They celebrate important spiritual events with an increase of Divine remembrance and intensified worship, because the Divine power of the ritual Prayer allows one to comprehend the spirit of the specific rituals one celebrates. Therefore the Divine blessings of these specific nights of celebration are multiplied and inexhaustible. This is what God pleases most: We turn to Him in the most precious sacred moments of our lives. Do we not celebrate the festivals with the One Who brought them to us to enrich and elevate our lives? Do we not wish to share these blissful moments with our Beloved? Do we not want to spend time in the Presence of the One Who brought these precious nights and festivals to us? For example, the most valuable hour of the week, the Friday Congregation, called the Prince of Days, *sayyid al-ayyam*, signifies the peak of celebration for the believers; it is the perfect proof of God's infinite mercy raining over His congregation. When the worshippers complete the ceremony with the two units, they are able to get a sacred taste of these precious sacred moments; they are able to take a share from the treasuries of light from the heavens. Another example, with the performance of the *Tarawih* Prayers every night of the fasting month, worshippers are able to experience the soul of Ramadan and become able, if God wills, to breathe the light of the Divine revelations. What is the mystery to be able to live the fullness and richness of these events of Islamic celebrations? Allah endows certain months, days, nights, and hours with a special excellence. He opens the doors of the heavens at these sacred moments and therefore Divine blessings and mercy are overflowing. In order for the worshipping congregation to catch the spirit and to become part of Allah's Divine bounties and grace, they must enter the ritual Prayer at these very specific times where the door of the heavens are wide open and receive infinite heavenly nourishment.

The ritual Prayer is surrounded, accompanied, and furnished with all and everything a religious practitioner needs to perfect his spirituality, namely, the ritual ablution, listening to call of Prayer, reciting the Fatiha, and reciting the verses of the Qur'an during *qiyam*, reciting the benedictions of the Prophet. If we omit *Salah*, we lose the prostration, *sujud*, we lose the salutation on the Messenger, *salawat*, we lose the prayer of glorification (*tasbih*), and we will be deprived of the personal supplications, *dua*. When we neglect *Salah*, we lose the light of our spirit, we lose cleanliness, we lose freshness, vitalization, renewal, strength, we lose the spiritual ascension of our spirit, we lose eternal salvation, we lose spiritual healing, we lose the light of the Holy Attributes, we lose eternal happiness, we lose the highest *muhabbat*, love and affection, we lose the sweet breath of the Hereafter, and we lose the grace and blessings of eternal conversation with the Exalted One.

Performing the True Prayer

The Holy Qur'an states: "*Those who are constant in their Prayer*" (al-Ma'arij 70:23).

Rumi says: "*Thus the jurisprudent explain the form of the ritual Prayer: You begin it with 'God is greatest' and you end it with 'Peace be upon you.' But the Sufi explains the spirit of the Prayer: The ritual Prayer is union with God such that none knows him who performs it but God Himself. The precondition for the form of the Prayer is purification with water. But the precondition for the Prayer's spirit is that you turn your eyes and heart into blood for forty years through the spiritual combat of the jihad, and that you pass beyond seventy veils of darkness and come alive through the Life and Existence of God.*

"*You say; Night and day I perform the ritual Prayer. How is it, O brother, that your words themselves are not a ritual Prayer?*"

Prayer is internal: 'There is no Prayer without the presence of the heart,' as the Prophet said. However, you must necessarily perform it in external form, with physical bowing and prostration. Only then you gain full benefit and reach the goal. 'Those who are constant in their Prayer' (al-Ma'arij 70:23). This is the Prayer of the spirit. Prayer of the external form is tem-

porary; it is not everlasting because the spirit of this world is an endless ocean. The body is the shore and dry land, which is limited and finite. Therefore, everlasting Prayer belongs only to the spirit. The spirit does indeed have a bow and prostration; however, bowing and prostrating must be manifested in external form because there is a connection between substance and form. So long as the two do not coincide there is no benefit. As for your claim that form is secondary to substance, that form is the subject, and the heart is king; these are relative terms" (Fihi ma Fihi, 38).

There are two kinds of worshippers; the ones who are unaware of what they are doing during their Prayer, that is to say, they do not know the significance of the ritual. The performance of their Prayer is mechanical, dry, and lifeless. There are the ones of whom our spiritual master commented: "*He who truly prays is certainly an imam, because there are angels praying behind him.*" Junayd al-Bagdadi said: "*The color of the water is the color of the cup that contains it.*" The truth accords with the state in which one finds oneself. The Lord appears in accordance with our need for Him, with our knowledge of Him, with our submission towards Him, with our longing for Him, and with our awareness of Him. The Exalted One says, "*I am according to how my servants think of Me*" (Divine *hadith*). A verse from the Holy Qur'an: "*There is nothing that does not glorify Him with His praise (proclaiming that He alone is God, without peer or partner, and all praise belongs to Him exclusively), but you cannot comprehend their glorification*" (al-Isra 27:44). Each mineral, vegetable, and animal, in its own way, worships its Creator more than men do, for none has a will of its own. But the human being, the most elevated and valuable creation of the Almighty, is given the gift of free will along with the gift of knowledge of all the Divine Names and Attributes. Therefore he is tested by his ability to choose. This is his honor, and in the same time, his danger. He can raise himself towards the heights of the realms of Allah's proximity or he can fall to the lowest of the low, which indicates the degree below the animals. If we try to understand Allah's words to us: "*I am as My servant thinks of Me; I confirm Myself to the opinion the servant has of Me,*" we might show much more effort to reach a state of clarity of vision and purity of being which will enable us to pray the true Prayer. The All-Merciful tells us: "*Woe to those worshippers (denying the Judgment), who are unmindful in their Prayers, who want to be seen and noted (for their acts of worship)*" (al-Maun 107:4–6).

During his performance of *Salah,* how can a worshipper realize the ascension of his spirit? The secret is that we have to be transported by the love we feel for the All-Merciful and the love we feel for the one who brought the *Sharia,* the canon law of Islam to humanity, Prophet Muhammad, peace and blessings be upon him. It is our irresistible wish, need and love for the Divine that becomes the leading force while praying. For all worship activities, especially the ritual Prayer, the ultimate wisdom lies in the fact that the worshipper has to enter the Prayer with need. Need is the answer to resolve the relationship with our Lord of all the worlds. It is the need for sacred awareness, for intimate conversation, for oneness, for unity, for embracement, love and affection, which is nothing else than the need for the truth. We have to show heightened love for the one who brought this greatest of all Prayers to us. The more we love our blessed master, the more we try to imitate his noble behavior, the more we listen and learn from him, to the degree we try to resemble him, the more the quality of the performance of the ritual Prayer will be increased. There is a direct relationship of the ritual Prayer to the glory of the universe himself. Due to his inner treasury of goodness, which is symbolized by his noble character, the peak of spiritual fulfillment of the ascension was given to humanity. Thus, abundant love for our blessed master will nourish the inner treasury of *Salah.* To the extent we show sincere efforts to enter his heart, to the same extent its performance will be beautified and revived. How much we try to become the dust in his footsteps in following him, to the same extent a truthful prostration will be granted. As much as we share the sorrow and sacred concern of our blessed master, as much we cry for him and with him, as much as we tremble for him and with him, to the same extent we might be favored to smell the sweet scent of the All-Merciful's nearness during the performance of *Salah.* We have to prove our love to him as he gave up all he has for us! True love is shown in trying to follow his example, trying to resemble him in all our thoughts, feelings, behaviors, and actions. His concern should become our concern, so we will share his tears, his sadness, and his joy. All of the wonderful qualities the Messenger of God possesses are within us. Through sincerely loving him, yearning for his beauty, we have the possibility to get closer to his supreme degree of existence. Our most sincere intention should be to imitate his noble character, to adopt his fine qualities, his perfect behavior. When we are able to reach some beauty of character, some light of wisdom, it will be like a spotless mirror in which the eternal light of Allah shines at us.

Most believers cannot take advantage of the spiritual treasury of the ascension during the performance of *Salah*. A Divine condition has to be fulfilled in order to become worthy of the exalted experience of the *miraj*, namely, we need to clean our inner self from greed, envy, arrogance, ambition, laziness, and ignorance. Allah the Almighty does not allow the idol worshippers, liars, the insincere, the hypocrites, the ambitious, and the heedless ones to enter into His Divine Presence. The Paradise of intimacy cannot be experienced with a heart filled with idols and filled with the trash of the world. In order to reach proximity with the Majestic One during Prayer, the believers' hearts must be cleaned, with their tears of regret, from distortion, falseness, hypocrisy, sins, idols, and the low desires of the flesh. In order to experience a spiritual ascension, God's gift of the heavenly ascension must be returned by our "giftlessness." The giftlessness to our Lord means to offer ourselves to Him in complete poverty and nothingness, unconditionally offer all that we have and are, and the offer must be sincere.

Thus *Salah* is designed to reach the ultimate station of self-annihilation. This is why according to a *hadith*, the ritual Prayer is called; the ascension of the believer, *miraj al-mu'min*. In that sense, the *miraj* carries a contradiction; the worshipper's gradual extinction generates in the same time his elevation: He is raised by God as he lowers himself. This paradoxical nature of the *miraj* is described by Muhyiddin ibn Arabi: "*At the end of this miraj, the ascension, man is reduced to the indestructible Divine secret which was lodged in him at the beginning of time by the breath of the Spirit breathed into Adam's clay. Then the even and odd come together, He is and you are not. He sees Himself through Himself.*" Thus within the performance of *Salah* the worshipper will be totally overwhelmed by his Beloved up to his own annihilation in Him. He gets consumed by the love he feels for Him and by the Almighty's love for him. He loses his will in the Will of the One he worships. This is true worship. Only Allah is left in the heart of the worshipper. The ultimate fulfillment is reached when the worshipper has attained the secret vision of "*the light of my eyes.*" This sacred state is described in a tradition of our noble master: "*If you are not, you see Him.*" Truthful worship is achieved where the worshipper is absent, leaving all place to God. Where true love resides, all creation dissolves. Nothing can compare with the sacred taste, the spiritual pleasure of dwelling in His Nearness. This explains that neither in his daily life, nor in any other form of worship, but during the performance of the ritual Prayer, our blessed master experienced the highest delight of which he commented: *"The freshness of my eyes is given to me in Prayer."* With this tender loving statement of adoration, our blessed master reveals to the followers of his community, what beauty and great joy he found while praying. In Arabic the expression 'the freshness' meaning 'the coolness' of my eyes, signifies intense pleasure.

Only poverty allows nearness to our beloved Lord. On that blessed night, the Almighty had the following conversation with His beloved. He asked His Prophet: *"My beloved, what did you bring from amongst your community?"* Our noble master replied: *"O my Lord, I brought something that You do not have."* God said: *"O My beloved, what do I not have?"* Our master replied: *"O my Lord, the only thing that You do not have is poverty. This is what I have brought to You."*

The ritual Prayer can only be truly performed if we reach the state of selflessness. Only through freeing ourselves from worldly attachments, we will become an empty receptacle for Allah's gentleness and mercy. If not a single particle of the world remains, Allah will rush towards us and give us His Nearness. He will close us with the robe of sainthood, His most beautiful Names and Attributes. Rumi comments: *"What is the miraj of the heavens? Non-existence... The religion and creed of the lovers is non-existence. As long as you have not died and become living through Him, you are a rebel seeking a realm for your copartnership with God. Kill your cow of your ego as soon as you can, so that your hidden spirit may come to life and awareness! I have been so naught in Your Love's existence that my nonexistence is thousand times sweeter than my existence. What sort of Beloved is He? As long as a single hair of love for yourself remains, He will not show His Face. You will be unworthy of union with Him and He will give you no access. You must be completely repelled by yourself and the world and be your own self's enemy, or else the Friend will not show His Countenance. So when our religion resides in a person's heart, it stays right there until it takes his heart to God and separates it from everything unworthy."*

Allah the Exalted exclaims: *"My servant, if you wish to enter the sanctuary of My intimacy, do not pay attention either to this world or to the higher world of the angels, not even to the higher realms where you may receive My Divine Attributes."*

The true Prayer is the Prayer of the heart, where the material self is combined with the spiritual self. Especially with the ritual ablution, we can learn about the external aspect linked to the inner reality, the total ablution. The outer cleanliness is merely the washing of the face, arms, head, ears, neck and feet. The inner ablution is cleaning oneself from the filth of the world, one's inner being, one's imperfections, and one's heedlessness. It means purifying oneself of the egotistical attributes of hate, envy, hypocrisy, worldly ambition, stinginess, arrogance, etc. When the worshipper puts utmost attention to the required time, the intention, the *takbir*, the *qibla*, the prerequisites before entering the Prayer, he can arrive at the place of spacelessness and timelessness, facing the eternal direction, witnessing the eternal beauty of his beloved Lord.

The secret is to go beyond. Only then we will hear the unheard and see the unseen. Only then we will be able to hear the angels' wings flattering, see the angels' smiles, hear the sound of footsteps in Paradise, and hear the angels' writing. Our blessed master, at the night of the ascension, is reported as having said: "*This night I was raised to the heavens. I reached such a level that I could hear the squeaking sounds of pen's writing.*" Our beloved master was raised to such heights, that he could hear the squeaking sounds of the Pen of Power, writing the destiny of the universe.

We have to be aware that when we pray this universal Prayer, *Salah*, it is ourselves who give space to it; it is ourselves who give time to it, and it is ourselves who give life to it. It is ourselves who evaluate its worth or lower its worth. Let's never forget that we are the performers. We have to be to the greatest degree thoughtful, alert, and attentive. In this most excellent of all rituals, we approached nearest to the Divine, and experience the most precious moments in the Presence of our Lord of Majesty and Bounty, the treasury of the moment in the Presence of the King. We have to contemplate the meaning of the Divine verses recited, give time in order to open the horizon of sacred awareness, give Divine efforts to expand our breast and breathe into the furthest corners of our being. Allah has given us eyes, ears, tongue, and mind. In the ritual Prayers, the senses have to be used on high gear, to their fullest capacity. Only a wholehearted concentration will bring us to the Eternal Presence. The highest Divine rewards are given to those servants who worship neither because of their longing for Paradise nor from fear of Hell. They worship purely for His sake. All what they do, they do it for His sake. They will enter Paradise and will receive the greatest honor conveyed by the Lord of Bounty and Majesty, an unrestricted view of His Beauty.

Having received the honor to belong to the Prophet's community, the five pillars of the *Sharia* are given from the All-Merciful without having paid any price. Thus we received the heavenly gift of ascension, we received infinite illumination, and we received the Divine revelations of the Holy Qur'an, without having showed any human efforts. Therefore we have to ask ourselves, what did we do to deserve this greatest of all Prayer, *Salah*? What did we do to earn the honor of the spiritual ascension? What are our efforts? How did we earn the privilege of the pilgrimage and the glorious month of Ramadan, which is the month of light? It is absolutely crucial for believers to show some efforts, to show some love in their devotion, to show some pleasure of faith, to show some gratitude. The sincere followers from the community of Muhammad should draw utmost inspiration, heightened sensation of faith, deepest gratitude, and love of submission in the performance of *Salah*. They must realize that if they lead a life of stagnation and boredom, completely disinterested for the Divine realities, it is impossible for them to travel and move forwards. Forget about travelling upwards, the vertical ascent, the *miraj*, one cannot advance even one step ahead, horizontally, if one carries heavy loads of worldly goods. To walk on the path of truth, we cannot afford to be blind and deaf. We cannot overfill the stomach when others are starving from hunger and thirst. We cannot celebrate gossip. We cannot live with a constant repetition of ruthless greed. Rumi says: *"Your boredom and indigestion is from lack of hunger, not from the repetition of words."* People prefer to walk around dead, when they could fly around in the heavens of Divine bliss. People prefer their own pain, when the keys of Paradise of eternal happiness have been given to them. People prefer to stay in boredom and baseness, when they are offered the heavenly ascension in this earthly life. The thickness of the head, the narrowness of the heart is the problem. People are full of self-importance, whereas our biggest treasure is pure modesty and nothingness. This means, we fail to sincerely believe, we fail to see the hidden treasure; in other words, we lack humanity.

We do either experience frustration, sufferance, distress, or we are residing in the Presence of the Lord of all the worlds. Islam is the sacred awareness of the Lord of all the worlds and the experience of the infinite goodness of the mercy for all the worlds. Allah the Almighty did not bring any sufferance or punishment to humanity. In the contrary, He brought the religion of Islam to remove all human sufferance and calamities. Whatever rule, condition, law, principle Allah the Almighty brought for humanity is for the sole purpose of preventing human sufferance. Our noble master was trying to take people out of Hell, but they threw stones at him.

The night of the ascension is the night of the good news, the infinite bounties and favors from our Lord of Majesty and Bounty. It is the night of the good news of eternal happiness for the community of Muhammad. To conclude, what is the ascension? To reach, in one breath, the realms beyond corporal existence with the help of Buraq, the heavenly mount of love, and the wings of sacred intelligence of the Archangel Gabriel.

For all believers of Divine unity, the Masjid al-Aqsa represents the place where the noble Prophet ascended on his heavenly journey, the *miraj*. The religion of Islam carries the Paradise of intimacy of the supreme love discourse, the highest intimacy with God, the ascension, the *miraj*. The worshipper experiences the reality of the conversation with the Everlasting, *Al-Baqi*, the Eternal One where he witnesses the Divine Beauty of God. He experiences the blessed delight of our blessed master who exclaimed: "*The freshness of the eyes is given to me during Salah.*" After the Ka'ba, Allah's house in Mecca, and the Masjid an-Nabawi, the Prophet's mosque in Medina, the most sacred place is the Masjid al-Aqsa.

The real Ka'ba is not in Mecca, it is the human heart. The Almighty proclaims: "*I do not fit in the whole universe, but I fit into the heart of man.*" When we look at the believers, living in the present modern societies, we can observe that some hearts are occupied by evil, diabolic forces, false gods, idols, hypocrisy, backbiting, greed, and spiritual sicknesses. Instead of jewels of character to prevail and reside in their hearts, instead of making room and clean the heart of its spiritual sicknesses so that the Majestic One can become their Guest, we can observe that the most precious and valuable creation of man, the heart, has become invaded and occupied by dark, evil forces. When the Ka'ba of the heart is occupied with the trash and dust of the world and therefore remaining in the darkness of unconsciousness, the believers cannot experience elevation, excellence and ascend with their souls to the realm of God's nearness, the *miraj*.

Supplications

"O Lord, let us pray Salah before Salah is prayed over us. Let's shed tears before it is too late and we will shed tears of regret at the Day of Resurrection!

O Lord, smash the cage of self-existence, deliver us from the day to day concerns of worldly thoughts, worldly desires, worldly activities, and worldly occupation. Deliver us from the suffering of self-centeredness. Bring us to rest, to peace and tranquility. How I wish to let go of myself, to deliver myself, give everything away what belongs to myself, forget myself while praying, make myself dead in supplication! I wish to get a rest of myself and just listen to the silence of the heart's speech. The only time a feel comforted and peaceful in myself is the moment of prostration. At this very moment all movement ends, the world stays still, the universe closes his mantel over me, I arrived at the bay of His tender care and loving protection.

How much my heart wishes to say amin! I am burning with all the limbs of my body, with all my senses, with all my cells of my being to join the Divine chorus of angels; amin! How much I wish to be part of the river of tears of amin sayers. The heat of my wish breaks my heart into thousands of pieces. I am dying, I am only longing. It is the eternal secret, the soul, which woke up to the eternal life hearing the sweet sound of its original home, the covenant of the Alast, because it joined the heavenly chorus of uncountable other souls saying amin! Yes indeed you are my Lord! I feel that my own tears are crying out and shedding tears of longing to be with the tears of other amin sayers. It is the soul, the eternal secret of our Lord, longing for itself!

The meaning of the Prayer niche, the mihrab is to direct ourselves to what we love. The qibla of the unbeliever is a full table of food, the qibla of the lover is You! We wish that You become our sole concern, our sole love, our sole comfort, our sole direction. O Lord, make us to be lovers of the mihrab! We wish not only to love You in words and supplication, we wish to express our love in directing ourselves to Your holy house the Ka'ba, and increase our longing, our heat, our desire for the performance of the most glorious of all Prayers, Salah. We wish to arrive at the place where we wait impatiently with burning longing for the next performance of Salah, the eternal rendezvous with You.

How can we gain understanding of qiyam, ruku and prostration? How can we dive into the ocean of their secret treasury? If we are not freed from the restrictions of transient life, how can we taste self-annihilation within prostration, how can we feel fear and love for You during qiyam, how can we bow our head towards You during ruku and excluding every-thing else? First, before anything else, before we become worthy to receive Your help, before we become worthy to receive Your guidance, before we become worthy to wish and plead from You, we have to ask ourselves; where is our need for the Divine realms of everlastingness? Where is our need for the sacred taste, where is our need to become earth, to get extinguished, to crush our selfhood? Where is our need to get lost in the ocean of Your mercy? Where is our affection for You, our intense yearning for You? O our Lord, You do not bestow anything without need. As our blessed master said: 'Knock on the door of hunger!' First we need to have the dream for the sweet taste of Paradise, the desire for intimate conversation with You. We have to long for the vision of beautiful appearances of angelic beings. All these heart wishes are compromised in the desire for the most excellent of all Prayers, Salah! Once we will feel the profoundest of all longings for the heavenly ascension towards You, we will feel, so You will, the irresistible attraction of the Power of Your Majesty and Beauty.

O Lord, fill our heart with humility and contentment, so that qiyam, bowing and the prostration becomes a Divine bliss and a celebration. Dur-ing qiyam the Companions were rubbing their bodies with such force against each other that their close tore apart. Therefore we ask You to let us feel the total melting with each other in qiyam like the Companions, unified as one body of loving brotherhood. As we will be lined up standing at the day of Resurrection fearful in front of Your Majesty, during the ritu-al Prayer in qiyam, we wish to feel this most precious Day of all days, fear-ful and trembling. O Lord, as qiyam represents the rehearsal for the Here-after, trembling before You becomes a necessity! Qiyam without modesty is invalid. Qiyam without fearful discipline is invalid. Qiyam without the physical expression of servanthood is invalid. Qiyam without humbleness, without poverty, without thankfulness is invalid. O our beloved Lord, You bestow on us the infinite treasury of the Fatiha, the seven Divine verses, in which miraculously the whole Qur'an is contained. Each verse contains a bottom and shoreless ocean of knowledge and meaning. It is Your order to recite this inexhaustible, constantly unfolding, infinitely flowing Divine vers-es 40 times a day. It is Your order to be immersed in contemplating the infi-nite wisdom of the Fatiha 40 times a day. Let us be attracted by the irre-

sistible power of Your Words. Let us get consumed by the beauty of Your light. Let us be in admiration, wonderment, awe of the perfection of the Divine revelations.

O Lord we beg You while bowing, in ruku, to give us the taste of leaning towards You with the exclusion of everything else together with Your sincere servant. We wish to express bowing to no one else than You, not accepting any kind of worldly authority and power. When we prostrate in self-effacement, let us melt with Your loving servants. Within the prostration we wish to become lifeless earth. We wish to extinguish ourselves and become nothing, smash the cage of self-existence and become dust before Your Majestic Presence. Prostration without contentment is invalid. Prostration without humility is invalid. Prostration without thankfulness is invalid. Prostration without surrender is invalid. Prostration without love, longing, admiration, without tearful regret, sorrowfulness is invalid. We wish to get lost, to dissolve, to get annihilated in the sea of Your gentleness and mercy, do not deprive us from the taste of the sweet scent of Your Nearness! O Lord, where else than in the prostration it is an absolute necessity to free ourselves from ourselves. Therefore we ask You and beg You to take us away from ourselves. Free ourselves from this mundane, meaningless, empty life and let us drink from the richness of the infinite Divine source, let us taste eternal happiness and eternal beauty. May the touching of our heads on Your most humble earth give us a breeze of its purity and modesty!

Modern life lost its charm, blessing, its dynamics. The flow of life is lost. The harmonious, peaceful breath is lost! We are suffocated, stagnated; we are deprived of breathing the universal harmonious flow of life. We wish to breathe the sweet scent of Your sacred Words. Let us become part of the Divine flow of Your revelations. Let us be part of Your Divine breath of mercy. Breathing Your Words is light on light. In one rakah, one Prayer set, let us flow through Your Name, let us flow through each letter of Your Name, let our body say Your Name; Allah! Let the power of Your Words revitalize our hearts towards eternal freshness, the eternal spring. Let our hearts get excited by the treasury of meanings. Let every Word we recite contain abundant praise!

May what we pronounce with our lips become a reality in our being. May the words we pronounce find life in our hearts. May the words become like seeds and find growth in the soil of the heart and blossom into a tree of loving harmony. May the state of our hearts find its expression in our conduct and speech. May the longings and desires find their language of Divine admiration towards You. May the heart's wishes become a poem, a supplication of burning affection towards You.

The knowledge we gain of You, the recitation of the holy verses of the Qur'an, have to illuminate the face of our soul. If Your Attributes and Names have no effect, if Your Words of Truth have no effect, if the Divine wondrous hymns and poems have no effect, we will be deprived of their meaning, their luminous brightness; we will be deprived of the light of Your guidance. Therefore O Lord, we wish most of all for a heart full of contentment for You! We wish a heart which melts in love in front of Your Divine beauty and perfection, a heart which continuously sheds tears of admiration and gratitude, a heart which feels constantly inspired to serve, to run, to work, to struggle for Your sake, a heart which feels restless, uncomfortable not being able to fill every moment of its life to do works for Your sake."

Zakah (The Prescribed Purifying Alms)

What you do to people, you do to God!

In a Divine *hadith*, Allah the Almighty says: *"Be merciful to your fellow beings, so the angels in the heavens might be merciful to you, too."*

The Holy Qur'an states: *"By no means shall you attain righteousness unless you give (freely) of that which you love; and whatever you give, in truth Allah knows it well"* (Al Imran 3:92).

Rumi says: *"In the religion of love, all things must be sacrificed."*

Martin Luther King says: *"We learned to fly like birds, we learned to swim like fish but we did not learn brotherhood."*

Charity is an obligation. Every year each Muslim is obliged to give one fortieth of his liquid assets to other Muslims in need. Charity is for one's material being, one's belongings. It is designed to purify our possessions and makes them lawful. It balances out the material self, possessions, status, goods, and the relationship with one's fellow beings. It cleanses the heart of impurities, the low qualities of arrogance, possession, and greed. Charity means literally to cleanse or to increase. To give alms is for the purpose of cleansing one's belongings of those impurities that entered them while they were being earned and causes them at the same time to increase. Wealth is like water, if its flow is obstructed, it becomes brackish, and if it flows, it becomes sweet and fresh. Charity is exactly opposite of an unrestricted greed and a disproportionate arrogance. Charity is the consciousness that all property and wealth belongs to Allah the Almighty. The act of almsgiving means therefore to give one's wealth back to its Owner. We have to ask ourselves; which goods we give to whom? The meaning of charity is not to own nothing in this world and give everything away; it is owning things of this world without being attached to them.

The great Caliph Ali was asked: *"O Imam, zakah means giving what percentage of what? What is the rule in Islamic law?* He said in reply: *"To those who are mean or stingy, it means giving one fortieth. But to us, it means giving everything."*

A wise man said: *"For everything we possess, we have to pay a price. Therefore the human being needs to pay charity. Charity of the body is the ritual Prayer and fasting. The charity of possessions is to pay one fortieth. The price for love is never ceasing to give and to give and to give."*

They asked our blessed master what is the best of action for a believer, and he answered: *"To rectify amongst people."* In another occasion he said: *"To be beneficial to His creatures."*

Abdul Qadir al-Jilani teaches a very important fact concerning charity: *"Whatever is given for this purpose passes through the hands of Allah before it reaches the one in need. Therefore, the purpose is not so much to help the needy, for Allah is the Satisfier of all needs, but to let the donor's intention be acceptable to Allah."* He describes the compassionate consideration a believer should show towards his fellow beings: *"He accepts even a little, but he gives very much. He accepts what is bad and worthless, but he gives what is excellent. He accepts defective articles of merchandise, but he always gives in full measure."*

In a noble tradition our master tells us: *"Generosity is a tree. Its branches spread out over the globe. Whoever grabs one of these branches will lift up his companion and take him to Paradise. Greed, avarice, parsimony, and stinginess are a tree that grows in Hell."*

When we truly give, we receive more than we give; when we truly help, we will be helped more than we help. To master the art of giving means to experience the secret of living, loving, and serving for Allah's sake. The noble Prophet said: *"The one who gives from his sustenance receives more from God than he gave."* The essence of true charity is living in His Name, doing all service for His sake, and showing unconditional love in one's behavior and actions. This noble character feature includes not showing the slightest sign of expecting any reward for one's good deeds. The humble servants endowed with the beauty of such a character trait will earn Allah's approval. The All-Merciful will meet all their needs, and they will find themselves in the position that others need them. The Qur'an states: *"Is the recompense of excellence (in obedience to God) other than excellence?"* (ar-Rahman 55:60) and *"For those who do good, aware that God is seeing them, is the best (of the rewards that God has promised for good deeds), and still more"* (Yunus 10:26).

Love, humbleness, generosity, kindness, patience, and selflessness towards humankind are the essence of charity. The inheritors of such excellent character traits do not wish any spiritual rewards for their devotions and voluntary actions for themselves, nor do they hope for Paradise, nor do they fear Hell. They intend to sacrifice all their good deeds to the sinners and disobedient believers. They do not keep anything themselves. Whatever they possess reaches immediately the ones in need. They do never accumulate wealth. They know that God is the Owner of all properties, of his belongings, his family, and his own life. Therefore they are infinitely generous. They do know the art of *"the left hand does not know what the right hand gives."* Such believers are soft, humble, and tender like the earth towards their brothers and sisters, and towards the unbelievers they are heroically courageous, powerful, and sincere. This attitude radiates from the inheritors of the noble feature of self-sacrifice.

Love manifests itself in giving. The greatest act of love is giving yourself. Who else but the beloved of Allah, the mercy sent to all humanity, is the embodiment of the purest love and compassion? No other Prophet showed such infinite love and concern for his own community. The glory of the universe represents the strongest light of guidance in living love and affection for each other. He illuminated our earthly existence with his abundant compassion and generosity towards all existence. In other words, he showed us how to live in this world for others. We learn from the Messenger of God that the secret of love is to satisfy the needs of others while being indifferent to one's own needs.

Islam is the religion of love. It is absolutely victorious in the sense that it does not make any distinction between country, race, status, or color. Islam makes no difference between human beings because we are all created by our Creator and have therefore all the same value before God Almighty. Beggar and king, poor and rich, women and men are equalized. Especially the pillars of fasting and charity generate this awareness of compassion and mercy and inspire the believers to live after this truth. If one does not adopt the awareness of charity, one will fall into the danger of seeing other races, countries, populations, and colors as inferior, or start to see other races as superior, envying them and worshiping their wealth. Charity, on the other hand, opens up the awareness of justice, brotherhood, and equality and enhances a deep reverence and respect towards all fellow beings, nature, and the universe.

The essence of charity necessitates to give preference to the well-being of others, although one is under great troubles, namely to give more value to the suffering of one's sister or brother than one's self. To help human beings, one has to forget one's own needs and troubles. Abu Bakr, who lived the peak of self-sacrifice, said: "*Taking pains to remove pains of others is the true essence of generosity.*" In other words, the suffering of our fellow human beings all over the world has to become the suffering of all people. In the religion of Islam, there are such heroes of faith; they keep their truthfulness even under threat. Their affliction causes them to fall even deeper in love with their Beloved. The secret lies in the preference of God's Will over one's own, never to pursue anything opposed to His good pleasure.

It is not what you do; it is how much quality you give to the performance of your actions. It is not how much you pray, the quantity; it is how you pray, the quality. It is not how much you serve; it is how much love you show while serving. To give charity without love is ugly. To give without love is living in hypocritical terms, showing disrespect towards the poor, the destitute. For example, reciting the Qur'an without love is equal as showing denial of the truth that is on your lips.

There are three stages of surrendering your life to Allah. The first stage is surrendering your possessions, your property, and your money. The second stage is your family, your friends, and your children. The third is surrendering one's own self, meaning body, health, mind, status, affection, heart, and soul, which is expressed through servanthood, *ubudiyah*. Consequently, the very art of life is giving oneself totally. When we do not love the noble Prophet and Allah the Almighty more than anything in this world, even ourselves, our faith is not complete. In this respect the Qur'an states: "*Say: 'If your fathers, and your children, and your brothers and sisters, and your spouses, and your kindred and clan, and the wealth you have acquired, and the commerce you fear may slacken, and the dwellings that you love to live in, are dearer to you than God and His Messenger and striving in His cause, then wait until God brings about His decree. God does not guide the transgressing people (who prefer worldly things to Him, His Messenger and striving in His cause, to truth and true happiness in both the world and the Hereafter)'*" (at-Tawbah 9:24). The same principle is uttered by the noble Prophet: "*One's faith is not genuine unless one holds him dearer than family, possessions and all else.*"

Concerning the relationship with Shams al-Tabrizi, Rumi commented about the educational effect the sincere friendship had on him: "*I learned from Shams to feel cold with the ones who feel cold and to feel hungry with the ones who feel hungry.*" This statement shows that it was not only spiritual knowledge he learned from Shams, but the noblest feature of self-sacrifice. The wisdom of sharing with the ones in need was precisely one of the principal reasons why Rumi fell in love with Shams to such high degrees.

The pillar of charity is given to work on one's consciousness in relation to all of humanity, to the planet earth, and to the universe. Charity increases the sensitivity towards all of creation and enhances the consciousness of responsibility for servanthood. One utterly valuable source of knowledge in this respect is given with the Qur'anic verse: "*Return to your Lord, well-pleased (with Him and His treatment of you), and well-pleasing to Him. Enter, then, among My servants (fully content with servanthood to Me)! And enter My Paradise*" (al-Fajr 89:28–30). In order to enter His Paradise, God makes us know that there is a Divine condition involved. He says: "*Enter among My servants,*" which means His Paradise is earned within His servants. God wants to show us that true love reveals itself through being useful to each other. It is easy to become a preacher, a learned religious academic, a professor of theology, but it is not easy to become a true servant.

The supplication for the well-being of others is the charity of the self. True supplication means self-forgetfulness to the point of one's annihilation in the Worshipped One. Personal supplication is an excellent way of learning how to think, to feel, to plead for other people. We learn the art of living for others; we learn the art of giving.

There are several degrees of ethical behavior towards one's fellow beings: I have and you have, I do not have and you do not have, I do not have but you have, and I have but you do not have. In that case, we should adopt the behavior that "what I have" shall be for others. More precisely, we must be utterly concerned by the fact that our brother does not have and we must do our best to find a solution for him. This human virtue represents one of the highest ethics of a believer.

In the religion of Islam, there are three main conditions to reach the perfection of faith; to wish for your neighbor what you wish for yourself; to love the noble Prophet more than anyone else, even yourself; to love each other for Allah's sake. If we do not fulfill these conditions, we do not even reach the station of true belief. Each one of the community of Muhammad is living under these Divine conditions, knowingly or unknowingly.

Correct behavior means to treat people according to their level of understanding. Loving a human being in a true way was expressed by Dostoyevski, one of the famous Russian writers, who said: "*To truly love a human being means to be able to see him in the way God meant him to be.*"

Self-sacrifice is the very essence of man, the very dynamics of life itself. Without the charity of the self, love becomes fake. Without adapting the noble features of heroic generosity, real love does not exist. The way of self–sacrifice is the way of generosity, the way of the perfection of compassion and love. Self-sacrifice, the charity of the self in the fight for the truth brings forth the fruit of *marifa*, sacred wisdom. Supreme self-sacrifice is called heroic generosity, *futuwwat*, derived from the term *fata*, or beautiful young person. It is further defined as youth and chivalry, chastity, trustworthiness, and loyalty. Chivalrous brotherhood in medieval times was a sort of religious brotherhood, having the highest ethics of help, showing total consideration for the weak and poor. The essence of *futuwwat* is considering others first, especially the ones in need, the helpless, showing kindness, goodness, and loving the ones who are weaker than you. It means honoring them, giving courtesy to them, showing kindness and politeness. It means showing respect towards the poor, the beggars, the weak, and the oppressed, and showing honor to the slaves. The true owners of chivalry resemble precisely the Companions of the Prophet, because they are not afraid to get hurt, tortured, mistreated, sick, or even killed. They showed patience when injustice was done to themselves, they fought for the rights of other people although their own rights were violated. They were kind to people who hurt them. They answered only with goodness to anyone who treated them badly. They were fair to everybody without expecting fairness in return. They did not resent others although others resented them. They forgave whatever injustice people did to them. They wished well for everyone even their enemies. They were content with poverty. They covered the faults of their fellow beings. They never asked to be helped or comforted by Allah even though they were tortured or in great danger. They had nothing left to eat or wear, but they still gave away their very last pieces, within their greatest troubles they continued their worship like nothing happened. They were immune to what happened to them, insensitive to pain because they are filled with the highest love for Allah the Almighty and Prophet Muhammad Mustafa, peace and blessings be upon him.

We have to ask ourselves, what are the highest ethics of man? What is the inner wealth of the religion? What is the treasury of being? What is this miraculous force which makes sultans become slaves, wealthy people into servants, ignorant, vulgar people into saints, and murderers into virtuous believers? How can beggars gain dignity, and slaves gain honor, and poor people gain respect? The answer is that these are the people who carry power as well as generosity in themselves, leadership as well as modesty, ownership as well as kindness, high intelligence as well as submission, authority as well as mercy, wealth as well as humbleness. Only and only the miraculous unification of such character features makes the whole of man. This is the final, ultimate treasure obtainable for every human being in this world, the glorifying oneness of being. The eternal bliss of enlightenment of being... The holder of these virtues can save humanity from moral ruin and destruction. These are the people holding the pillars of this world. Due to them God protects the inhabitants of the earth. These men shine with their light of unity throughout the world. It is through this light that the world is maintained, and if it is extinguished, the gradual disappearance of the world will take its course. These beautiful personalities produce luminous fruits to be tasted by all of humanity.

Let us see if we just find a handful of people with these miraculous character features in this world and let's see if we find some people who are willing to listen and learn and have the capacity to receive their enlightenment. When do we give up being happy in the hellish prison of this world? When do we give up to desire what is worst for us? When do we give up running away from what is good for us? When do we finish exhibiting our ambitions? When do we stop the game in the circus of this world? When do we start to fill and serve the truth instead of filling our own pockets and serving our own egos? When do we start to see that servanthood is our honor, that nothingness is our capital, that poverty is our wealth? When do we realize what is beneficial and what is of harmful for us? What is our loss and what is our gain? What is human abasement, what is human elevation? What is our refuge, what is our salvation, and what is our destruction? What is our freedom, what is our imprisonment? Until the rulers, authorities, kings, ministers, political leaders, corporate owners, doctors and professors have become the servants of their people, there will be disharmony, war, and corruption in our world. As stated by our noble Prophet, *"The real leader of a people is the one who serves them."* The superiors have to serve their inferiors. The wealthy have to support the poor. This is what the world needs the most now. This is the solution for the current problems.

Poverty draws one to Allah. Poverty protects one from desiring the world. The ultimate wisdom lies in seeing the state of sorrow as a friend, poverty as pride, need as a blessing and capital, that is to say, loss as gain. Thus to the degree of one's helping and serving the poor, one will participate in the good that goes to them, one will have a share in the purity of their beings, and one will have a share of the eternal flow of Divine grace. Serving the needy means participating in the nearness they possess to the One and Only. As beauty needs a mirror to be seen, the beauty of good deeds needs the weak and destitute people. That is to say, the poor are needed for generosity to appear. Bounty looks for beggars. Generosity reflects itself in the mirror of the miserable and lonely. The poor are mirrors of God's mercy and generosity. Generosity is an attribute of God. Every moment of our lives on earth we witness His unconditional favors, blessings, bounties, and mercy flowing towards His creation. Therefore, generosity is the essence of true humanity, it is the beauty of being, the heights of faith. This most excellent quality is such a light that when an unbeliever sees true generosity in his fellow being, it might give him the inspiration to enter true belief. We learn from studying the Prophet's life that unbelievers entering into the presence of the noble master, they became believers in one instant because they experienced the overwhelming treasury of goodness of the noble Prophet. They were completely shattered by the light of his graceful appearance and behavior. Their egos were totally broken in one moment, and they could not help to give immediate witness to belief.

A wise man said: *"Futuwwat is a treasure obtainable by climbing high beyond all the highest mountains of the world; what business have those who fall tired even on a smooth road with such a treasure?"* Junayd al-Baghdadi said: *"A loyal, truthful one changes states at least forty times a day (in order to preserve his personal integrity), while a hypocrite remains the same for forty years without feeling any trouble or unease (over his own deviation).*" The highest degree of faith is to be ready to sacrifice everything for the sake of Allah, in service of the truth of the religion. It is reported in a tradition: "*O Lord, send us back into the world, so that we may repeat our martyrdom. Then send us yet again, that we may be martyred once more. O Lord, we implore you to let us taste over and over again the joy we know in our moment of martyrdom.*" What is this pure joy they feel? Only the ones who taste know! We learn about truthful martyrdom from the example of the magicians. After having seen the true miracle of Prophet Moses, peace be upon him, with his staff, they admitted their belief in the One and Only. Having pronounced their faith in Allah, the tyrant Pharaoh threatened to cut off their hands and feet and hang them up with the rope if they would not give up their belief. They answered in peace and tranquility: "*Do we not return to our Lord anyway?*" We also learn this virtue from the noble Companions of our blessed master. After having fought a war, some were lying severely wounded on the battlefield. When the war was over, a Companion came to help in order to cure the wounded bodies lying scattered on the field. He heard voices crying for water and approached one warrior lying severely injured on the field. In the moment he tried to quench his thirst, he heard another voice calling for water. To his astonishment the wounded Companion lying in front of him refused to drink the water and told him to rush to quench the thirst of his brother first. So he left the first warrior and went over to the next, and he found himself in the same situation again hearing another voice and was told by the second warrior again to give preference to the other brother. This repeated itself three times, and when he tried to give water to the third Companion, he died in his arms. So he went back to the second wounded Companion and saw that he had also become a martyr, and when he reached the first martyr, he was lying already dead.

A sincere believer who reaches the state of selflessness is bankrupted to the world. He has become a "living martyr." Bankruptcy to the world brings spiritual vision. Through selflessness, Allah's mercy can be activated. Giving up the attachment to the world is rewarded with the news of eternal life. Self-sacrifice, the charity of the self in the fight for the truth brings forth the fruit of *marifa,* sacred wisdom. Burning in the fire of endless efforts to reach the Beloved turns the fire into a rose garden of the heart. Cleaning and purifying the mirror of the heart from egotistical qualities reveals the beauty of the Divine light. It is a duty for the believers of Divine unity belonging to Prophet Muhammad's community to search in the desert of worldly existence for the water of life.

The ultimate wisdom is this: Whatever we do to people, we do to God. Whatever good we do to His creation, we do to Him. When we serve people, we serve God. In serving Allah, we are proving our trust in Him, our love for Him, and we are showing our thankfulness to Him. All good deeds done for Allah's sake will rise to heaven. On the Resurrection Day, we will be judged by the good works we have done in the world below. The noble Prophet asked his Companions what the state of a bankrupted man signifies, and they answered that it is someone who lost his money and his goods. Then our blessed master explained: "*A man who falls into a state of bankruptcy is someone who lost all the religious practices he has done in his life, although he performed them continuously and all times, on the Judgment Day in front of Allah. The reason for his total loss lies in gossiping and therefore bringing spiritual harm to his fellow beings.*" Perfect belief is not reached by just obeying the commandments of Allah. It is through the treasury of goodness, the noble character features; it is through the human quality of compassion, generosity, kindness, and love.

Tears

Rumi says: "*Since Adam escaped God's rage by means of shedding tears, the words of a penitent person should be his tears. Adam came down to earth crying, lamenting and being sorrowful. As you are fond of bread (the food of this world) how will you ever appreciate the pleasure of tears (of a lover)?*"

A sincere believer endowed with the responsibility of servanthood and with a universal consciousness, which is the consciousness of charity, will spend his life in tears. How much man exercises self-sacrifice, to that degree he will cry. Tears are the manifestation of the inner world, an expression of the inner treasury of love and affection, a physical appearance of the spiritual reality of man. The more we weep, the more we are able to grow towards spiritual maturity. Tears are a token of Divine love for our Lord of all the worlds and our prince of the universe, the mercy for all the worlds, Prophet Muhammad, peace and blessings be upon him. The tears of true love are not shed for any purpose. They are not shed because of losses in this world or failures in this world. Tears of the heart have such a power that one drop can extinguish the fire of Hell.

Tears shed for Allah's sake have such a great spiritual impact that they are able to remove the veils that cover the glorious truth. Participating wholeheartedly with our tears in the events of the lives of our most beloved Prophet, his family and the Companions will shorten time and distance of 1,400 years into nothing. Tears will revitalize the historical events. They can reproduce the Divine scenarios and bring us to such closeness that we are miraculously transported right into them. It means that the sorrowful tears of a weeping heart bring us beyond time and space, and we can experience and participate in the event such as Karbala, the place where the martyrdom of the Prophet's family took place, as if it were today. The martyrdom of Husayn, the grandson of our blessed Prophet, is regarded as the saddest spiritual event in Islamic history. Consequently, a weeping heart of a true lover participates with his whole being in the reality of the spiritual nature of all events, whenever and wherever they happen. Only a heart which feels love for human beings can cry. Tears cannot flow if we are attached to our desires for the world. We need to reach a general state of human vulnerability, a state of humility, of admitted incapacity and insufficiency, which will soften the heart and fill it with love and mercy. Such tears are the tears of affection and compassion. They are pearls and with such tears He will become our Friend. Thus the Almighty will let us weep the tears of longing for Him and tears of longing for His most beloved Prophet, his family and the venerable Companions. Such tears are pearls that will unify us with the weeping tears of all His lovers. This is the highest Divine bliss a soul can experience, the tears of longing for the Majestic One shared with all the weeping lovers, all over the world. A life without weeping turns into a life of frustration, disappointment, suffering, dissatisfaction, depression, and loneliness. The crucial point is that the mind has to be connected with the heart, the intelligence with tears, love with knowledge, and servanthood with sacred awareness. Human nature becomes whole and reaches spiritual maturity with the knowledge of humility, with the intelligence of a merciful mother. The Lord of Majesty and Bounty, at the creation of man, breathed His breath of compassion and His creatures came into being. He fashioned us with His Holy Names. He is the Most Beautiful and the Most Generous. Our blessed master is the noblest of all men, the pride of the universe. He represents the treasury of pure modesty. He is the reason for creation, but he does not attribute anything to himself.

Intelligence has to be connected with the tears of the heart and the treasury of love and affection has to find refinement and purity through the illumination of the mind, otherwise the human being cannot breathe the breath of eternal life. Sheikh Abdul Qadir al-Jilani gives us exquisite imagery for the precious values of human tears: *"If you do not place your forehead of urgent need upon the soil of admitted incapacity, and if the tears of sorrow do not rain down from the clouds of your eyes, the plants of your delight will not become verdant in the orchard of daily life. The gardens of men will not become fecundated to suit your purpose. The branches of patience will not put forth the leaves of contentment and the fragrant perfumes of intimate friendship, nor will they bear the fruits of the nearness."*

Rumi says: *"Till the cloud weeps, how should the garden smile? The weeping of the cloud and the burning of the sun are the pillars of this world: twist these two strands together. Since the searing heat of the sun and the moisture of the clouds keep the world fresh and sweet, keep the sun of your intelligence burning bright and your eye glistening with tears."*

The tears of the heart are of two kinds: the tears of sorrow, which are the tears shed in the face of human suffering, and the tears of joy, which are the tears shed in the face of Divine beauty. A sincere servant of Allah always slides between those two states, as he always slides between love and fear of God. The tears of joy bring us in a state of admiration, wonderment, amazement, and awe. Man is created to witness Divine beauty. The act of creation is an act of beauty. When the beauty of the light of God's Majesty shines from the purified mirror of the heart, when the perfume of intimate friendship pleases the heart, when the pouring of inexhaustible treasures from the heart is witnessed, the tears of utter joy will be shed. When the soul hears the sweet sound, when the soul hears intimate loving whispers, when the soul receives the sweet taste of awareness, when the soul perceives the beauty of His Face, how can it not weep? The tears of sorrow are the tears resulting from the sacred concern one feels for humanity. One weeps due to witnessing of human tragedies. One cries with the crying pictures of poverty. Tears shed for the love for one's fellow beings are tears shed for Allah's sake. One of the greatest unifying links is the tears that flow due to the inner witness of human tragedies and miseries. These are the tears of sorrow and of helplessness; they are shed due to the feeling of incapacity in front of the immensity of human tragedies. One is moved by what one sees to such extent beyond supportability that one's heart shatters into pieces and overflows in weeping and wailing. Such tears represent a token of sacred love for all humanity. They become our most precious sacred capital because they bring us closer together. Today, vulnerability, harm, and damage have reached their peak. Some people are hurt in the deepest centers of their hearts. Their injuries passed far over their own bodies, taking over their thoughts, feelings, consciousness, mind, and heart. We see bulldozers erasing everything people possess; their houses, their belongings, their families torn apart. Only the clothes on their bodies are left. We can witness a market place full of people killed in one moment by the pressing of one button, reaching out even to the mothers who carry growing embryos in their wombs. We witness whole populations, tribes, and villages cut off from the rest of the world, held prisoners in their own land, on their own properties, earned by the sweat of their own hands. Not to become completely brokenhearted to see the level of despair shows human irresponsibility, ignorance, and a lack of character. Especially in today's world, a sincere believer lives in a state of deep sorrow, sadness, and humility. This is his true nature, his original being, the ideal as he was created: modest, soft, tender, humble, and kind. He realizes his incapacities, his nothingness, and his imperfections in the Presence of God's All-Embracing Power. Such weeping creatures become the beloved of Allah. He honors them with His Presence.

Sadness is one of the highest character features of a believer in the eyes of Allah. A heart equipped with this quality will be honored with His Presence. The feeling of sorrow and compassion for humanity will draw us close to God. It is God's gift to His servants who try to show servanthood to their Creator, who do everything in their capacity to serve Him. Actually the highest of all favors Allah bestows on His servant is His love and contentment for them and when God loves His servant, He fills their hearts with sorrowful weeping for His sake.

Unfortunately, there are people whose hearts are remaining closed even under severe examination and great suffering. They become aggressive, frustrated, and miserable. They do not realize that misfortune, calamities, sickness, and sufferance cause sadness, and this state will purify themselves of egotistical attributes. True sadness cleanses one's heart of the low qualities of arrogance, possession, and greed. In that sense, sadness revitalizes the heart, providing that the sadness is of sacred nature.

If we participate in the misfortunes, the oppression, or the injustice of our brothers, we feel sacred sorrows. If we feel bad about our own insufficiency, our imperfections, our mistakes, and our sins, we feel sacred sorrows. The value of sadness is measured by to the degree of the awareness of one's human failures and by the ability to turn to one's Creator for help, forgiveness, guidance, and protection. That is to say, true sadness will help us realizing our human state of helplessness, weakness, and need in front of our Lord of Majesty and Bounty, and so God willing, seek refuge and shelter in Him, the All-Merciful and the All-Compassionate. A wise man said: "*Sadness or sorrow is like a ruler. When it settles in a place, it does not allow others to reside there.*" The wisdom we can draw from this statement is that sadness is covering the whole being and has therefore a healing effect. The sacred sorrow is nothing else than the pain of separation felt as creatures in this world from our beloved Creator.

Prophet Adam, peace be upon him, was the first human being created and is regarded as the father of sorrow due to his fall from Paradise, the separation from his Lord. He cried for 40 years. The Prophet Jacob, peace be upon him, cried for the loss of his son Joseph the same length of time. Furthermore, Prophet Moses, peace be upon him, experienced unbearable hardships during his life with the tyrant Pharaoh, and Prophet Abraham, peace be upon him, with the tyrant Nimrod. Prophets Noah and Jesus experienced deep sorrow due to the unbelief of their people. All of the Prophets were continuously in a state of sadness because they were not able to carry out the Divine revelations without the greatest threats from unbelievers and enemies.

Muhyiddin ibn Arabi said: "*No reward that a human being can receive for his achievements can compare with the felicity awarded to whoever shows compassion to humanity.*" Compassion and mercy is the essence of being human. The sky yields rain and the earth flourishes. A heart full of love and compassion for humanity will become soft, and a soft heart will continuously weep for Allah's sake. The tears for Allah's sake will nourish the earth, and a tree of loving harmony will grow. That tree will be beneficial for all humanity; its fruits will nourish the thirsty and needy souls pleading for help, sustenance, shelter, friendship, brotherhood, and love. Compassion can save us from selfishness, arrogance, and power hunger. We have to reflect on what it means to do service to the needy. Allah says: "*I am with those whose hearts are broken for My sake*" (Divine *hadith*). This is one of the principle teachings of the religion of Islam. Allah is with the sorrowful. Allah is with the oppressed, with the lonely, with the orphans, with the miserable; that is to say, Allah is with the ones who are in need of Him! To serve the needy is to serve the expectations God has of His servants. To help His creation, to be useful to His creation, is to help realizing the goal of His creation. It is reported that God's Messenger said: *"When one of you looks at someone who is superior to him in property and appearance, he should look at someone who is inferior to him."* He also said: *"Seek Me among your weak ones, for you are given provision, or are given help, only by reason of the presence of your weak ones."* Ali said: *"As much as one is deprived by one's own family and friends, as much one might receive help from strangers."* As much as one shares the sufferance, the tears, the loss with others, as much as there is Divine inspiration.

Sorrowfulness was a state of our blessed master to the extent that he is described as "the Prophet of sorrow." Thus, a moral responsibility arises for everyone who belongs to his community. The noble Prophet came to this world for no other reason than as a mercy for the whole world. So should we not share his concern and show mercy and compassion to our fellow beings? The ones who share the sacred concerns of our blessed master will certainly inherit his character traits and begin to resemble him. What a great honor to those who are able to shed tears with him, the most beloved of Allah. No other human being suffered so much like our blessed master. No other being experienced so much sadness. No other being shed so many tears. No other Prophet felt such concern for his community. He was sent to spread mercy to the whole world. The sadness he felt was due to his utter care and compassion for the whole humanity. He tasted the greatest sorrows from the unbelief and hostilities of his enemies and the torture and killing done to his believing followers. His sorrow was never for himself, it was the sorrow for his community who lived in poverty and desperation. What terrifying human tragedies he had to witness! Once Aisha asked him what was the saddest event in his life and before he answered he uttered, *"Ah! Ah!"*, and she felt immediately sorry to have asked him. He answered: *"I entered the city of Taif and went first to visit some relatives of third degree. When I entered, three young people came and sat in front of me, and I explained to them that I was chosen by God to be His Prophet. Then they started laughing, and the first one said: 'If you are a Prophet, I will tear the cloth of the*

Ka'ba like a thief.' The second one said: "If you are really a Prophet, how can you talk to me like you are a simple person, and how can I talk to you as if you were a simple person?' The third one said: "Of all the population of Mecca, how come you have been chosen, a person having no education, an orphan with no profession?" After this darkest encounter, these relatives spread the news of the conversation to the village and told our blessed master a surprise would wait for him. When he left the relative's house, the greatest terrifying experience in the Prophet's life happened, namely the children of the village threw stones at him. After this incident, covered full of blood, Archangel Gabriel asked him if he wanted God to destroy the whole city. But the mercy of the universe asked God to forgive its inhabitants, because of all the inhabitants of the city of Taif, there might have been some people ready to receive Divine guidance and become believers. A tradition shows the gravity of our blessed master's overflowing concern for us: *"I see what you do not see and hear what you do not hear. If only you knew with what the heavens creek and groan. In fact, they must do so, for there is not even the space of four fingers breadth in the heavens where angels do not prostrate themselves. I swear by God that if you knew what I know (with respect to God's Grandeur) you would laugh little and weep much. You would avoid lying with your wives and cry out unto God in the fields and mountains."*

Ahl al-Bayt: The Prophet's Family and the Blessed Companions

There is a flowing river; this river is constantly flowing from the core of human illumination, the venerable *Ahl al-Bayt*, the Prophet's family, and the supreme examples of the four caliphs and all the Companions. To do service to the religion of Islam is to do service for the community of Muhammad, the most honored of all communities. The most honorable man in this universe, the pride of humanity, our blessed Prophet, and the most honorable people are the members of his family and his venerable Companions. So to serve his community means to serve his family and the Companions, because they were direct recipients of our noblest master's words, behavior, and actions. They inherited his noble character. They suffered the sufferance of Islam, and they lived the joy of Islam because they breathed the sacred scent of the Divine revelations. Anything they did was an expression for their need of love for humanity and the love for the noble Prophet and Allah the Almighty. The *Ahl al-Bayt* and the Companions are the champions of truth.

Allah the Almighty first created the light of Muhammad. He fashioned a tree named the tree of certainty from that light. He adorned the Prophetic light with ornaments of white pearls formed in the shape of a peacock and set it upon a tree. Allah then commanded this sacred bird to look to the four quarters, and he could see that four lights had been created. These were the lights of the four caliphs, Abu Bakr, Umar, Uthman, and Ali, may Allah be pleased with them. Thus, their station is beyond our comprehension. After our blessed master and his family, they are Allah's most dignified creation; they are the chosen ones to guide all generations to the truth with their illuminated character. They are the heroes of self-sacrifice. They gave all possessions, property, belongings, their family, even their own lives for the service of the religion of Islam. Such abundant self-sacrifice is very particular to the religion of Islam. This highest degree of submission is born especially in our Prophet's universal religion because our blessed master represents the pure servant to all human beings and the pure slave of his Lord. The generosity of the Companions is of such infinite glory, it extends towards all existence, like Allah's Mercy and Compassion extends towards the whole universe and all that it contains. They reached such a level of purity attributing nothing to themselves, not even their own goodness. They never did anything for any reason, neither for ulterior motives nor expecting results or Divine favors. They only wished to conform to the Divine Will and please their Lord of Majesty and Bounty. The religion of Islam demands comprehensive responsibility and unconditional submission. The Companions carried the full responsibility for their belief on their shoulders and many of them paid the price with their lives. They were pure receptacles of the inner meanings. The purity of their hearts could give inner witness to the truth. As soon as they were hearing the newly revealed Qur'anic verses from the lips of the noble master, they spend all their time, their efforts, their attention in order to penetrate into their deepest layers of meanings in such intensity, sincerity, until the revelation became part of their lives.

The birth of Islam was possible because 150 people were sustaining the religion of Islam for 12 years. These were the members of the Prophet's household and the four caliphs and the venerable Companions. They were the holders of the light of Islam. Without their sacrifices the religion of Islam would not exist on earth. The universal religion of Islam was brought to all humanity by Prophet Muhammad, peace and blessings be upon him.

The religion of Islam spread throughout the whole world by the first believers through the love for the noble Prophet. That is to say, the family of the beloved Prophet and the venerable Companions gave birth to the religion of love. Giving birth to the religion of Islam means giving birth to the perfection of God's Light. As much as the Prophet called people to the light of God, as much as the Prophet invited people for the religion of unity, *tawhid*, to the same degree the unbelievers would humiliate him, throw stones at him, threaten him. For the followers who believed in the Prophet it meant that their lives turned into a battle field. Most of them got beaten up, tortured or killed after confessing to the religion of Islam. Especially for Fatima and Khadija, these constant hostilities from the Arab elite became part of their lives. Thus both of them had an active role in trying to decrease the threats from the unbelievers in whatever way they could act like a shadow of the blessed master, constantly on his side. They were offering their friendship to the newly initiated believers, helping them materially as well as morally. Fatima in an internal way, Khadija on the social level...

The essence, the core of Islam is lived by the Companions. They represent the perfection of the religion of Islam. If we wish to reach true belief, we have to study the lives of the Prophet's family and the venerable Companions. We have to look into the sky for those stars of Divine guidance. In order to be able to perceive their light, we have to occupy ourselves with the heightened ethical behavior of the Companions. Thus through studying the enlightened examples, we are able to gain awareness of who we are, of our true human nature, the way God meant us to be. The noble Prophet said: "*My Companions are like the stars in the sky. Whichever of them you follow, you will find the true path.*" How do we attain the nearness to God? Through the beloved of God, the honor of the universe, Prophet Muhammad, peace and blessings be upon him. How do we reach closeness to our blessed master? Through the ones who were near to him, through the ones who loved him. If one wants to become a true believer, there is no other way than to align one's self behind the Prophet's family and the Companions of the noble master.

To understand the treasury of Islam we need such heroic figures like Asma, Bilal, and Khadija. It is not enough to pronounce the affirmation of unity and the profession of faith with one's lips. Love needs action. It needs people like Abu Bakr and Hamza. Rumi states: "*In the religion of love, everything has to be sacrificed.*" Believers of Divine unity are obliged to fight in the name of the Messenger of Allah against selfishness and their low desires. The truth cannot be given for nothing. Love needs people like Abu Bakr and Asma.

Sumayya was the first martyr in the religion of Islam. When the Companions gave the news of the martyrdom to our noble master, he responded: "*The work of the infidel, the unbelievers is finished! If Sumayya would have said yes, we would have ended up in desperation. Now such a magnificent sun is rising that the work of unbelievers is finished. All of you take the good news!*" Before the venerable black slave, Bilal, one of the noble Companions, joined the community of our blessed master; he had to experience the most severe torture from his owner. He was asked to deny the Prophet's religion under unsupportable pain, but he kept exclaiming: "*Ahad, Ahad!*" The penetrating sound of Allah's Attribute of oneness was cutting clear through time and space, reaching the glorious realms of eternity. What wisdom did the exalted slave Bilal show us with his determination, bravery, and heroic endurance? He simply said: "*Allah exists, and I do not exist without Him*" and "*I gave little, but I win all and everything, I win immortality!*" We have to learn from the noble presence of Khadija who could not stay at home in the shadow once the Prophet had to leave the house and she exposed herself in the burning heat of the sun. She said: "*Until the Prophet returns home, I will not return home as well. As long as the Prophet has to be under the shining sun, I will not sit in the shadow. It is not in my control. My heart does not let me stay home. Once my beloved master will retire in the shadow, only then I am able to go inside.*" Each work in this world if it is done with the awareness of the responsibility for servanthood is sacred. The art of being a servant needs an intense struggle of the heart. The Companions and the Prophet's family showed us that executing duties, carrying responsibilities for the sake of God are of sacred nature. They demonstrated how to carry the weight of Divine responsibility, how to carry the Divine trust. They showed us how to fight on the way of truth without expecting any rewards. They demonstrated an unbroken faith, never ceasing to continue to strive, although they were in greatest difficulties. They combined their struggle, their efforts with heightened joy. Their hearts worked to the highest gear. In their hearts, human faith got symbolized, faith got kept eternally alive.

Whoever is in search of Fatima, Ali, Hasan, Husayn, and the Companions will not be able to find them in books about their lives, listening to their stories, saying the dry words of loving them, but in their own service to the religion of Islam, in their self-sacrifice, in the sacred efforts helping to satisfy the needs of humanity. In other words, through the works of service for the religion of Islam, believers might be able to reach the heroes of self-sacrifice. This is exactly the wisdom we can draw from studying their lives, namely service without giving from one's substance is of little value in the eyes of the Almighty. It is through the love and the service we show towards our fellow being that we find Divine approval and therefore find access and closeness to the purest of the pure, the highest of the high, the most beautiful of the beautiful, the Prophet's family and the Companions. We have to try to resemble and adapt their most worthy qualities of heroic generosity towards all humanity, their unconditional love, and their abundant servanthood. This means the more we show self-sacrifice, the more we show service, the more they will enter into our hearts. We have to work in the trade of Divine love. Our sweat, our tears, our trembling, and our struggling in the way of the truth will be a token for the love we have for our honor of the universe and his family and the Companions. The more we will give from our substance, the higher price we pay, the higher will be the honor of seeing their beauty with the secret eyes of our hearts, and we might be honored, if God wills, to drink some drops of Muhammad's light and earn some portion of the Paradise of intimacy with our supreme Lord of Majesty and Bounty. Our lives have to be devoted in search of the lives of the Companions. A verse from the Holy Qur'an: *"Say: 'I ask of you no wage for it (for conveying God's Religion to you, which will bring you this favor), but (I ask of you for) love for my near relatives (on account of my mission)'"* (ash-Shura 42:23).

There are countless traditions demonstrating that the four caliphs are the possessor of the highest level of faith amongst all human beings. Ali ibn Abu Talib, although being the door of knowledge, said in utter humility: *"If you teach me one letter, I become your slave."* When the enemies tried to kill our beloved Prophet, that night Ali was told by our master to sleep in his bed, so when the enemies came to murder our blessed

Prophet, they would find Ali in his place. Thus, he waited patiently in the Prophet's bed to be killed. When the enemies came, they found Ali and let him live. As soon as the enemies left, Ali was eager to rejoin his beloved master, who was on his way emigrating from Mecca to Medina with his caliph Abu Bakr to avoid being killed by his enemies. Ali walked rapidly for many days and nights without ceasing through the desert so that his burning heart could rejoice with his beloved master as soon as possible. When he finally arrived in Medina, he embraced his enlightened master, but his feet were covered in blood from the burning sand of the desert. His heart burned with so much longing for his beloved Prophet, he did not even feel the bleeding wounds on his feet.

One day a poor relative knocked on his door. Fatima opened and he told her that he was in desperate need for food and she immediately gave him whatever she could find in the household. In the later evening, Ali came home and Fatima told him about this beggar. As he listened to her a profound sadness came over him. He exclaimed: "*Ah! Ah! How could I not become aware of his situation? I could have given him before he had to come to beg from us!*"

It is an absolute condition in the religion of Islam to give in secrecy. We learn from the venerable Ali, who was made a martyr by the cruel Ibn Muljam. Before the funeral, while they were washing his blessed body, they discovered bruises on his shoulders and they asked his two sons, Hasan and Husayn about the cause: "*Every night when people were sleeping so nobody could see him, he carried heavy loads of food for the poor and put them before their doors.*" Exactly the same beautiful behavior went over to his son, Hasan who was martyred as well. He used to go frequently at night with his face covered so that no one could recognize him giving food to the poor, leaving it at their doors. Once he had passed away from that day on, the poor people noticed that there was no food left at their doors. They realized that no one else than our beloved one could have been the mysterious donor.

The following tradition about the Caliph Abu Bakr demonstrates the highest example of self-sacrifice. From time to time the beloved Prophet called his Companions and caliph to himself, suggesting that everyone should give some charity to the poor. Two or three days went by, everyone returned except Abu Bakr. Finally, the caliph walked into the presence of our dearest master with a small piece of cloth and some date leafs to cover his almost naked body. Everyone was astonished at his strange appearance, and he said pointing to the small wrappings around his body: "*O my Prophet, nothing is left except these!*" In this moment, the Arch Angel Gabriel appeared, dressed in the same way and said to our Prophet: "*When Allah witnessed the great charitable act of your Caliph Abu Bakr, he ordered all the angels in heaven and myself to dress in the same manner, and He ordered me to report that He is well pleased with your beloved Companion, and He asks, is Abu Bakr satisfied with Me?*" When our caliph heard this great news from the All-Merciful, he fell into a state of complete ecstasy, opened his arms towards the sky and whirled around, and with each turn he said: "*I am content, I am content!*" In another tradition, God made Abu Bakr see Hell and its tortures. From the sight of it, he was terrified to such an extent that he begged God to make his body big enough to cover all of Hell so that no one would be able to enter.

One day, the blessed Messenger sat together with Abu Bakr, Umar, Uthman, Ali, Fatima, and Aisha, may Allah be pleased with them. Suddenly he started to weep to such an extent that it became too hard to bear for his Companions. Approaching his beloved Prophet, Abu Bakr asked gently: "*O Messenger of Allah, why do you cry?*" He answered: "*There will be a very long and difficult way for my community, there is a heavy load on their shoulders and a lot of sins. They will be judged, how can I not weep?*" Abu Bakr was very affected and he replied: "*O my Prophet! Keep your heart in joy. In order to lighten the sins of your community, if God gives me the permission at the Day of Judgment, I will take half of their sins on my behalf.*" Upon this utterance, the Messenger made a supplication for Abu Bakr, praising, loving, pleasing, and caressing his heart. After the Messenger turned to Umar and said to him: "*O Umar, you listen to the words of Abu Bakr. What will you do about my sinful community?*" Umar gave the following response: "*I do not have the strength of Abu Bakr. If God gives me the permission, I will carry one third of the sins of your community.*" The Messenger made a supplication for Umar, praising, loving, pleasing, and caressing his heart. After the Messenger asked Uthman: "*What will you do about my sinful community?*" Uthman, may Allah be pleased with him, gave the following answer: "*I cannot do as much as Umar did. If God gives me the permission, I will carry one fourth of the sins of your community.*" The Messenger made a supplication for Uthman praising, loving, pleasing, and caressing his heart. After the Messenger turned towards Ali: "*O Ali, what will you do about my sinful community?*" Ali gave the following answer: "*If God gives me the will, I hold both sides of the Sirat bridge and I will hinder that the rebellious community goes to Hell. If the situation will get worse, I will go into the fire for each one of them.*" The Messenger made a supplication for Ali praising, loving, pleasing, and caressing his heart. After the Messenger turned to his wife Aisha: "*O, Aisha, what will you do about my sinful community? You are their mother. For the children, mother's mercy is needed.*" Aisha said: "*In the presence of Fatima, I do not need to say anything.*" Fatima gave the following answer: "*You are a mother; it is not suitable to talk first in the mother's presence.*" Then Aisha said: "*How can I talk first in the presence of the one our blessed master, who said, 'Fatima is a part of myself?'*" Fatima said: "*How can I speak in the presence of the one the Messenger, who said, 'When you will not see me anymore, you will receive half or one third of the religion from Aisha?'*" Then Aisha said: "*I swear by God, I will not speak first!*" Fatima turned to the Messenger and said: "*O my father! I will stay in front of the scale on the Judgment Day.*" Our noble master replied: "*O Fatima, the pupil of my eyes! What will you do with my sinful community?*" Fatima answered: "*When the sins are heavy and if God gives me permission, I will take Hasan's poisoned shirt and I will put it on the right (good) pan of the balance. If it will not be enough I will add the bloody shirt of Husayn. If again it will be not enough, I will take off my scarf from my head and I will tie my hair. In order for the community to increase the heaviness of the good pan of the scale, I will put my scarf as well. I will wait until the weight will intensify and outweigh the sins of the community.*" Upon this, the Messenger made a supplication for Fatima praising, loving, pleasing, and caressing her heart. He turned to Aisha: "*O the mother of believers, what will you do about my rebellious community?*" Aisha answered: "*That Day when there are so many to intercede there is no need for me!*" The noble Messenger replied: "*O Humayra, if there would be need for you, what would you do?*" Aisha said: "*It is not appropriate to tell you.*" The noble master: "*Tell us O Humayra! Or tell it to Abu Bakr.*" As Aisha insisted still not to speak on the Messenger's advice to tell Umar, Uthman, Ali, the Messenger asked again: "*O Humayra! All right, who do you wish to tell it then?*" She said: "*I will tell it to the Almighty,*" and she left and went to another room and took off the scarf. She rubbed her hair and face on the earth begging God the following way: "*O my Lord! You honored me to be the mother of believers, I asked You for motherhood, love, mercy and affection from my heart and You accepted my plead. You placed love in my heart! For sure, all of the mothers cannot be content if their children will go to Hell. O Lord, do give the permission that they will enter Paradise. But, if it has to be, I will go with them to Hell!"* While supplicating, she cried due to the love for the believers. In that moment, an intense sound came from the heavens. Gabriel came to the Messenger and said: *"O Prophet of mercy! God sends you His salams and says: 'O Muhammad! Tell Aisha: 'You are the wife of the Prophet. How can We send you to Hell, it is not suitable for you to burn in the fire. To separate the mother from the child is not right either. O Aisha! May your heart stay in comfort. On the Judgment Day, we will reach all your children and you will enter Paradise with them. We will seat them on an angelic thrown and put an angelic crown on their head. 'Their Lord will favor them with the service of a pure drink'"* (al-Insan 76:21).

Such are the noblest character features, their station of intercession, their profound love and affection, their supreme servanthood, their most excellent behavior, and the overflow of the sacred compassion of the Prophet's family and the Companions!

May Allah, the Most Merciful, who created such magnifying exalted noble saints, give all believers the opportunity to regain the capacity of their hearts, the inner potential, the purity, the magnifying power, the treasury of love. May He allow us to regain the sensitivity like that of the venerable Companions. May He allow all of His servants to become a precious, unique drop and melt into the eternal current of oneness and love.

The human being, what a great hero, he can keep straight whatever happens to him! He is such an original, the unique, supreme, and most precious creation of Allah. He is composed of millions and millions of particles which miraculously work together and make a whole. The greatest miracle of creation is the mystery of man. He comprises the whole universe in himself. He is a living miracle. Rumi describes: *"The core of every fruit is better than its rind; consider the body to be the rind, and its friend, the spirit, to be the core. After all, the human being has a precious core; seek it inspired by the Divine breath."* Unfortunately believers of Islam have lost courage, bravery, chivalry, straightforwardness, and loyalty; that is to say, they have lost truthfulness. The actions of Muslims need courage to put their ideals in action whatever the cost and to show sincere servanthood and heroic generosity to the Almighty under all circumstances. God answered to Moses about the most worthy virtue of chivalry: *"It means that you are able to return yourself to Me as pure or untainted as you received it from Me."* This highest level of faith is attributed to no one else than the venerable Ali, the personification of bravery, truthfulness, and heroic generosity.

Supplications

"Our reward is not our good deeds, high numbers of worship activities, if we gain some success in Your Eyes, it is through what we have brought to the path of truth, how we have contributed to the religion of Islam, namely how we have served Your book, the Qur'an, how we have served Your needy creatures, how we have served Your saints and friends, how we have to be able to touch the hearts of the lonely, oppressed, innocent, and sick creatures, how much we have contributed to spreading the truth of Islam. O Lord, let us live a life of being useful for Your religion and for Your creatures!

Bestow on us the universal consciousness that all believing servants are brothers and sisters of the Hereafter. Help us to embrace the whole of humanity as one community. O Lord, make us feel like a family of loving brotherhood. We ask you to bestow on us a universal consciousness and feel the loving embrace for all of humanity. Make us feel the honor, favor, and worth of belonging to the community of Your beloved Prophet that You bestowed on us. O Lord, make us aware of the meaning and worth of sending him as a mercy for the entire world! Let us become receptive towards his inexhaustible blessings, his all-loving, tender care for us. Let him be the curer of all our spiritual wounds. Let him be the remedy of our broken hearts. Let him give comfort to our distressed hearts. Let him nourish our needs for beauty, love, mercy, and compassion. Let us be part of his supplication: 'O Lord, we need You, we need You.' Let us become part of his supplication: 'O Lord, make me live as a poor person, make me die as a poor person, resurrect me as a poor person.' Let us be part of his supplication: 'O Lord, increase my marveling at You.' Let us feel his nature, the treasury of pure modesty. Let us take part in his inspiration to love, in his admiration towards You. Let us be part of his grace of intimacy with You.

O Lord, You are All-Caring and You are All-Loving! All is in the hands of Your loving concern. You are with the broken-hearted! You are the protector of the orphans, the needy, the widows, and the poor. You are the Friend with the lonely, the sick, the weak, the poor, and the destitute. You are with the ones who are in need of You, who offer themselves to You in total want. You desire the ones who desire You. You love the ones who love You. You say: "My love, My existence is their love for Me." The highest love is the love You have for Your creatures. We wish to take refuge in Your loving care for Your creation. We wish to participate in Your Presence with the broken-hearted! We wish to be part of Your flowing mercy and compassion towards them. Let us prove our trust in You by serving Your creation.

Experiencing hardship in this world means facing You, facing You means turning towards You, turning towards You means taking refuge in You, and taking refuge in You means being saved from all threats, attacks, hostilities, and whisperings of the devil the accursed. Taking refuge in You means becoming immune to the attacks of the ego, one's lower nature, lust, desire, bad habits, and heedlessness. Taking refuge in You means to put things in their proper places, namely to become aware that all things happening to us come from You. O Lord, whatever tragedy, calamity, or suffering may befall us, help us to willingly accept up to the point of being pleased with You.

O Lord, help us to see the wisdom of the catastrophes threatening the world. Help us to see the wisdom of earthquakes where within some seconds the earth swallows up masses of people. Help us to see the reason for human suffering. Why are all these great disasters happening? Why does the world experience such an increase of suffering, turmoil, disaster, and devastation? I know, the more we know You, the more the sufferance ceases! All the worldwide disasters are caused by our heedlessness, our spiritual blindness, our ignorance, our forgetfulness. Our worthless, profane, superficial life caused us to forget You. O Lord, with Your help, we will wake up from our sleep of ignorance. May the endurance of turmoil and suffering bring us back to our lost identities, may we regain our human worth and dignity because the more we endure calamities in this world with patience, the more You increase and spread Your endless mercy and blessings throughout the whole world.

We have to plead to You due to our insufficiencies, shortcomings, and irresponsibilities. You are the Sustainer, the Satisfier of all needs. You are the Forgiver; You are the Veiler of our sins. Our heedlessness towards the needs of our brothers and sisters all over the world can cause much harm. Our ignorance towards the people in need all over the world might enhance their suffering and calamities. Nothing stays by ourselves, as our blessed master says in a tradition: 'If you give true guidance to a human being, it is as if you give eternal life to the whole of humanity.' O Lord, we plead with You, make us aware of our shortcomings, our irresponsibilities and increase our sensitivity, respect, and compassion towards our fellow beings all over the world. Bestow on us a universal consciousness.

O Lord, relieve the suffering of the poor, give sustenance to the poor, give richness to the poor, give shelter to the poor, give protection to the poor. We know, You are the Curer of all ills, You can bring salvation for all distressed souls in this world. May our tearful supplication of utter helplessness in the face of human tragedies be a token of the love, sorrow, and compassion we feel for them. We ask You to send Your blessing, Your Mercy, and Your grace as a healing comfort for their soul! Send armies of angels with their blissful presence comforting them. Clothe the naked, needy, and the poor with the robe of sainthood, Your most beautiful Names and Attributes. May our heartfelt supplication of helplessness be sufficient as we have no means to help otherwise."

Supplication with the Tongue of Impotence

"How can we feel content if we cannot embrace the truth and embrace the whole of humanity? How can we feel content if the noble character of Prophet Muhammad, peace and blessings be upon him, did not spread all over the world into the hearts of all believing servants? How can we feel comfort and well-being if human sufferance does not cease, the torture, oppression, the injustice, the tyranny does not cease? How can we feel at rest if the community of Muhammad do not respect and live after the Divine rules of worship and the Divine rules of behavior? O Allah, Your most beloved Prophet felt every sufferance of his followers in his blessed heart. He worried for all humanity. He trembled even for the people who came in later times, our present time, and one thousand four hundred years ahead!

I have nothing to say, my tongue is tied in impotence from the overwhelming fullness of my heart. I overflow of sadness witnessing innumerous souls in desperate need, loneliness, helplessness, and destitution, innocent, crying pictures of poverty, blood, sweat, and tears. I see shoes torn apart, I see clothes torn apart, arms torn apart, flesh torn apart, I see personal belonging without owners scattered in the streets, I see houses torn apart, I see mosques torn apart. My tongue is tied in impotence, I lost my speech to You from seeing the wholeness split into thousands of parts.

My tongue is tied from the feelings of insufficiency towards You. My weakness becomes heavy; my loneliness is a clear-cut isolation from the rest of the world. You see my state; it is enough for me that You see my condition. My state is my supplication to You! I cannot speak anymore. My tears of incapacity speak, the trembling of my breast, the burning longing of my searching, the pain of my head, the tears of sorrowful lamentation speak. My scattered heart tells infinite tales of my irremovable imprisonment, my soul is lamenting witnessing the miserable condition of human beings in complete innocence, hundred thousand people forcefully displaced, deserted, paralyzed, stranded in a nowhere land with nothing left.

O Lord of all the worlds! We are successors to Adam. We are the children of Abel, the martyr. We are the ones who bear witness to tawhid. We are human beings who accepted the mission and calling of Your Prophets. We are Your friends. We are Your caliphs. We belong to the community of the mercy for all the worlds. We are the descendants of the universal architect of the foundation of the house of tawhid of Prophet Abraham, peace be upon him. We are the followers of the dust in the footstep of all the Prophets. We belong to You; You are closer to us than we are to ourselves. We belong to the religion of: 'Iyyaka nabudu wa iyyaka nastain.' We belong to the religion of the glorified prostration and the most exalted experience of the miraj, the ascension, through which we received the Paradise of intimacy with You. How unfortunate that we have shattered and spoiled the presence of the Divine in this world. We have not been truthful followers. We have not paid unto You a goodly loan. We have not been able to assume the Divine trust. We did not carry the Divine trust. We did not follow in the footsteps of all the Prophets. We did not understand the bloodshed of the martyrs of Husayn and Hamza. We did not see the beauty of their heroic self-sacrifice. Instead with a devilish, animalistic ignorance, we blow ourselves up in the crowded area of market-places, brutally murdering innocent civilians and think we can earn the ticket to Your Paradise.

We have to ask ourselves; what did we do that all these bombs are dropped on the world of Islam? We have to ask ourselves, does our laziness open a way to the increase of tyranny in this world? Does our actions and behavior have an effect for the acceleration for the happening of the Day of Judgment? Does our insufficiencies to cope, to help, to serve, to support actively the community of Muhammad increase the suffering, poverty, sickness of the helpless, poor, needy, and innocent of this world?

O Lord, when we are stuck with three meals, how can we resemble Hamza, Husayn, or Bilal? O Lord, turn the imprisonment of the population of Gaza, who live under occupation in all levels of life, into the beauty of a spiritual seclusion! May their isolation from the rest of the world turn into the Paradise of intimacy with You!

O Lord send all over the world the ones who believe in You wholeheartedly the merciful Prophet Joseph, peace be upon him. Through his radiant being, may he save us all from the darkness of unconsciousness of the pit. May we become a king like him governing our own human kingdom.

O Lord, we are finally not alone with ourselves anymore. We are unified with the hearts of the community of Muhammad. We became part of their suffering; we shed tears of sorrow along with their tears. We supplicate and plead to You along with their pleading for help, protection, peace, and healing."

The Inner Witness to the Events of the Present World

Prophet Muhammad, peace and blessings be upon him, said: *"Islam began strange, and it will become strange again just like it was at the beginning, so blessed are the strangers"* (*Sahih Muslim*, 1/130). When asked who those blessed strangers were, he answered: *"Blessed are the strangers who restore what the people corrupt of my Sunnah"* (*Sunan at-Tirmidhi*, 2630).

Jose Marti: *"When others weep blood what right do I have to weep tears?"*

Bediüzzaman Said Nursi: *"Yes, be hopeful! The loudest and strongest voice in the coming upheavals and changes will be that of Islam!"*

Human history repeatedly shows us that humanity does not change until it is forced to do so. Today, the events in the political scenarios are starting to bear a spiritual character, they are gaining spiritual significance. How? History started the process of purification. Humanity is experiencing the rehearsal of the Day of Judgment. An awakening takes place, a spiritual resurrection takes place. Humanity is experiencing the end of times. Man slides between truth and falsehood. Time has started to speak to mankind. It is time for the truth behind the truth. It is time for the ultimate Truth. Major lessons for all mankind can be drawn. The Almighty is teaching His closeness to humanity. Ignorance and heedlessness get washed away. People on a worldwide scale have started to face each other. The universal consciousness gets enhanced. Hunger, material bankruptcy, tyranny, deprivation, misery, exploitation, war, calamities, poverty, death, torture, and oppression is experienced. Therefore the need for the truth is brought forth. As a result, higher awareness, wisdom, mercy, and compassion is being revealed.

Moreover, it has to be mentioned that not just the political events are gaining spiritual significance, today modern science is giving evidence for belief, respectively, God's revelation gets confirmed by the modern scientists. The higher awareness of the mystics meets in a harmonious manner with the new discoveries of modern scientist. On the one hand, the universe can be tested mathematically and on the other hand, religion can be scientifically explained. The process of human history unifies rational science with sacred wisdom, that is to say, modernity meets eternity. History brings union and closes the circle.

If we adapt the consciousness of unity of brotherhood, the consciousness of responsibility of servanthood, we become aware that our time carries the stamp of charity like no other time. It is the end of times, carrying in its womb the heaviness of sorrow and pure need. There is an alarming truth within our modern societies: the increase of refugees all over the world, hundred thousands of people displaced, unwanted, abandoned, thrown out of their homes, culture, countries, and separated from their own families. The refugees, the orphans, the immigrants, the destitute, the lonely, the homeless, the surprised, the terrorized, the widows, the prisoner of wars, the victims of earthquake, typhoons, and tsunamis... stripped off all worldly, became completely naked, waiting for our help, waiting for our supplications, waiting for comfort, embrace, warmth, waiting for homes, cloth, food, water, waiting for schools, education... These human tragedies demonstrate that a great part of the world's population has become totally incapacitated to live a normal, civilized life, just waiting, sitting displaying need. These are the orphans of the modern world. It is as if they wait to be judged, living the rehearsal for the Day of Judgment! As we learn from the Holy Qur'an: "*Did they feel secure from God's designing (against them some unexpected affliction)?*" (al-A'raf 7:99).

Our present time resembles the time when our blessed master started to receive the Divine revelations in Mecca. The first believers arrived in a state of total helplessness, left without bread and water, thrown out of their own homes, threatened with torture and threatened with death.

They were forced to immigrate and became refugees, homeless, suppressed, separated from their work, their surroundings, and their own families. Through the economical rulers drunk with power and arrogance Mecca turned in a place of tyranny, hostility, and hatred. Are Africa, Palestine, Syria, Egypt, and Iraq different today?

Our blessed master was an orphan alone in the desert—no father, no mother, no education, and no wealth, so he turned only to his beloved Lord for help. Whoever is left alone in the desert of the modern societies is like him. The poor, neglected, suppressed, sick, lonely, and destitute of today's world have no one else to turn to with their needs except God, the sole source of power, support, and help. The existence of orphans and refugees has not ended at all. To the contrary as we see, they are increasing in number every day. The world is staring at us with the eyes of poverty and need, destitution, and loneliness. Great parts of the world's population become spiritual orphans. These are the poorest of the poor, the most naked of the naked, because they lost everything. They are the refugees displaced from their homes and country to a nowhere land, or starved to death because of the brutal oppression of political tyrants. To understand our blessed master is to understand the state of an orphan, the state of the unlettered Prophet, the state of an immigrant. To be with him is to share his need and his poverty. As he said: "*My state is utter need, my poverty is my pride.*"

The most important action for believers is to take refuge in God Almighty. The world today shows pictures of crying need. Today, this need became unstained and pure because nothing is left other than Him. Even if we are far away from the state of refugees, far away from having lost our homes, families, and goods, we should adapt the consciousness of being orphans in this world, being helpless in this world, being pilgrims in this world, and being immigrants in this world. We have to recognize our total dependence on Him and try to shape our lives accordingly. Doing so, all things will be resolved, and we will live the peace and tranquility of the Qur'anic verse: "*God is well-pleased with them—and they are well-pleased with Him*" (al-Maedah 5:119). Let's supplicate to our Lord and ask Him to increase our need towards Him and help us become aware of our dependence towards Him.

The greatest victory is to gain unity, *tawhid,* and the greatest loss is the loss of unity. In our present time, unity, wholeness, togetherness, oneness, and embracement have vanished from people's lives. The virus of separation and division has taken their place. Unity is extinguished as a name, as a reality, as an attribute, as a power, and as a human link. In the present time, we can observe the splitting up of families, the division of societies, the division of countries, and the division of continents. All is at war with all, people destroy each other, and there is an increase of sectarian violence, aggression, threats, terror, and corruption. On one side, great cosmic war, one continent is at war with the continent, half of the world is at war with the other half of the world. On the other side, I see the microcosmic war, the tiniest fraction is at war with the tiniest fraction, families are at war with families, tribes with tribes, family members are at war with family members, neighbors with neighbors, community members are at war with community members, corporations members with corporation members, sects with sects. It is human dispute, argument, aggression, opinion, arrogance, a war of words, which shows that we lost common belief and therefore we experience the greatest tragedy of all, the separation of hearts.

Scientists split the atom apart and the atom bomb got invented. Oppenheimer, one of its inventors, warned that: "*If atomic bombs are to be added as new weapons to the arsenals of a warring world, or to the arsenals of the nations preparing for war, then the time will come when mankind will curse the names of Los Alamos and Hiroshima. The people of this world must unite or they will perish.*" We witness today an earthquake of material and spiritual nature has shaken humanity to extremes. We are smitten with heavy destructive forces all over the planet. A global malaise is spreading through the world's arteries. We live in a time where corruption, abuse, falseness, distortion, injustice, perversion, exploitation, and aggression have reached their peaks. People abused their trusteeship with God. People abused nature, they abused human relations, and they abused the Divine order of the cosmos. We live in a humanitarian crisis. God took away the values of security, health, trust, order, comfort, and peace.

As long as poor people do not get good treatment, as long as the people of power and superiority wish to keep controlling the people inferior to them, as long as beggars do not receive attention and respect, as long as the powerful exploit the helpless, as long as there is child prostitution, child labor, and child trafficking, as long as mothers and fathers

sell their own children, as long as there are innocent children held in prison indefinitely, as long as the innocent get victimized, as long as there
are millions of people forcefully displaced, as long as there are millions
of victims of civil wars, as long there is an election for new government,
but instead of voting it becomes a war, as long as there are foreign pri-
vate contractors trample over the poorest people on earth and with their
rootless greed and reduce the conditions of their lives to the lowest levels, depriving them of the most fundamental sustenance like drinking
water and electricity, as long as black people are rejected and enslaved
because of their color, as long as the terror of poverty remains and the
desperation reaches such heights that a mother sells her own child for
slavery and sexual abuses, what should we say? What can we do?

The suffering of our fellow beings all over the world has to become
the sufferance of all people. Human misery has to bring people together.
The problem the whole world is facing has to unify all of humanity. Not
to feel the injustice to brothers and sisters in another part of the world,
not to feel sadness for the sick and poor, is human irresponsibility. A
heart insensitive to human misery in the rest of the world, not sharing
the sufferance in active help, charity and supplication, is in fact a dead
heart. Witnessing the sufferance, oppression and injustice of one's fellow beings has to fill one's heart with compassion and sadness. Sufyan
ibn Uyayna says: *"God sometimes has mercy on a whole nation because of
the weeping of a broken heart."*

Holding life sacred is the absolute condition for the functioning of a
healthy society. With the absence of this awareness and attitude towards
creatures and creation, human beings will head into moral, social, and
religious decay. Selling one's own children represents a human tragedy
on a much bigger scale than smuggling drugs and weapons, business corruption, lying, and stealing. Does not the today's human tragedies resemble the time of Prophet Moses, peace be upon him, where the tyrant Pharaoh buried the male children alive?

We have to show care and love for others, we have to give to the
ones in need below our material level, being concerned to serve them, as
well as receiving from the ones above our spiritual level, being concerned to learn from them. In other words, we have to spend our sustenance, materially and spiritually, in Allah's cause. We have to give up the
reasoning of the lower senses; we have to soften our hearts in order to

get receptive towards Divine realms of everlastingness, His beauty, and perfection. If we know God as the All-Merciful, if we receive mercy as His gift, we will leave aggression, rivalry, ignorance, arrogance, power hunger, and envy. If we become the possessor of higher awareness, how can we do what we do, respectively, kill, terrorize, hate, and tyrannize? Human beings, especially today, have to acknowledge that they cannot answer people's threats by threatening them. We should not dispel darkness with darkness. We cannot fight evil by doing evil. We should not answer people's attacks by attacking them. We cannot answer people's hatred by hating them. We should not dispel hostility with hostility. We should dispel darkness with light. We should fight evil with goodness. We should forgive our enemies whatever they do. When we do not forgive people for their misconduct, how can we ask God Almighty to forgive us? This is Divine policy, we should try to adapt the following behavior: What we wish for ourselves, we have to wish for our fellow beings, otherwise our faith is not complete.

The greatest problem people have in today's societies is not so much the possession of money; it is more so obsession with position, status, power, authority, and rank. This attitude creates purposeful relationships, profitable relationships, and calculative relationships instead of servanthood. It is the worst cancer spreading into the hearts of people destroying the inner life of man. What is left is animalistic behavior, power hunger, greed for superiority, obsession for ownership, pathological desire to control other people. All these deformations of human character happen through the absence of love. All the great religions God sent to humanity were given for the purpose to teach justice among people. Only through the triumph of love can people find peace, justice, righteousness, and equality with each other. For when man is leaving worldly status and honor, he will be able to gain the station of servanthood.

Some statements from an American newspaper: "*When we look at Iraqi people, they are now facing an 'everyday apocalypse,' a complete security meltdown in which crime and terror flourish. Bush's war has created the greatest humanitarian catastrophe of our time. Not only 700,000 dead, millions more maimed or traumatized for life, and an entire country reduced to rubble, but the assassination of teachers and intellectuals went into high-gear. Archeological sites, museums, and anything else connected to Iraqi cultural and historical identity is under relentless attack. The attacks on holy sites and mosques have persisted to this day. There is a conscious effort to destroy all the religious symbols and monuments which bind the people together in the shared experience of a common faith! The same sinister forces which are inciting the sectarian violence are trying to remove all sense of brotherhood and spirituality. Their objective is to "wipe the state clean" and rebuild the entire society according to their own corrupt policies."*

Why are there such division, splitting, distance, hostilities, separation, enmity, and dispute? Why is there such an increase in oppression, terror, and war? Why is there such an occurrence in different opinions and mentalities? What happened? We become each other's enemy, we are in war with each other, we kill each other, and we throw bombs on each other's mosques and churches. What is this sufferance, this misery, this oppression, and these invasions? There are hundred thousands of people held innocent in jails, why? Countries are demolished, civilizations are ruined, states are destroyed, and populations are extinguished. Communities, societies, families, friendships are collapsing. Conscience, morality, faith, psychology, mind, and hearts are demolished. In other words, in our present societies we witness the ultimate tragedy; human feelings are extinguished within the hearts of man!

However, we are not hopeless. If we turn to the All-Merciful with the purity of intention and the spirit of devotion, if we strive in His cause and for humanity's good with collective philanthropy, and if come together around high human values, it is possible to achieve a global peace.

The Fasting and the Holy Month of Ramadan

S awm is one of the five pillars of Islam in the ninth month of the Muslim calendar. The meaning of *Sawm* is to abstain. In this month, Allah has made it compulsory that the fasting be observed by day, and he has made the *Tarawih* Prayer a *Sunnah*.

The Holy Qur'an states: "*O you who believe! Prescribed for you is the Fast, as it was prescribed for those before you, so that you may deserve God's protection (against the temptations of your carnal soul) and attain piety*" (al-Baqarah 2:183).

When the month of Ramadan arrives, the Divine Throne, the Sublime Seat, and all the angels proclaim the good tidings to the Community of Muhammad: "*Good news, O Community of Muhammad! Congratulations to you!*"

Prophet Muhammad, peace and blessings be upon him, is reported having said:

"*If my community realized what Divine grace there is for them in Ramadan, they would beg their Lord to let the month of Ramadan fill the whole year. For all good works are rewarded many times over during this month. Worship is accepted, supplication is granted, and past sins are forgiven. In Ramadan, Paradise falls in love with my community.*"

"*Paradise is divided into four groups for my community; those who recite the Qur'an, those who guard their tongues against foul speech, those who feed the hungry, those who keep the fast in Ramadan.*"

"*On the first day of Ramadan, Satan and the infidel jinn are clapped in irons. The gates of Hell are shut.*"

"*On the first night of Ramadan, the Lord of Majesty gives the call: Is there no one to love Us, that We may love him? Is there no one who wants Us, that We may seek him? Is there no one seeking Our forgiveness, that We may pardon him in honor of Ramadan?*"

"*On the first day of Ramadan, a breeze blows from beneath the Divine Throne. The rustling of the leaves of Paradise produces a musical sound more harmonious than anyone ever heard.*"

We know these heavenly melodies were heard by our blessed master at the night of the ascension. Our master reports that the *houries* pray on hearing these modes: "*O Lord make us the mates of Your servants who earn Your pleasure by fasting in this blessed month.*"

Each night of Ramadan, Allah calls His servants: "*Has no one a wish that I may Grant it? Does no one repent that I may grant his repentance? Does no one seek forgiveness that I may pardon him?*" Every day in Ramadan a million people deserving torment are delivered from the fire. This continues until the first Friday, and on that day a million of people deserving torment are pardoned every hour. On the last day of Ramadan, another million people obtain Divine pardon for every single individual pardoned up to that time.

On the day of Resurrection, the Almighty will embody the month of Ramadan in a beautiful form and take it into His Presence and Ramadan will prostrate itself. The Lord will say, "*Come state your need!*", and it will say: "*O Lord, let me intercede for those who respect me, grant me this right of intercession!*" Then the Lord of all the worlds will reply: "*Be an intercessor for those who respect you, observe you and know what you deserve.*"

God gives us the good news about Ramadan; the smell of the breath of the one who fasts is sweeter to Him than the fragrance of musk. With a truthful fast, the so called bad odor is transformed into the manifestations His Attributes of compassion and mercy.

Ramadan is the month of the birth of the Holy Qur'an. The entire month of Ramadan is in essence a celebration of the revelation of the Qur'an, which is described as a "*A guidance and mercy for those devoted to doing good, aware that God is seeing them*" (Luqman 31:3). Ramadan celebrates God's Mercy by which He sent a guiding light with the Holy Qur'an that leads human life towards the path of goodness and virtue. For this reason Ramadan is called the month of light, affecting the fasting believers with its sacred attraction and power.

Prophet Moses, peace be upon him, the converser with Allah, used to spend time at Mount Sinai. One day he asked his Creator to reveal Himself to him, and God answered: "*You shall not see Me! Moses, how can you see My beauty when there are seventy-thousand curtains between us?*

You are incapable of seeing Me. But near the Resurrection I shall give a month as a gift to the Community of My beloved Muhammad. That month shall be called Ramadan. To that community that fasts during that month, I shall so manifest Myself at the time of breaking fast, whereas between you and Me there are now seventy-thousand veils, but there will be no veil at all between Us and the fasting community of Muhammad at the time of breaking fast."

A significant conversation took place on the night of ascension, which sums up the comprehensive treasury of the glorious month of Ramadan. The exalted Lord said to our noble Prophet: *"Do you know the reward due to a servant of Mine if he fasts and keeps silent to please Me?"* Our master said: *"My Lord, I do not know."* So the Exalted One explained: *"The reward for fasting, keeping silence, and not talking too much is wisdom. The legacy of wisdom is spiritual knowledge. The end of spiritual knowledge is closeness to Me. I have three rewards for anyone who conducts himself to please Me and earn My Divine approval; I shall teach him such knowledge that no ignorance will remain in him. I shall give him such intelligence that no forgetfulness will remain in him. I shall give him such affection that he will love nothing other than Me. That servant of Mine will have his heart so full of My love that there will be no space in it for any other. I love those who love Me. I also cause them to love My servants. I make them kings of the heart."*

The Glorious Lord mentioned to Prophet Moses, peace be upon him, some of the bounties He had granted the Community of Muhammad: *"Moses, I have given the community of Muhammad two lights, so that two dark shades may not harm them."* He then asked: *"What are these lights You have given to the community of Muhammad, O Lord?"* Allah replied: *"One is the light of Ramadan and the other is the light of the Qur'an."* Prophet Moses, peace be upon him, asked: *"My Lord, what are these two dark shades?"* The Glorious Lord answered: *"One is the darkness of the tomb while the other is the darkness of the Day of Resurrection."* The tomb of one who recites the Qur'an is illuminated by the light of the Qur'an, so he does not see the darkness of the grave. The light of Ramadan will not leave the believers in darkness on the Day of Resurrection. True worship is generated in the domain of selflessness and in the domain of the angels; it is the conjunction of light upon light. Ignorance and heedlessness belongs to the domain of the ego and Satan; it is darkness within darkness.

Mankind is in this world in order to cultivate the trade for the Hereafter. The wisdom of the fast of Ramadan is to enforce the cultivation for the Hereafter. Respectively, the experience of fasting is to obtain Divine approval with intensified worship and service. Ramadan is the month of joyful obedience, loving surrender, and pleasure in faith. It represents an extremely profitable market for the trade of the Hereafter. It is a brilliant holy festival where we celebrate the heights of true belief, the loving universal embrace of brotherhood. Sincere believers can earn His contentment, His pleasure, His approval; they can earn the innumerable bounties of Paradise, rewards, and Divine favors, which are exclusively given in Ramadan. The heavens are at our disposal, the Divine treasures are opened. Paradise adorns itself with beauty for the community of Muhammad. The entire universe and all that it contains, all the angels celebrate in honor of this month. Allah closes the gates of Hell. He looks on His servants with compassion in this month. When they offer supplication, He addresses them saying: *"O My servant, from you supplication, from Me acceptance. From you the question, from Me the answer. From you the request, from Me the pardon and forgiveness."*

The month of Ramadan is one of the Almighty's most excellent creations. He holds this month in greatest esteem and made it into the sultan of all months and into the month of light. This glorious month represents, therefore, a Divine treasure beyond comprehension with inexhaustible blessings. Allah created this exalted month in order to show His love for His believing servants, and to show His mercy and forgiveness to the fasting believers. The members of the community of Muhammad receive the gift of the perfection of His Divine light in Ramadan. So we can name this month, with the infinity of Allah's Names and Attributes, the month of mercy, the month of forgiveness, the month of sacred communication, the month of obedience, the month of affection, the month of oneness, the month of Divine guidance, the month of the community, the month of togetherness, the month of embrace, the month of spiritual nourishment, the month of the Divine favors, the month of Divine grace, and the month of brotherhood. In return, the believers get an opportunity to show their love and thankfulness to their Lord by performing the true fast, the most excellent fast, namely to be with their Beloved excluding everything else, so that only the love for Him remains in their hearts. That way they fulfill the goal of the fasting month and the goal of life on earth and arrive at the level of: "*God is well-pleased with them—and they are well-pleased with Him*" (al-Maedah 5:119).

All five pillars are given to prepare oneself for the day of Resurrection. As Jalal al-Din Rumi says: "*The spirit of all knowledge is only this; to know who you will be on the Day of Resurrection.*" Being hungry, thirsty, and naked, the believers get reminded on this day where they wait to be judged by Allah. One of the greatest fears is the fear of waiting for one's judgment on the day of Resurrection. It is more frightening and burning than the fire of Hell. Everyone will ask, what will become of me? To shorten this profoundest fear, our beloved master will intercede for all human beings and plead with Allah: "*Forgive O Lord these servants of Yours!*"

To deprive oneself of eating, drinking, and sleeping is one of the most rigorous experiences human beings can experience because one reduces one's most central life functions to a minimum. Without giving one's body food and sleep, one cannot survive. Therefore, hunger is the most effective teacher to learn about one's base nature and one's human needs. The experience of fasting also represents a perfect cure for impatience and lack of endurance. God's Messenger relates that God Almighty asked the carnal self: "Who am I, and who are you?" It replied: "You are Yourself, and I am myself." However much God punished it and repeated His question, He received the same answer. But when He subjected it to hunger, it replied: "You are my All-Compassionate Lord; I am Your helpless servant" (Nursi, *The Letters*).

Ibn Arabi comments: "*If hunger were for sale in the market place, spiritual aspirants (al-muridun) should purchase nothing else!*" There is a famous utterance from the mercy for all the worlds: "*Knock on the door of hunger.*" Hunger generates the absolute need of creatures for their Creator; hunger burns away impurities and clears the way to the Lord of Majesty and Bounty. It is the thirsty who look for water, it is the needy that plead, pray, cry and ask for salvation. Hunger is our supreme teacher for all spiritual sicknesses. It is a remedy for all human distress, calamities, fears, and depression. In Rumi's words: "*Spend less time seeking water and acquire thirst! Then water will gush from above and below. Indeed, hunger is the sultan of remedies. Place hunger in the soul—regard it not with such contempt! Hunger makes all unpleasant things pleasant—but without it, all pleasant things are rejected. Hunger keeps on coming to you from your healthy constitution and burns away indigestion and boredom.*"

When a man gains the ready cash of hunger, his organs and members become married to constant renewal. God has given hunger to His elect so that they might become mighty lions. No physician gives pills and medicine without an illness—I will become totally pain so that I may reach the Remedy. When love's heartache leaves the breast for an instant, the house becomes a tomb and all its inhabitants grieve. I wonder at that seeker of purity who flees cruelty at the time of polishing. Love is like a lawsuit and to suffer cruelty is the witness; if you have no witness, your lawsuit is lost."

A wise man said: "*True comfort is freedom from the desires of the lower self! Your prison is your own lower self. As soon as you escape from it, you will live in the comfort of eternity.*" Fasting is the method to free oneself from the tyranny of one's lower self. In other words, what makes you free is the abundance of what imprisons you. The wisdom of the fasting month is this: Do not fill your stomach with food, so you might see the light of wisdom within yourself. To become the king of your own heart is the result of true fasting.

The month of Ramadan is specifically designed by the All-Merciful to heal ourselves from physical and spiritual sicknesses. Fasting is a treasury of healing. A fasting practitioner who has attained his physical and spiritual health has attained the consciousness of responsibility.

"To fast from the world" brings us paradoxically closer to the world, penetrating into the dynamic of human life on earth. It brings us closer to ourselves, it brings us closer to our fellow beings, and therefore it brings us closer to our Lord. It is the fast in the world from the world in order to increase love for the Lord. This is the treasury of fasting, the healing from the terror of selfishness, from the lower desires of the flesh, from the darkness of unconsciousness.

The true fasting equips oneself with a true vision of how things really are. It increases and illuminates the inner horizon of sacred awareness. The fast with all our senses, feelings, mind, and heart will enable us to distinguish truth from falsehood and eventually generate an awareness which enables oneself to discriminate the smallest particle of good from the smallest particle of evil. True fasting works within the deepest layers of human existence because it reduces one's primary life activities to a minimum. Fasting moves the chemistry and the hormones of the human body to such an extent that all fuzziness, indifference, silliness, confusion, absentmindedness, denial, doubt, opinion, and disbelief gets removed and washed away from the mind, the feelings, and the heart.

Holding the fast properly means holding oneself or restraining oneself. Holding oneself means being in control of oneself and being in control of oneself means becoming aware of one's oneself. Being aware of oneself means becoming aware of God. Once the power of control is established, one will be able to submit and submitting oneself in all matters of life will bring sacred awareness. That is to say, the degree of one's consciousness of Allah is given in proportion to the degree of one's submission.

The root of all sicknesses is attachment to the world, and the healing from all sicknesses is to be attached to the Hereafter. The most effective method to heal and detach oneself from the world is through hunger and need. With the help of fasting, one learns to say no to the world and yes to the Hereafter, respectively, one becomes impoverished by the world and enriched by the Divine Presence. Thus, fasting lowers all things that belong to the world and heightens all things that belong to the Hereafter. In this respect, our noble master reports in a tradition: "*When the month of Ramadan starts, the gates of mercy are opened and the gates of Hell are locked and the devils are chained.*"

Fasting teaches us to control and decrease our love for comfort and enforces us to increase our love for poverty. It means stripping off our material being, shedding off the heavy weight of the world, removing the thick veils covering our soul, and breaking the idols of the heart. Fasting combined with heightened worshipping activities during this month can bring us to a place where we become able to rediscover our roots, find our true self, in absolute need. This is true fasting, to become in need, longing, desire, and poverty in front of His door, with tearful supplications and intimate conversations.

Fasting expands our breast, the seat for love and affection, and heightens the horizon of sacred awareness. It brings the mind and heart together because they are equally stimulated and nourished through each other. The heart finds satisfaction through perpetual nourishment with the light of the Qur'an, Prayer, supplication, almsgiving, and works of service. The intellect finds enlightenment and eternal bliss in contemplation, *sohbet*, remembrance, and tearful supplications.

Reducing our lives to working, sleeping, and eating means to sink into the biological level of existence. If we wish to save ourselves from the dangerous and low places of human existence, we have to discover the thirst of our soul. To become aware of the soul's thirst is to become aware of oneself. Obviously we suffer a great lack of sacred thirst in our mundane lives. Therefore, we are confronted with the problem of how to revitalize the sensitivity of hunger and thirst of our soul. The answer lies in the unfortunate fact that the soul is not attracted by the Water. Man veils the light of his own sun by the cloud of his unconsciousness. Thus fasting is the perfect means to wake up from unconsciousness and ignorance. Fasting effectively increases our sacred thirst; more precisely it increases the need for the truth. In order to understand our true nature and find the purpose of our lives, we have to occupy ourselves with God. We have to drink from the water of life, we have to eat from the banquet of the Heavens, and we have to experience the heavenly ascension. There is no reason that fasting is given to humanity other than it enables us to realize the eternal secret of human existence. If we do not build our lives on belief, we will be lost in moral decay, disorder, and ignorance. In other words, we will lack true humanity.

Ramadan is an annual training program to refresh the performance of our worship obligations: to rebuild our human relationships, to reestablish our good contacts, behaviors, actions, and intentions, to rediscover the joy of belief, to renovate the strength of sacred consciousness, to revitalize the feelings of compassion, generosity, humility, and love for the poor, hungry, and needy. Ramadan reawakens our soul, heart, spirit, mind, and feelings and reestablishes justice, peace, and harmony between human beings. Ramadan is a source of wealth in terms of character, faith, and illumination.

Fasting is equal to reconciliation. If fasting is taken serious, one has to go through all the registers of good and bad deeds throughout one's passed year. It is a renovation of one's inner condition, investigating what needs repair, what needs cleaning, rearranging, rebuilding, revival, what needs to be erased, what needs to be forgotten, what needs to be remembered, what needs to be thanked for, and especially, what needs repentance.

Fasting reinforces, strengthens, revitalizes what is valuable in ourselves. It is an inner reawakening of the components of what is human in ourselves, that is to say, it strengthens our humanity. What is the most valuable thing in us? It is our spirit, breathed at the time of creation of man with the Breath of the All-Merciful. To become aware of our spirit means to become aware of the thirst of our spirit. The spirit itself only gains value for us, in terms of our quenching its sacred thirst. Thus the fasting month is an excellent opportunity to nourish the spirit with worship and service. In Ramadan we have to set the table of the Heavens. This table is covered with the food of angels, the verses of the Qur'an, remembrance, ritual Prayer, fasting, and glorification of His Most Beautiful Names, with supplications, contemplation, and service. A satisfied soul shines with the beauty of its Divine light and will ascend towards the eternal realms of nearness towards the Lord of all the worlds, freed from the restrictions of the body. Further, fasting helps remove forgetfulness. The modern man is hopelessly caught up in the business of the world and forgets his sacred source. He becomes a stranger to himself. The power of this holy month will help human beings to rearrange their lives and rediscover their place in society and within their families, their place at work, in politics, in economics, in their country, and most of all Ramadan will help us revive and strengthen our relationship with our religion. Further, fasting works on human fear. It tranquilizes, harmonizes the inner organs, and gives comfort and peace to the mind and heart. The majority of people are holding onto worldly dignities, they are holding onto their rank, power, status, wealth, and possessions. They have a terrifying fear of losing their rank in society and what they possess. Fear is one of the basic human instincts; the fear of the unknown, fear of losing, fear of poverty, fear of human misery, fear of sickness, fear of loneliness, fear of sufferance, and fear of death. This is the wisdom of fasting, to let go of one's worldly ambitions, to give up feeling pride for one's status, for one's wealth, for one's superiority and to replace it with the feelings for compassion and love with the intention to serve the needy and poor. Fasting helps to lower the worldly fears and heightens the fear for Allah the Almighty. Once the worshipping believers are able to give up the fear of losing worldly dignities and ownership and on the other side begin to fear losing the Almighty's good pleasure and love, they will be able to walk firmly on the straight path, the *sirat-al-mustaqim*.

The essential wisdom of fasting is not merely physically restraining from food and drink, but the total commitment to the spirit of fasting. In the first stage, one concentrates on the fast with the senses: the fast of the nose, the eye, the ear, and the tongue, of which our blessed master said: "*A Muslim is he from whose tongue and hands other Muslims are safe,*" and "*Whoever does not give up backbiting, lying speech and acting on those lies and evil actions, then Allah will not accept his fasting.*" Thus one continues the fasting with one's extremities, the fast with one's hand, and the fast with one's feet. Thus the fasting with the five human senses and the extremities is exercised in order to prevent oneself from touching, smelling, seeing, talking, and listening to unlawful things. Once we undergo the training of our senses and extremities, we become ready to rise towards the higher levels of purity. In order to arrive at this ultimate level, we need to go through the fast of the mind, which is avoiding thoughts other than Allah, constantly remembering Him. Then we concentrate on the most important fast, the fast of the heart. This is accomplished by completely denying the world and its attraction, by suspending occupation with the world and cutting off all the attachments to it in order to break the false idols which occupy our hearts, so that nothing but God the Majestic can be received as our Guest in the clean and empty hearts. This is the level of the pure Self. Our organs will become a holy channel where Allah can act through us. The Divine tradition is then realized: "*When I love a servant by the voluntary acts he does, I become the eyes with which he sees, the ears with which he hears, the feet with which he walks, and the hand with which he grasps, and the tongue with which he talks. I become the strength in every part of his being.*" It means that all the fast which is done in addition to the fast with our bellies, the fast with our minds and hearts, represents an act of love. The servant tries with his own firm determination and uninterrupted struggle to approach his beloved Creator with voluntary acts of worship and service. He is full of longing and desire for union and therefore wholeheartedly submitted to his Lord of Majesty and Bounty. In other words, the secret of the month Ramadan is to experience the silence of the heart's speech. In this way, Ramadan becomes the treasury of intimate conversation. The sincere devotees who reached the sublime station of the perfect fast take such intense pleasure in obedience and submission, that hunger becomes their food. They attain the angelic attributes, feeding their spirit unceasingly with recitations, remembrance, Prayers, glorification, contemplation, and supplication. These devotees are able to experience Paradise on earth. They feel eternal comfort together with the most honored of all communities, the community of Muhammad, because they inhale the sweet scent of remembrance, day and night, without interruption.

Prophet Muhammad, peace and blessing be upon him, said: "*The one who fasts has two satisfactions. One is when he breaks his fast at the end of the day. The other is when he sees (his Lord).*" The whole wisdom of fasting lies in this teaching of our beloved master. There are uncountable levels of fasting, from the first level of exclusively fasting with one's stomach and the ultimate fasting of truth is the fasting which is not limited to the month of Ramadan, nor by any other time. Abdul Qadir al-Jilani explains in his discourses the different levels of breaking the fast. In the first stage, the believer experiences the pleasure of eating at the time of *iftar*. In the following stages, the pleasure of fast breaking is experienced in seeing the new moon. The ones who know the inner meaning of fasting experience the joy of breaking their fast the day when they will enter Paradise and partake of the delights therein.

The month of fasting is designed to turn the life of the believers upside down. Within one year, the religious practitioners are usually living a worldly life of regularity. Thus in Ramadan, this way of life turns into the way of life of the Hereafter. We have to consider the fact that the majority of believers throughout the whole year live in a state of moral and spiritual degeneration, exercising careless, heedless behavior with their bodies, senses, emotions, souls, hearts, and minds. Eleven months of dirt are gathered and in consequence the same amount of darkness is spreading into their hearts. In other words, people waste their lives away for eleven months, living in ignorance by which feelings, thoughts, speech, behavior, and actions become sullied by the dirt of worldly ambition. The qualities which elevate, purify, illuminate, and beautify human nature are neglected and thrown backstage, and what is worthless, low, insignificant takes the center of attention. In consequence, physical and spiritual sicknesses occur. It is precisely the power of the fasting which is able to reverse this disharmonious life style. The cleaning of the material self is easy to do, but the cleaning of the inner world, the spiritual self, is very difficult, because the spiritual sicknesses are engraved and imbedded in the deepest interior of our selves. For example, for the majority of people, the state of distortion, decay, corruption of their mental faculties, their intellect, human consciousness, psychology, and subconsciousness is the reason for a misinterpretation of reality. Rumi gives us an excellent description: *"You think you escape from torment and suffering, but your thinking is torment's fountainhead. Because of the darkness in your eyes, you imagine that a nothing is something. Your eyes can be made healthy and illuminated with the dust of the King's doorstep. He who is fortunate and is confidant of the mysteries knows that cleverness is from Iblis and love from Adam. Sell your cleverness and buy bewilderment! Cleverness is opinion, bewilderment vision."*

People usually have a spiritual defective understanding, a distorted view of the world and themselves. The mind produces fantasies, illusions, primitive games to satisfy the ego; their thoughts produce false pictures of the world in order to serve the sensual desires. Nevertheless it is precisely through the discipline of fasting that we get a chance to wash the polluted eyes in order to regain clean eyes. If we train ourselves wholeheartedly with the excellent teacher of hunger, the eye of weakness can turn into the eye of discrimination. The eye of wretchedness can turn into an eye of righteousness. The distorted eye can turns into a clear eye. The defective vision can reach a clear vision. The corrupted, distorted view can turn into a truthful consciousness. Confusion, irritation, chaos, and disorder of the mind find regulation, tranquility, harmony and clarity.

If the desires of our lower selves do not leave us, we cannot receive the sacred love from Allah. As our noble master said, *"The greatest enemy among your enemies is your (carnal) soul."* The month of fasting is precisely given from our Creator to help us conquer this enemy. Fasting helps us to oppose the animalistic desires like anger, fighting, aggressiveness and negativity in one's emotions, thoughts, words, and actions. Our bad habits are very hard to oppose because they are engraved in our body. Gluttony, excessive sleep, idle occupations, gossip, uncleanliness, laziness, heedlessness, and sensuality have become part of our personality. The Companions asked the beloved of Allah about the shortest way to reach Paradise, and he answered with just with one phrase: *"Do not get angry!"* To be victorious in refraining from breaking out in anger and aggression, not reacting with harshness and tension, not shouting or raising one's voice, is a clear sign to be able to control one's negativity and temper. To be able to control one's temper is one of the most difficult tasks for human beings. It requires all-comprehensive wisdom because it means to have control over one's nervous system. It needs spiritual intellect and heightened awareness. It needs the greatest efforts of patience, endurance, sincerity, and truthfulness. It is the essence of religious and ethical behavior. Prophet Jesus, peace be upon him, tells: *"Love your enemy."*

We are the key and the door for personal salvation, but at the same time we are its hindrance, its obstacle. The cage of existence, our body, prevents us from spiritual development, but at the same time, it is our means to reach the One and the Only. Thus it is through suffering that we can decrease suffering. It is through the experience of sickness that we can eliminate sicknesses. This principle is especially effective in terms of fasting. We fast in the world from the world. We fast with the body to overcome the body. Through the physical struggle, we can transcend our physical limits. Through our temporal, limited existence, we can realize our true existence. Thus we cure ourselves with our own selves. Once we can overcome the material self, we gain access to the true, spiritual self and reach selflessness. We have to see the world as a plain of the Hereafter. The fruit of eternity and sacred harmony are only earned through the struggle in daily life. Struggling makes one witness the Sacred Essence. This principle is also applied in the use of time. With the exact use of time we can reach timelessness, respectively through utmost precision in time, we can transcend time and space and reach the realms of infinity. In other words, the education of the body through fasting is nothing other than making matter subtle, and the heavy light, striving towards cleanliness and purity. In short, the body has to become refined by our own efforts up to the point of transforming it into a holy instrument, through which God Himself can act. This is a principal teaching of Islam; it teaches the wisdom that suffering is our remedy, hunger is our food, pain our salvation, nothingness is our gain.

Our blessed master said: *"Poverty is my pride."* The state of poverty our blessed master describes is the highest stage human beings can acquire. Poverty is the essence of the religion of Islam; it is the essential message of our beloved master, it is his basic quality, his main feature. True fast can only be performed when the state of poverty is reached. The ultimate goal of fasting is therefore to become poor towards the world, to empty oneself of selfhood in order to earn the eternal richness of Divine Presence. Poverty compromises all other most worthy features of the believer because it demands self-sacrifice. This sublime state of selflessness generates true humility, loving submission, bewildered admiration, infinite generosity, absolute contentment, and security, and most of all, pure servanthood. We have to know that the imprisonment in our bodies prevents us from becoming aware of our spirituality, the sacred reality within ourselves. To free oneself of the limits of mundane life, we must work on the way of spiritual poverty. If we are not freed from the restrictions of transient life, there is no taste of self-annihilation. As Rumi says: *"The miraj to heaven is non-existence."*

Ibn Arabi describes two ways of reciting Qur'an: *"In the one, the servant recites the Qur'an in God's Presence. In the other, it is God Who recites the Qur'an for the servant."* The majority of Muslims make fasting into a priority during the month of Ramadan. But actually it is the reversed way. We celebrate the birth of the Holy Qur'an with fasting. The holy month was given as a Divine gift to honor the night of power where the Divine revelations descended to humanity. Thus the wisdom of fasting is given to heighten our spiritual sensitivities and become receptive for the Divine revelations of the Holy Qur'an and to become part of its flow. One has to reach the capacity where one will become able to draw Divine guidance from the light of the Divine revelations of the Holy Qur'an. Our blessed master said in a tradition: *"The verses of the Qur'an, the wise and wondrous poems of love and sounds and voices of yearning, illuminate the face of the spirit."* The spirit of Ramadan is the Divine revelations of the Holy Qur'an. That is why the month of Ramadan is called the month of lights and the sultan of the months. Ramadan is like a palace, within which the believers celebrate the sultan of all nights, which is better than a thousand months. Therefore the believers fast, pray, recite the Holy Qur'an, give charity, and supplicate in order to give appropriate respect with the beauty of their abundant devotions.

In this sacred month, the sincere servants actually celebrate true belief and the joy to belong to the community of Muhammad and celebrating the belief in Divine unity, and celebrating the unity of brotherhood. For the lovers, this holy month offers the opportunity to celebrate the honor of carrying the title of "the member of the community of Muhammad." Therefore Ramadan represents the festival of the community of Muhammad. Millions of fasting believers share the light of faith, the light of the Divine revelations, the light of unity amongst the religious brotherhood of our noble master, Prophet Muhammad, peace and blessings be upon him. The Holy Qur'an has to become part of our lives; it has to become our nature. The month of Ramadan is precisely a perfect opportunity to train oneself in making the Holy Qur'an the central focus point of one's life. That is to say, to wholeheartedly occupy one's self with the Divine revelations. The believers are created for the sole purpose, to bow to the Truth day and night. This is the gift of the holy month Ramadan, the whole world is turned into a Divine stage for the fasting community, where we play the most honorable role of believing servants.

In Ramadan, we get a change to save ourselves from the modernization of our daily lives. Today's societies work on dehumanizing human nature. People lack truthfulness, wholeness, integrity, grace, and blessings. Modernization is like a virus which spreads throughout the whole world. This virus is called materialism, capitalism, or secularism. People's daily lives are built on consumerism, devoid of spirituality. They never forget to feed their bodies. They utterly exaggerate in eating, sleeping, and talking. They suffer from boredom, emptiness, indigestion, and baseness. The month of Ramadan reverses this disproportionate lifestyle and enforces the exaggeration in worship, service, remembrance, and supplication.

Modern man lost the true purpose of his life. He is deceived by his ego and his senses. He is deceived by the attraction of the world. He suffers from self-importance, self-centeredness. His life degenerates either into an animal or a machine. He has become a stranger to himself to such an extent that he turns into a tyrant, a monster, or a corpse. He lost spirituality, togetherness, oneness, and brotherhood. The worst loss is the loss of the Divine unity, *tawhid*. In that sense, fasting is an antidote against the virus of profanity, secularism, capitalism, materialism, ignorance. It is an offence against the modern world; it is a shield, an antivirus. It exterminates the material values of selfishness. It is an antidote against the splitting up of religions, the dividing of countries, the separations of tribes, the fight between friends, the gap between upper and lower classes, the breaking up of couples, the splitting apart within societies, and the degeneration of families. The modern man lives in danger: The sicknesses of his heart can cause his spiritual death. Ignorance, heedlessness, and darkness of unconsciousness is equal to a spiritual suicide.

If the secret of the month of Ramadan is smelled with the nose of good fortune, if the heart is softened to such extents that its owner becomes senseless, incapacitated, helpless, and smashed into tiny pieces in the sea of regretful tears, then the heart understands that this month is the month of supplication to the Ever-Living and the Self-Subsisting! For the sincere servants in the fasting month, the world turns into the plain of Arafat. It is the headquarter of all hearts, it is this most excellent plateau where beams of light shone back and forth like a fuse from earth to heaven and heaven to earth, where the spiritual calls go back and forth, "*O my Lord, O my Lord!*", and "*My servants, My servants!*" The plain of Arafat bears the symbolism of the eternal rendezvous of the invoker with the Invoked, the worshipper with the Worshipped, the lover with the Beloved, and the seeker with the Sought. If fasting is understood to turn oneself wholeheartedly to one's desired Lord, renouncing the world and what it contains, renouncing one's lower desires, appetites, and ambitions, then we can step on the plateau of Arafat, the plain where the fruits of *marifa*, the most exclusive wisdom, are plucked, where the comfort of eternity is felt. Then we can pronounce loving whispers from our hearts towards our Beloved Lord.

Allah the Exalted made a promise long before the creation of the world: "*My Mercy encompasses by far My Wrath... I forgive you before you ask forgiveness from Me.*" A friend of Allah, Sahl al-Tustari describes the quality of repentance: "*When God loves a person, He makes this person's sin appear great and opens to him the door of repentance. This door opens to the gardens of intimacy with God. When He becomes angry with a person, He makes his sins appear very small in that person's eyes and He punishes him with a variety of calamities; but because the person is unfortunate enough to see his sins as small, he does not take advice and the result is frustration and disappointment.*" Repentance done with sincerity is a light from God, opening up the doors of Allah's mercy and forgiveness and purifying the inner being. The All-Merciful created the month of Ramadan in order to show His compassion and forgiveness for the fasting community, which manifested in the Holy Qur'an with the Almighty's often repeated Names, *Ghafur* and *Rahim*, the All-Forgiving and the All-Merciful. Through fasting, believers find to the door of repentance, which is held wide open especially in the exalted month of Ramadan from where Divine grace and inexhaustible blessings flow. In the spiritual development of man, repentance is the first step, and the rising of every succeeding level is again obtained through repentance. As the goal of fasting offers the healing from one's spiritual sicknesses and the opportunity for self-renewal and the final purification and thereby cleansing oneself of everything other than God, the fasting believers need total commitment to the plead with their Creator for forgiveness. Without feeling regretful, we cannot reach true humanity. Without repentance, we cannot reach the treasury of love. If repentance is not felt by the heart, it is worthless. Repentance means to establish a humble relationship with one's Creator as His creature, with one's Lord as His servant. True repentance means to cut the ties to the world and turn wholeheartedly to one's Creator in tearful supplication. True repentance is asking for God's mercy. The business in this world, the goal of human existence in this world, is to learn to take refuge in the Lord of all the worlds, to take refuge in God's mercy from His punishment, to take refuge in His pleasure from His wrath. Only taking refuge in God brings creatures to the nearness to Him. In that sense, true repentance means to take refuge in Him from Satan, the accursed, from the temptations of the world, from the heaviness of one's body, from the demands of one's ego. One has to recognize one's sins, imperfection, mistakes, and heedlessness. One has to feel regret, remorse, and shame for one's bad habits, negativity, fighting, anger, idle occupations, excessive sleep and eating, greed, and arrogance. True repentance means to fear and love Allah. There is outer repentance and inner repentance. The former is pronounced by the tongue of the common man. The latter is done with the heart which necessitates cleaning one's heart of all worldly desires, idols, spiritual sicknesses, dirt, and dust and replacing it with the Divine love for the All-Merciful.

True repentance has to be connected with human tears, that is to say, repentance is hardly effective without shedding tears of sorrow and regret. Tears of repentance open the door of helplessness, need, poverty, and modesty. The truthful repentance creates shame, *haya*, and shame is the awareness of love. Tears can open the horizon of awareness for the recognition of one's servanthood and one's total dependence and need for God. There are pearls far more valuable than the pearls one can find in the deep sea. These are pearls running down the cheeks; these are the human tears. Only and only in the life of this world tears can run down the cheeks of human beings. Man has to regain the capacity to cry tears. It means to water the desert of worldly existence with our tears of admitted incapacities. It means to soften our hearts with modesty, shame, and humility.

The Qur'an states: "*They (Adam and Eve) said (straightaway): 'Our Lord! We have wronged ourselves, and if You do not forgive us and do not have mercy on us, we will surely be among those who have lost!"* (al-A'raf 7:23). Rumi comments: *"When God wants to help us, He turns our inclination towards lamenting (and repentance). How fortunate is the eye that cries for Him and how auspicious is the heart that burns for Him. Wherever there is running water, there is greenery; wherever there are running tears, there is the Mercy of God. If you want such tears then take pity on those who shed tears; if you desire mercy, take mercy on others"* (*Masnawi*, I/817–822)*"The outer dirt can be cleaned with water, but the inner dirt keeps on increasing; it can be cleansed only by water of the eyes when it becomes manifest"* (*Masnawi*, III/2092–2093). *"Beware! Don't desire your dog-like selfhood alive for it has been your bitter enemy for ages. Pour dust on the head of these bones if they hinder the killing of the dog (of selfhood). You have shed tears for others, weep for yourself for a while, because it is due to the crying clouds that the boughs and trees become green and the candle burns brighter with tears"* (*Masnawi*, II/474–480). We need God like a baby who cries for milk.

The Holy Qur'an states, *"Surely God loves those who turn to Him in sincere repentance (of past sins and errors), and He loves those who cleanse themselves"* (al-Baqarah 2:222). The additional heart of this work of repentance is consistency. Sincere believers should never leave their plead for repentance to their Creator through their whole lives. Even the beloved of Allah, the purest and spiritually most elevated of all creatures, used to ask forgiveness seventy to hundred times every day. A sincere believer never leaves the state of repentance because he lives in the consciousness of always residing in God's Presence. He is taking refuge in the All-Merciful at all times and in all places; therefore, he is never unaware of his insufficiencies and nothingness in front of God's Greatness and Perfection. When sincere devotees forget Allah for a single moment, they immediately repent and feel urged to take a great ablution in order to wash themselves clean from their moment of heedlessness, whereas the majority feels the necessity for repentance only when they are sinning. Furthermore, a heart exercising continuous repentance is living with the fear and love for its Creator. Such a heart will be guided by Allah the Almighty and become wakeful and alert at all times in all places, not sliding and deviating even for one millimeter from the Straight Path.

Some examples of the supreme value of sincere repentance: Bahauddin Walad, a well-respected scholar, comes from Kayseri to Konya in order to train Rumi. He makes him enter three times in a row the profoundest spiritual discipline of the retreat, *halwat,* in order to grow into the Divine Presence. When Rumi completed this long-lasting seclusion, his master asked him about his ascetic experiences. Rumi reported to his master the following: "*At the end of the seclusion, I asked Allah the Almighty to forgive me. Then I heard a voice; 'I forgive you, I forgive you, I forgive you! Again I asked Allah to forgive the community of Muhammad and I received the same answer three times.*" The wisdom we can gain from the highest disciplinary efforts of 120 days of seclusion from Rumi, who is one of the greatest saints who ever lived, lies in the sole concern; to be forgiven by his Lord.

We know that one of the most important celebrations of the Islamic calendar is the Night of Absolution (or Salvation). This celebration stretches over three nights in which our blessed master throughout the whole nights until the morning asked forgiveness from his Lord for his most desired community. Allah the Merciful granted forgiveness in the first night for one third of his community, in the second night for two third, and in the third night for all of the members of his community.

Our blessed master will not wish to enter Paradise at the Day of Judgment before his beloved Lord forgives every single soul of his community and grants them entry into Paradise.

Four people consulted our spiritual master. Each one with different problems and questions, but his answer was always the same: "*Repent before the Almighty!*"

We know that Prophet Adam's most excellent virtues were the qualities of shame and repentance. After being expelled from Paradise and arriving on earth, he felt utter shame and felt the urge to repent at once and he cried for 40 years asking for forgiveness.

We have to consider that we cannot ask Allah's forgiveness if we do not forgive our fellow brothers and sister. Actually one of the best actions for the believers is to forgive enemies although they might do harm and act unjustly. How can we ask forgiveness from the All-Forgiving, the All-Merciful if we do not forgive our brothers? Everything is conditional. If we thank Him, He will increase our prosperity. If we give charity, He will increase our wealth. If we trust in Him, if we take refuge in Him, He will give us all comprehensive protection, support, and help. If we are patient, kind, forgiving, and compassionate to human beings, God will answer with the same attributes we show towards His creatures. His love and His care for humanity are infinite. This was the most exalted behavior of our blessed master, Prophet Muhammad, peace and blessings be upon him, during his whole life. May Allah allow us to adapt his noblest behavior.

The Messenger of God says: "*It is not allowable for a Muslim to keep apart from his brother for more than three days.*" It shows that believers are not allowed their resentments to go on more than three days. It is a big sin to hold one's anger towards a person more than three days. The religion of Islam holds brotherhood above all.

The true fast is the fasting with Prophet Adam, peace be upon him, walking with him in the desert of worldly existence in the burning sand under one's feet, with the flame of love in one's heart, the heat of search in one's breast, and the streaming tears from one's eyes, wandering and searching restlessly for the Exalted One, like Adam, drawn by the pain of separation. In other words, our fasting efforts have to connect us with the first human being, the father of mankind. Our fasting has to draw us to walk in his footsteps, because he was searching for love, he was searching to regain the love, forgiveness, and contentment of Allah the Majestic with his tearful repentance. Our father had no eyes and ears for the world; his life was a fasting life. His life signifies true abstinence, true asceticism. He was made to leave the exalted station of Paradise where the angels prostrated to him and was made to descend on earth. He felt the pain of separation and asked His Lord for only one thing, His forgiveness and His mercy. Nevertheless, the pain of separation was not caused by the loss of Paradise or the loss of the company of the angels. His true loss was the loss of his Beloved. Therefore, if the fasting is not a fast from the world for the sake of increasing love for the Lord of the worlds, our fasts are lost efforts and struggles. The result is only some good meal at the time of fast breaking, nothing more. The opposite of fasting is not luxury, wealth, status, or ownership, as the opposite of poverty is not richness. Wealth, glamour, and luxury are the absence of love, which means, the opposite of fasting is the absence of the sacred love for the All-Merciful. Fasting from the world is gaining the treasury of love and sacred awareness. True asceticism is staying in retreat alone in intimacy with one's beloved Lord. Remaining in the pleasures of the world signifies the separation from one's Lord. The wisdom we can draw from our father is that love is only sold in the house of human grief, hardship, efforts, and fasting.

To conclude, fasting means cleaning, and cleaning means to fulfill two conditions: repentance and *muhabbat,* higher love and affection. It is the heart which has to be cleansed with these two attributes. This is the wisdom of Adam. Repentance opens the door of helplessness, need, poverty, and modesty. It opens the horizon of awareness for the recognition of one's servanthood and one's total dependence. The recognition of one's mistakes, insufficiencies, incapacities, heedlessness, weakness, and imperfection is the crucial point where love starts.

It is through fasting that the feeling of mercy and compassion for the poorer classes of people, the underprivileged, the oppressed, and the needy get enhanced. Fasting increases the sensitivity for one's fellow human beings; it opens up the awareness of one's brothers and sisters in the whole world. Of all the favors and bounties given by the All-Providing, Ramadan represents the gift of unification. For 30 days and night, the whole world of believers is worshipping the Lord of all the worlds, thereby practicing universal love. Gradually, as the fasting days follow each other, human beings feel an increase of loving embrace towards each other. The more one fasts, the more one feels closer to fellow beings. It is a miraculous feeling of shared love of brotherhood, spreading throughout the fasting crowds across the whole world. Additionally, millions of believers pray in congregation every night after the fast breaking, the most unifying Prayers; the *Tarawih.* Performing this Prayer means to experience the soul of the holy month of Ramadan. Sharing the infinite blessings of this Prayer, the worshippers all over the world melt into one body of loving brotherhood. Thus through the feeling of universal love in this sacred month, the devotees attain the awareness of poverty, the awareness of injustice, the awareness of sickness, and oppression. In other words, they become sensitized towards human suffering. They learn to share the pain, calamities, and the miseries of their fellow beings. This state represents one of the sublime treasures of Ramadan. In fact, one of the sacred conditions of this holy month lies precisely in the fact that the fast has to be connected with good works and service which benefit society. Therefore it is highly recommended, that one gives alms, during this month. As Allah's mercy, forgiveness, and favors flow in abundance during this noble month, so should the fasting believers increase their generosity, compassion, and love towards their fellow human beings. Thus, by trying to perform the duties of servanthood in this noble month, the worshipping believers will return the Almighty's given favors and bounties. This is the beauty of this month, they get a chance to prove their love for the One and Only.

When we study Abdul Qadir al-Jilani's life, we become aware that the ultimate fasting, which is fasting from the world and its inhabitants, brings us to the unimaginable heights of sacred illumination and wisdom. From early childhood, the saint heard voices while he was studying or playing with other children saying: "*You are not created for this!*" Then he saw a vision of pilgrims on the plain of Arafat. After this profound spiritual experience, at a very early age, Abdul Qadir al-Jilani felt compelled to ask his mother for permission to leave his school and family life in order to go on the spiritual journey in search for the path of truth. At the first stages of his journey, when he was going to enter the city of Baghdad, Khidr appeared to him and prevented him from entering, taking him to the desert outside of the city where he remained for 25 years. Abdul Qadir al-Jilani himself reports: "*During my stay in the desert, all that appears beautiful but is temporal and of this world came to seduce me. Allah protected me from their harm. The Devil, appearing in different shapes kept coming to me, tempting me, bothering me, and fighting me. Allah rendered me victorious over him. My ego visited me daily in my own form and shape, begging me to be its friend. When I would refuse, it would attack me. Allah rendered me victorious in my continuous fight against it. In time I was able to make it my prisoner and I kept it with me all those years, forcing it to stay in the ruins of the desert. A whole year I ate the grasses and roots I could find and did not drink any water. Another year I drank water but did not eat a morsel of food. Another year I neither ate, nor drank, nor slept. All of this time I lived in the ruins of the ancient king of Persia in Al-Karkh. I walked barefoot over the desert thorns and did not feel a thing. Whenever I saw a cliff, I climbed it. I did not give a minute's rest to the comfort to my ego, to the low desires of my flesh.*" As we know from his speeches, discourses, and books, after the intense training of asceticism in the desert, his spiritual knowledge came gushing forth like a river.

The salvation of man lies in renouncing the mortal world and all it contains. The most effective method to completely withdraw from one's environment is to adapt the state of asceticism, live a life of seclusion. The conscious and continuous efforts of fasting bear the essence of asceticism. Seclusion means, therefore, fasting from the world, respectively excluding all and everything that belongs to the world. Isolating oneself completely from one's environment, retiring from the superficiality of mundane life for a specific period of time, mostly 40 days, is called *halwat*. The treasury of *halwat* carries the seat of complete fasting, namely, one fasts from one's family, one's work, one's home, one's social life, cutting all contacts with the outer world. Staying in retreat is one of the most effective methods to reach spiritual perfection. All essential life activities are reduced to a minimum, especially eating, sleeping, and talking. The more one separates from outside, the deeper one will descend the inner world. The further the distance from the external realms, the material realms, and the closer one will approach to the internal, spiritual realms. One shuts the ears, eyes, and mouth from hearing, looking, and talking. One locks out all the things that belong to the mortal world and all the negative forces of the ego and the devil. One withdraws one's ugliness from one's beauty. One withdraws one's evil from one's good. One withdraws error and sin from one's faithfulness. In other words, one removes the low attributes of envy, hate, arrogance, stinginess, anger, and hypocrisy from his heart. Seclusion means spiritual wakefulness. With seclusion, one reaches the peaks of *taqwa*, piety. Seclusion means living in ritual cleanliness. Seclusion is a renewal of the self. Seclusion means exercising constant self-supervision. Seclusion means to cleanse one's self of the desires for worldly approval like status, rank, accumulation of wealth, and worldly success. The awareness one adapts in retreat is renouncing worldly ambition all together. The mercy for all the worlds said: "*The beauty of being a good Muslim is abandoning what is of no use to him.*" That is to say, the essence of seclusion is not to occupy oneself with the petty things.

Moreover, to seclude oneself does not exclusively mean to expand and deepen the spiritual dimensions of one's personality in order to strive towards inner purity. Nor does it exclusively mean meditation and exercising self-restraint, or attaining physical and spiritual cleanliness in order to find peace of mind and heart. The wisdom of retiring from the world is to dive into the ocean of Allah's Mercy. That is say, the goal and essence of asceticism is to be with one's Beloved! True asceticism means one practices profound discipline in order to grow into the Divine Presence. All senses are shut, only Allah is left. The Almighty declared to Moses: "*Those who desire to get near to Me have not been able to find a way better than asceticism.*" In other words, the path to Allah is the path of seclusion. Without seclusion there is no love. The great writer Farid al-Din al-Attar comments: *"The one who desires the love and friendship of Allah, without asceticism, he is false in the claim of love."* True seclusion culminates in the pleasure one feels to be in privacy with Him, to dwell in the Paradise of intimacy with Him. Rumi gives a perfect description of a true ascetic: *"One wise and sensible prefers the bottom of the well, for the soul finds delight in privacy of being with God. The darkness of the well is preferable to the darkness people because the one holding on to the legs of people has never been able to arrive with a head. One must seclude oneself from others, not from the Beloved. Fur is worn in winter, not in spring."* The present world itself has become a place of retreat because a believer today feels inwardly far removed from the environment he lives in. This state represents precisely a form of seclusion because every moment of his life he struggles to be in sacred communion with his beloved Lord, although he is bombarded with constant stress factors like superficial restless activity, material heaviness, chaos, distraction, emptiness, cheap talk, gossip, bombardment of the media, and so on. Living a way of life of retreat will become a way of life of the Hereafter. It means living the reality of: *"Your noise is my silence,"* as Jalal ad-Din Rumi said. Nevertheless, the true ascetic remains in retreat with his Beloved at all times, in all places. He never leaves His Company, even when he is together with people. He remains in retreat although he lives in wealth, luxury, and worldly possessions. He remains humble although he is superior in status and rank to other people. He remains poor although the world praises him as a king. The glory of the universe said: *"How fine is the property a righteous man has!"* Rumi comments: *"The water in a ship causes it to sink, while the water under it causes it to float."* The secret is remaining indifferent to the world and its pomp and glory while being in the world. The saint Busayri gives us a beautiful description concerning the fast of our most beloved of all hearts: *"Not to feel hunger, he wound a girdle around his belly; the stone's pressing upon his blessed stomach. Huge mountains wishing themselves gold offered themselves to him, but he that noble man remained indifferent to them. His urgent needs decisively showed his asceticism. For those needs were not able to impair his innocence. How could needs have been able to invite to the world the one but for whom the world would not have been come into being out of non-existence?"*

The last third of Ramadan, the last ten days, represent precisely a form of retreat, called *itikaf*. It is a voluntary act giving total concentration and respect towards the climax of the holy month, established by the Prophet himself. He used to perform *itikaf* in the last ten days of Ramadan and never left the mosque, stayed in retreat alone, and exerted himself in devotion. Especially the performance of the *Tahajjud* Prayer in the middle of the night in the last ten days of Ramadan represents not only the culmination of Ramadan, but one's total deliverance into the hands of God Almighty with comprehensive devotion. The glorious Prayer of *Tahajjud* bears the most perfect symbol of the day of the Resurrection. It represents the state of the Prophet himself. Within the participation of the flow of the Divine grace and blessings of these voluntary night Prayers, we can smell the sweet fragrance of his station. It is light upon light. The ones who have tasted know. For the fasting believers the last ten days, representing the climax of the holy month of Ramadan, offer the opportunity to perfect one's fast. One perfects one's inner cleanliness, one's asking of forgiveness, one completes the recitation of the Holy Qur'an, and one reaches the peak of one's supplication to the Lord of all the worlds. Furthermore, the Holy Qur'an is reported to have been sent down in one of the last ten days of Ramadan. That night is called the Night of Power, *laylatu'l-qadr*, and is described as being greater in blessedness and spiritual virtue than 1,000 months. Therefore, the treasury of *itikaf*, paired with the glorious *Tahajjud* Prayer and the Night of Power, is incomprehensible in its beauty and spiritual richness.

In order to become sincere in our thanksgiving, we need to know what we are grateful for, and we need the appropriate feelings of appreciation for the things we are thankful for. To thank Allah the Almighty requires the awareness that all things we possess, that all gifts we receive, that all knowledge we perceive, that all the Divine favors we taste are coming from Him. We owe nothing in this world, not even ourselves. Therefore all Divine bounties, favors, and gifts are a manifestation of the blessing and mercy from the Lord of all the worlds. For truthful believers, it means that their lives become lives of thanksgiving. Particularly the month of Ramadan represents the means to experience and express universal thankfulness. Through fasting, one becomes aware of the infinite bounties and favors of our Creator. How can we appreciate a glass of water and a piece of dry bread when our stomach is full? How can we appreci-

ate Allah's favors when we are rich? How can we realize the Divine bounties if we never experienced real hunger? How can we understand Allah's
gifts if we seldom experience need, desperation, and helplessness? This
is the value of this fasting month: to recognize Allah's bounties, to appreciate their worth, and show appropriate thanksgiving. For the fasting
believers a piece of dry bread becomes the greatest pleasure of heavenly
food. Therefore, the miraculous effect of fasting is felt from the top man-
ager of a business corporation down to the poor beggar equally.

The rewards for worship activities in the month of Ramadan are
thousand-fold. It is a specialty of the fasting month that the religious practices are to a great extent multiplied, level upon level. The practices of
Salah, the recitation of the Qur'an, the *Tarawih* Prayers, the *Tahajjud*
Prayers, *itikaf* in the last ten days, charity, asking forgiveness, supplication, and thanksgiving are intensified because they are increased in length
and number. Paired with fasting, the heart and spirit receives infinite
portions of spiritual nourishment. According to traditions, each word of
the All-Wise Qur'an has ten merits and will yield ten fruits in Paradise.
During Ramadan, each word bears not ten fruits but a thousand, and verses like *Ayat al-Kursi* thousands for each word, and on Fridays in Ramadan the merits are highly accelerated. On the Night of Power, each word
is counted as thirty thousand merits. According to the Qur'an, the Night
of Power is more auspicious than a thousand months which equals to
that of a lifetime of eighty years. Such are the Divine rewards and bounties, thousand and thousand times multiplied, in honor of this month. Our
blessed master tells us in a Divine *hadith*: *"If a person attends a learned
assembly in the month of Ramadan, for every step he takes he will be cred-
ited with the reward of one year's worship. That servant will be with me
beneath the Throne on high. If a person constantly prays in congregation
during this blessed month, Allah will give him a city of Paradise of the Day
of Judgment for each cycle of Prayer he has performed. That city will be
filled with the bounties of Allah."*

Said Nursi gives us an excellent description of the worth of fasting:
*"The factory of the stomach has many workers. And many of the human
organs are connected to it. If the instinctual soul does not have a rest from
activity during the day for a month, it makes the factory's workers and those
organs forget their particular duties. It makes them busy with itself so that
they remain under its tyranny. Also, it confuses the rest of the organs in*

the human body with the clangor and steam of the factory's machinery. It continuously attracts their attention to itself, making them temporarily forget their exalted duties. It is because of this that for centuries those closest to God have accustomed themselves to discipline and to eating and drinking little in order to be perfected. However, through fasting in Ramadan the factory's workers understand that they were not created for the factory only. While the rest of the organs, instead of delighting in the lowly amusements of the factory, take pleasure in angelic and spiritual amusements, and fix their gazes on them. It is for this reason that in Ramadan the believers experience enlightenment, fruitfulness, and spiritual joys which differ according to their degrees. Their subtle faculties, such as the heart, spirit, and intellect, make great progress and advancement in that blessed month by means of fasting. They laugh with innocent joy in spite of the stomach's weeping."

Supplications

"In this month, we ask ourselves, how much is the most precious of all books, the Holy Qur'an in our hands, on our lips, on our eyes, in our hearts? How much is the Qur'an in our lives? Is it just placed on a shelf in our houses or is there none at all? In this month, we ask ourselves, how much do we run to do good works? How much are we concerned to help our fellow beings in need? How much time do we reserve for the service of the poor and sick?

O Lord, we are in shame for the answer to this question. One of Your greatest servants, the venerable Abdul Qadir al-Jilani never slept at night for 40 years! He performed his Morning Prayer with the ablution he had taken to make his Night Prayer. He read the Qur'an every night so that sleep should not overtake him. He stood on one food and leaned against the wall with one hand. He did not change this position until he had read the whole Qur'an. When he could not fight sleep himself, he would hear a voice that shook every cell of his body. It would say "O Abdul Qadir, I did not create you to sleep. You were nothing. I gave you life. So while you are alive you will not be unaware of Us!

O Lord, in this fasting month, we came with dried out hearts in this desert of our world and wish to drink the water of life. We came with hearts filled with longing, desire for You!

O my heart who finds rest with fasting, what a miraculous blessings of healing! What a relief from these constant ego attacks, what a great comfort, what a freedom having cleaned the mirror of our hearts from the dirt and dust, what a benefit, what a present for my soul having made order and set the barriers for the human kingdom of the body!

O Lord, take away our ignorance and heedlessness and fill it with certainty of belief. Take away our forgetfulness and our confusion and replace it with constant remembrance and worship for You. Remove our idols, our cheap occupations, our defective visions, and our hypocrisy from our hearts and replace it with Your all-comprehensive wisdom, power, perfection and beauty. Take away the self from ourselves and replace it with nothing else than You! Become our sole Guest in our hearts. Fill our hearts with Your love in such a way that nothing else can enter. O our Lord, increase our sublime tendencies and decrease our profanity, increase our spirituality and decrease our materiality, increase our admiration and decrease our calculation. In this sacred month of Ramadan, we wish to make our spirituality the priority of our lives and throw our material life backstage.

O Lord, we usually make the most important things into the least important things in our lives. Seemingly, unworthy things take the center of our attention. We give importance to worthless things and we do not give any importance to valuable things. This is our human weakness, to stay on the wrong side of life! Instead of being busy with our failures and losses, we are busy with our gains and success. Instead of earning Divine approval, we are concerned with earning worldly applause. There is an endless list of misconduct. Therefore O Lord, we ask You to help us to remove this disproportionate behavior and help us to accomplish the ethics of the noble character of Your most beloved of all Prophets. We beg You to help us to deal with our imperfection within and without ourselves.

O Lord, release us from the world of appearances and reveal to us the worlds of the hidden, release us from surface worshipping and show us the worlds of the unseen, take away the defective perception and replace it with the true vision, take away our obsession with form and bestow on us the world of wonders, awe and mysteries, free ourselves from looking at ugliness and dirt and make us see Your beauty and perfection.

O Lord, release us from the attachment to the picture of the world. Release us from getting stuck at the wall of existence. Release us from getting caught by the illusion to take this world for real. Release us from the influence of the devil's deceptive perceptions of reality. Release us from our egotistical usage of the eyes of our head. Release us from the slavery to our five senses. How long do we want to stay at the surface? How long do we want to stop at the picture of this world? How long do we want to look at form? How long will we join the vision of the devil that looked at Adam and failed to see the inner Divine treasury of man and therefore refused to prostrate? If we fail to live the inner dimensions of the human being, if we fail to see the Divine beauty, if we fail to discover the secret treasure, if we fail to love, if we fail to recognize our worth and honor, if we fail to see the light of our own soul, if we fail to travel upwards, we will not only inherit the defective look of the devil, we will risk to be disobedient and start to show weakened submission.

O Lord, through the means of fasting we ask You to give us the opportunity to move away from the falseness, hypocrisy, corruption, ignorance, and heedlessness! Our lives caught the virus of modernization and we ask You in honor of this month to help us to fight the illnesses of profanity, secularism, capitalism, and materialism. O Lord, cleanse hatred, envy, indifference, levity, darkness of our hearts and replace it with affection, love, mercy, compassion, generosity, and brotherhood! O Lord, close us with the robe of firm belief."

Hajj (The Pilgrimage)

The wisdom of the pilgrimage is infinite; the merits of this rite are immeasurable. In a Divine *hadith*, Allah states: *"I created everything for you; I created you for Me."* To go on pilgrimage means to experience the state of belonging to Him, being His slave, His servant, His property, which corresponds to sacred phrase: *"I created you for Me."*

The pilgrimage is one of the most excellent worship rituals, furnished with eternal recipes to educate the full complexity of the human soul. The pilgrimage represents the key to eternal richness, the key for the treasury of the soul. The pilgrimage represents the lesson of one's lifetime; it signifies a program for human resurrection. The pilgrimage is a spiritual education for all mankind. It represents the greatest annual gathering in the world, in the history of mankind; therefore, it possesses limitless excellence. The pilgrimage represents the ultimate eternal rendezvous of the servant with his Lord. The pilgrimage symbolizes fighting on the way of truth. On the pilgrimage, one hunts the truth. The pilgrimage represents the call for the truthful death. On the pilgrimage, the conditions of being human get fulfilled. On the spiritual journey, the pilgrim fully surrenders his small will towards the Exalted One and becomes an instrument of His Divine Will. On the pilgrimage, one exercises the sacred recipe: "Die before dying." The pilgrimage offers, in its essence, the possibility to break out from the prison of worldly existence. The pilgrim's goal is smashing the cage of self-existence, smashing the inner idols of the heart, burning the veils covering the soul in order to become nothing, become poor of the worldly. The pilgrim has to undergo an examination of his will, an operation on his heart. Rumi says: *"If you remain in form, you are an idol worshipper. Pass beyond the form and behold the meaning! Proximity to God is not to go up or down—proximity to Him is to escape from the prison of worldly existence. Fear the existence in which you are now! Your imagination is nothing, and you are nothing. A nothing has fallen in love with a nothing; a nothing-at-all has waylaid a nothing-at-all. When these images*

have departed, your misunderstanding will become clear to you. Self-exis-
tence brings terrible drunkenness; it removes intellect from the head and
modesty from the heart."

The pilgrims are people of unity. On pilgrimage they walk in the footsteps of Prophet Abraham, peace be upon him, up to the seal of all the
Prophets, our blessed master. Let's play their role, let's walk where they
walked, fight where they fought, and supplicate where they supplicated.
Let's walk and hold hand with the hand that holds the hand with the
hand of the descendants up until the seal of all the Prophets, our blessed
master Muhammad Mustafa, peace and blessing be upon him. The pilgrims
have to adapt the consciousness of being Abraham seekers and Muhammad seekers and they adapt the consciousness that they are the children
of the venerable martyr Abel. The pilgrims carry on their shoulders the
inheritance of all the Prophets; they carry the responsibility of servanthood. The pilgrims are God's caliphs, the deputies of God on earth.

How can we see the Hereafter before death? By performing the pilgrimage... Whoever understands the mysteries of "die before you die" has
seen the Resurrection before the last trumpet sounds. So without adapting and living the mysteries of spiritual poverty, we cannot perform the
true pilgrimage and therefore we cannot see the Day of Resurrection.

In the life of this world, we should leave everything and run. A verse
from the Holy Qur'an: *"Let us flee unto God"* (adh-Dhariyat 51:50). The
pilgrimage is a physical expression of taking refuge in Him, fleeing unto
Him, running unto Him. The pilgrim actually runs away from the temptation of daily life.

The pilgrimage is a continuous prostration of the heart, a continuous ascent of the spirit, a continuous homecoming, a continuous rehearsal of the Day of Judgment. The elevation, the ascension, the resurrection,
is experienced within the crowds of pilgrims, the community of believers. The pilgrimage, representing the rehearsal for the Judgment Day,
means to experience the "crowdedness" of that Day. The Qur'an states:
"On that Day, when a person flees from his brother, and from his mother
and father, and from his spouse and his children" (Abasa 80:34–36). If the
pilgrimage is experienced as a rehearsal in which one judges oneself before
one gets judged, one faces oneself before one guest brought to the Divine
Court, one dies before dying, one will have truthfully experienced the ultimate Day. God willing, one will not to have to run away from one's own

kind. In that sense, the pilgrimage is to get ready for the Day of all days. The ones who can offer themselves in complete sincerity, have seen this day with the eye of spiritual poverty. They have found eternal comfort not just in this world, but in the intermediate realm of the grave and for the Day of Resurrection.

In the world left behind, one deviated from the straight path, one became sullied by the world's dirty games, and one gave up the truth and lived falseness. Whereas on the pilgrimage, one regains one's lost Paradise, the lost Paradise of Adam. On the plain of Arafat, the pilgrims attain the fruit of *marifa*, sacred wisdom. The treasury of the pilgrimage lies in the possibility to regain the lost self, regain one's humanity. The pilgrim regains health, regains the flow of the human breath, pure, untainted, unsullied by the dirt of the world. He regains the water of life, the brilliance of sacred awareness, the infinite expansion of the breast. He regains the honor, elevation, and worth of being created as human being. In Sheikh Ghalib's words: "*Look at yourself with joy, for you are the essence of the universe. You are the Adam, the pupil of the eye of the universe.*" Once having gained peace with oneself, one will be in peace with the whole of humanity and further become one with nature and the universe again. The ultimate gain and reward the pilgrimage has to offer is the greatest of all victories, *tawhid*, unity. All fear and grief leaves one's heart. One returns home, the home of one's origin, the home of the inner pilgrim. The Qur'an states: "*Is he (who derives lessons from God's acts in the universe, and so) whose breast God has expanded to Islam, so that he follows a light from his Lord (is such a one to be likened to one whose heart is closed up to any remembrance of God and, therefore, to Islam)? So woe to those whose hearts are hardened against the remembrance of God (and who learn nothing from His signs and Revelations)! Those are lost in obvious error*" (az-Zumar 39:22).

On the spiritual journey, we become able to live in the awareness that each day is a treasure, that every moment as a treasure. It means to celebrate the beauty and perfection of Allah, to celebrate the certainty of belief, to celebrate to be honored to belong to Prophet Muhammad's community, to celebrate the ascension of the believers, the *miraj*. One of the greatest longing of truthful believers is to be able to say wholeheartedly, with all the cells of the bodies, the first line of the Fatiha: "*All praise and gratitude are for Allah, the Lord of the worlds!*"

We have to be aware not to go on pilgrimage for the sake of personal gain. Rumi comments: *"The dervish that wants bread is fish on land. He has the form of a fish but he is fleeing from sea. He loves Allah for the sake of gain. His soul is not in love with Allah's Excellence and Beauty."* The secret and treasury of the pilgrimage is to realize the identity of "nothingness." On the spiritual journey, the pilgrims smash the cage of self-existence, wearing the shroud of death. When they enter the plain of the pilgrimage, they shave their heads off all the material attributes and they deliver themselves from the attributes of beasts, lust, greed, hate, and aggression. They deliver themselves from defect and ugliness, from the artificial cleverness of the devil, from doubt, argument, falseness, black magic, illusions, artificiality, hypocrisy, ideologies, and philosophies.

In order to experience a truthful pilgrimage where the proximity to Allah is reached, the pilgrims have to shed off their material possessions. Material heaviness hinders spiritual progress. One of the pre-condition of the pilgrimage is precisely the necessity to cut off the attachment to the world, leave one's status, possessions, rank, and family in order to be ready to undergo the true journey to the inner essence of the heart. The great Sheikh Ibn Arabi, who started his spiritual path at an early age, entrusted all his possessions to his father and told him to distribute them among the needy. When his father asked the reason for such an action, he answered: *"A servant of Allah, who has a claim of someone else on him, is incomplete in his servanthood in the proportion of his claim."*

The pilgrimage represents the absolute submission, the total self-sacrifice. Thus, the most desirable state of a pilgrim is adapting the state of an orphan, a martyr, a widow, respectively become Allah's orphan, refugee, and humble slave. This is what is meant to take refuge in Allah the Almighty. All loves for this world, especially for one's children, have to be extinguished. As the pilgrimage symbolizes one's spiritual death in order to be resurrected in Allah, one has to abandon everything what belongs to the world, sacrifice one's highest loves, desires, affection, needs, wishes so that only Allah will be left in one's heart to be loved and remembered. This is the meaning and the goal of the pilgrimage, the sacrifice of Prophet Abraham, his son Ismail, peace be upon them. Abraham had to cut the throat of his most heightened love for his son. Thus the pilgrimage signifies the sacrifice of all the things what is not the love for God. The Qur'an states: *"Your worldly possessions and your children are but a source of temptation and trial (for you); and God it is with Whom is a tre-mendous reward"* (at-Taghabun 64:15).

Worshipping God Almighty means to melt into the Divine Presence of the All-Merciful. In this world we are all guests of the All-Compassion-ate. But in order to realize the truth of these words, believers have to struggle, they need to work. But in contrast, by the fact that the Lord of Majesty and Bounty invites His servants to the pilgrimage, they receive the honor to become the guest of the All-Merciful without showing any efforts. In other words, with the pilgrimage, the Almighty invites the believ-ers to dwell in the ocean of His Mercy. The invitation from our Lord for the pilgrimage represents therefore an enormous Divine favor, thus, without paying any price, without showing any efforts, we are given the taste of the sweet scent of Paradise, we are given the miraculous trans-fer from the world into the plain of the Hereafter, we are given the bliss to dwell in the ocean of His infinite Mercy. Being a truthful guest of the All-Compassionate in this world combined with being His guest on the pilgrimage signifies the accomplishment of the true pilgrimage. In other words, our life in this world has to unify with the life of the pilgrimage. This is true for all the sacred pillars of Islam. When our lives become a life of pilgrimage, a life of charity, a life of praying, and a life of fasting, we will attain the fast of truth, the Prayer of truth, the charity of truth, and the pil-grimage of truth. The pilgrimage of truth is reached if one has exchanged the way of life of this world with the way of life of the Hereafter.

The abundance of what connects oneself with the world necessitates striving in God's cause and for humanity's good. The pilgrim has to show an unbroken, firm, sincere, and courageous attitude and intention for unconditional submission. It is his responsibility to be truthful to the *tal-biyah*, the pronunciation of the acceptance of the invitation for the pil-grimage: *"Labbayk Allahumma labbayk—I am present my Lord, all of me I am here, now, at your order."* He has to show absolute readiness for sac-rifice. In that sense, the pilgrimage represents the work with one's jugu-lar vein. The spiritual journey signifies going to the end, going to the end of one's existence. The heart of the work means going to the one's essence, one's roots, respectively, experiencing the end of one's life, experiencing the state in the grave, and experiencing the day of Resurrection. Only then the garden of Paradise will be revealed in our hearts. It means that the pilgrims have to hunt the truth. The truth is not easy to access. The truth is not given for nothing. Take refuge in Allah the Almighty cannot be done with supplicating to Him exclusively with our lips. The pilgrims have to offer all what they are, cleaning themselves of all ulterior motives. This is the ultimate goal of the pilgrimage. The heart in prostration, the eyes in tears, and the tongue tied in impotence before His Grandeur and Majesty. Advancing as far as the very moment of being thrown into the fire and advancing as far as the very moment of one's throat being cut. This implies to go as far as feeling the heat of the fire and feeling the knife on one's throat. If we go to the end, the knife does not cut, the fire does not burn. The water of Zamzam and the rose garden will be given as a Divine reward. Eternal life will be given, the glorious gratification of the rebirth.

By the fact that all existent things are created by God, all creation feels an irresistible attraction towards its Creator. The human souls emanating directly from God's Essence, He breathed into the bodies through His Merciful Breath, are dominated by the wish to return home, to reemerge with their origin, to rejoin their lost union with their Creator. This is the concept of God's creation. Nature, the world, the universe, and man are all striving to return to their Creator. All creation worships Him, desires Him, proclaims His glory, and strives for union with Him. In Rumi's words: "*All parts, whether moving or still, are reciting, 'To Him is the homecoming* (at-Taghabun 64:3).'" As long as we are not woken up to the awareness that we live a part of the whole existence, we cannot accomplish our human destiny; we cannot perform the true pilgrimage. The ones who know they belong to Allah the Almighty, have uncovered their soul of its veils and become able to feel its eternal longing. They feel the attraction of their soul longing for its Creator, for its original home. This longing represents the desire of creatures for their Creator and the holy desire of the Creator for His creatures. Rumi comments: "*As a result, love courses throughout the world's arteries. All movement and activity result from that original Love; the world's forms are but the reflections of its unique Reality.*"

The pilgrimage means facing oneself. How much one faces one's self means how much one becomes a pilgrim. Facing one's self means examining one's self. Examining one's self means taking one's self to account. Ibn Arabi said: "*There are three dangers that may keep you from examining yourself. The first is unconsciousness. The next is the imaginary pleasure you take in the deceptions of your ego. The third is being a slave to your habits.*" The first step on the path of spiritual healing is to repent and making account of one's self. The Messenger of Allah says: "*Make your accounting before it is made for you. Weigh your sins before they are weighed for you.*" The act of repentance implies the recognition that each individual on this earth carries spiritual sicknesses within himself which need cure. This is the meaning and goal of the pilgrimage. If we work in this way, it can bring the healing process of our whole being. God created man in such a wonderful fashion, he can become successful in treating himself, and he can become his own doctor. For every sickness, Allah gives us a cure. The pilgrimage is an excellent treasury of healing potential and it is given to humanity by the All-Merciful.

Going on pilgrimage means to save oneself from the life, narrowed down to four walls, and throw oneself in the desert of worldly existence in order to practice the wisdom of the Divine revelations, and make the lessons one draws from the Holy Qur'an into a part of one's spiritual journey. Instead of reciting the Divine verses, it is living their truth. That is to say, the rituals of the pilgrimage are given for the realization of the Divine verses and express them in action. The pilgrims have to melt and lose themselves in the truth of the religion of Islam in order to catch the scent of the Divine revelations. They have to dissolve with their bodies in the knowledge they possess, they have to penetrate into the deepest layers of the ocean of meanings. Rumi says: "*Pass into sight, pass into sight, pass into sight! One sight perceives only two yards ahead; another sight has beheld the two worlds and the Face of the King. Between these two is an incalculable difference; seek the remedy of vision and God best knows that which is hidden.*" In other words, the pilgrims have to sacrifice themselves for the sake of the truth of the Divine revelations of the Holy Qur'an. It is not the animal which has to be sacrificed, but selfishness, bad habits, desires of the flesh which have to be burned away, so the spirit of the Holy Qur'an can conquer the heart, thus the pilgrims will be able to be enlighten, humbled down in poverty and nothingness. It means to apply the sacred description of our blessed master: "*Die before you die.*" We can serve the Qur'an, comprehend the meaning of the Qur'an, and live the truth of the Qur'an, when the truths of the Divine revelations become alive in our inner world. As our great saint Rumi proclaimed: "*I am a slave of the Qur'an as long as I live.*" That way, we will get resurrected in the truth, we will get born anew. We will earn the title of the true pilgrim.

The Holy Qur'an came down for three principle reasons; to take inspiration to serve and to take inspiration for guidance, and to take inspiration for healing.

It is essential on the pilgrimage to adapt the consciousness that all pilgrims are one community. The Qur'an states: "*Humankind were (in the beginning) one community (following one way of life without disputing over provision and other similar things. Later on, differences arose and) God sent Prophets as bearers of glad tidings (of prosperity in return for faith and righteousness) and warners (against the consequences of straying and transgression), and He sent down with them the Book with the truth (containing nothing false in it) so that it might judge between the people concerning that on which they were differing*" (al-Baqarah 2:213). "*Your creation and your resurrection are but as (the creation and resurrection) of a single soul*" (Luqman 31:28). It is reported that the noble Messenger said: "*The believers are brothers and men of knowledge are like a single soul.*" The pilgrim's duty is to live the secret union of brotherhood. On his spiritual journey he has to align himself and melt with all the pilgrims into one goal, one color, one dress, one thought, one name, and one breath. The essence of pilgrimage is to become one single soul, one family, one community, one body, and one brotherhood. Leaving the world and entering the plain of the Hereafter bears the symbolism of leaving all differences, distinctions between people, nationalities, communities, sects, social status, or rank and unite in the love of universal brotherhood. The pilgrimage bears the symbolism of transferring from one's individuality to the oneness of community. What unify people are eternal values inherent in everyone. With the sacred ritual of the pilgrimage, Allah calls us to realize the unity of His Names and Attributes. If human life is devoid of His Attributes, human beings will become stranger to each other, misunderstand each other, get distant to each other, not greet each other, and struggle with each other. The separation of hearts is exactly what happens in our modern society today due to the loss of unity of brotherhood, family, neighbors, communities, social relations. The only way we can save ourselves from moral destruction is to follow the Prophets of unity. We are Allah's caliphs, the deputies of Allah on earth, we carry Allah's trust, and we carry the responsibility of servanthood. We are the creatures to whom the angels prostrate.

Through the mystery of belief, there is unity of brotherhood. The community of Muhammad is all believers of Divine unity. Togetherness, embracement, love, sharing, and brotherhood are all necessary elements for human survival, because they are food for the spirit.

The pilgrim has to melt, dive, and become part of the uninterrupted, endless, eternal flow with all the pilgrims' souls, flowing in the arteries of the cosmic order. It is the flow of Divine grace. This is the ultimate spiritual fulfillment, the attainment of unity. The pilgrim becomes Abraham, Ismail, and Hajar. The experience of the spiritual journey is to become a seeking traveler on the way of truth, walking in the footsteps of the footsteps of the friends and saints who walk in the footsteps of the footsteps until Prophet Abraham, up until Prophet Adam, peace be upon them. It means the pilgrims are walking in the chain of transmission and join the ones who have seen the ones who have seen the ones who have seen the Companions, which have seen Prophet Muhammad Mustafa, peace and blessings be upon him.

The wisdom of the pilgrimage is that the knowledge of the religion is a light. Islam represents the highest school of thoughts, the all-comprehensive, all-embracing wisdom of the Divine revelations of Allah. It is nor information, nor philosophy, nor dry knowledge. True knowledge is nourished by the light of Allah; it comes from the deepest regions of one's being, and it is the light of the heart, the eye of the heart which sees. It is the light of Divine inspiration. This knowledge is the knowledge of the way towards Allah, the *sirat-al-mustaqim*. It is the knowledge of Divine guidance. It is the knowledge of purification of mind and soul. It is the knowledge of self-sacrifice. It is the knowledge of our noblest master, the glory of the universe. It is the knowledge of humility. This enlightenment is available for every believer who goes on pilgrimage, because the pilgrim is a fighter, travelling on the way of truth towards the Almighty. This light is given within the rituals of the glorious pilgrimage from our Supreme Creator. This light shines in full splendor on the plain of Arafat coming from the masses of pilgrims; it is the light of faith! This wisdom is not acquired with any book or studies or lessons, it is only earned through the great struggle, the struggle with our own *nafs*, respectively this knowledge is only earned in the realms of the internal struggle. It is realized knowledge.

The way towards Allah is the way of sacrifice. The art of approaching represents therefore the greatest of all the arts. It is called *jihad*, the sacred internal struggle. The Messenger of Allah, having returned from a war with his enemies, tells us in a well-known tradition: *"We have returned from the lesser jihad to the greater jihad."* What he meant with the greater struggle is the war with the enemy within our own selves, the war with one's ego, carnal soul. Therefore it is called "the greater war," a spiritual combat. *Jihad* is the essence of the pilgrimage. It means cleaning ourselves of the evil, diabolic forces, the false gods, the idols who invaded and reside in our hearts, in order to enlighten the human essence and purify the soul. In other words, the abundance and detachment of what connects oneself with the world, necessitates *jihad.* The Holy Qur'an states: *"Those (on the other hand) who strive hard for Our sake, We will most certainly guide them to Our ways (that We have established to lead them to salvation). Most assuredly, God is with those devoted to doing good, aware that God is seeing them"* (al-Ankabut 29:69). *Jihad* represents the fight for *tawhid,* it is the struggle for unity versus setting partners to Allah, the diabolic forces of polytheism. It is the struggle against tyranny in order to gain justice. It is the fight against anarchy to gain law. It is the fight against slavery to gain freedom. It is the fight against carnal pleasures to gain spiritual elevation. It is the fight against wildness to gain civilization. It is the fight against deviation in order to gain righteousness. It is the fight against materialism to gain spirituality. These sacred efforts are comprehended in the eternal fight, the ultimate discrimination of the pilgrim; the truth versus falsehood, the eternal fight for *tawhid* versus *shirk.* The Qur'an states: *"Those who (truly) believe fight in God's cause, while those who disbelieve fight in the cause of taghut (powers of evil who institute patterns of rule in defiance of God). So (O believers), fight against the friends and allies of Satan. Assuredly, Satan's guile is ever-feeble"* (an-Nisa 4:76).

It is part of the ritual of the pilgrimage to throw stones at him which means the pilgrim has to confront himself and fight with Satan. This symbolizes the war one fights with one's inner enemies, the dark forces of the egos. In our daily lives, Satan is our biggest enemy, who uses religion in order to alternate religion. He wears sacred clothes, acts as friend and supporter, but serves his own religion of polytheism. He serves Pharaoh, Nimrod, Abu Sufyan, and Cain. Thus, on the pilgrimage, it is essential to confront oneself with the Surah Al-Falaq and the Surah An-Nas, as they are utterly useful for the spiritual journey. These last chapters of the Holy Qur'an bear immense sacred wisdom. Allah makes us aware of the greatest dangers we live in; He shows us the constant threats of dark and evil forces in everyone's life, the dreadful, horrific forces operating within and without ourselves.

The Surah Al-Falaq: *"Say: 'I seek refuge in the Lord of the daybreak from the evil of what He has created, and from the evil of the darkness (of night) when it overspreads, and from the evil of the witches who blow on knots (to cast a spell), and from the evil of the envious one when he envies"* (113: -5). These are the external enemies of the world, the one we see face to face, referring to people, friends, neighbors, societies. When we throw stones to the devil, we throw stones at *"the evil of the darkness (of night) when it overspreads,"* we throw stones to *"the evil of the witches who blow on knots,"* influencing destroying, thoughts, character, culture, feelings, knowledge, and we throw stones at *"the evil of the envious one when he envies."*

"From the evil of the sneaking whisperer (the Satan) who whispers into the hearts of humankind" (an-Nas 114: 4-5). These are our internal enemies, secret agents who try to deform our hearts. They work on the weaknesses of our egos, the low sensual desires, which show readiness, willingness without resistance to give into their demands, submit towards their evil suggestions.

"The evil of the darkness (of night) when it overspreads..." The evil forces working at night. That is why they have to be conquered by the sword of the brightness of the day, the light of the awareness of the day. These evil forces whisper magic, plant seeds of hate, make enemy from friends and friends from enemies, they paralyze the will of man, they destroy faith and determination, they destroy good intention, they destroy the togetherness of communities, and they make man deviate from the straight path. In order to fight distortion, degeneration, moral decay, disorientation of mind and heart, and spiritual emptiness, we have to be aware that the dark and evil forces are neither exclusively on the exterior nor interior as the two chapters of An-Nas and Al-Falaq provide proof. The enemy is everywhere and all-present, sometimes in our thoughts, in our intentions, in our actions, sometimes at work, mixing with our friendships, marriage, brotherhood, parenthood, and social relations. Satan and these evil forces have such power; they can paralyze ourselves and make us blind, death, and numb. They may distort our consciousness to such an extent that we see the truth as falsehood and falsehood as truth.

Humanity experiences throughout history the eternal dilemma of war. It started at the time of the creation of man. Satan became envious of the first created human being, Adam, and the envy of Cain towards Abel caused a murder. Rumi comments: *"The Forgiving God desired and decided in eternity to reveal and manifest Himself. But no opposite can be displayed without its own opposite, and the peerless King has no opposite. So He made a vicegerent, a possessor of the heart, to be the mirror of His Kingship. Then He gave him limitless purity, and produced his opposite from darkness. He made two banners, white and black; the one was Adam, the other the Satan of His way. Then the strife and war that came to pass between these two great camps. In a similar manner, Abel came in the second period, opposed to his pure light was Cain. Period after period, generation after generation, the two parties have continued to war."* Cain, who represents the eternal enemy of the human being, is described by Ali Shariati as follows: *"Indeed, there is this Cain with seven colors, seventy faces, seven hundred names, and seventy thousand strategies! He leaves but then he comes back, you throw him out the door, he breaks in through the chimney."*

We are the Almighty's vicegerents. We are carrying the Divine Trust. If we are believers of Divine unity, we owe Allah to go on pilgrimage. We owe Allah the consciousness of becoming a fighter for the truth. We owe Allah to fight in His way. That is to say, we owe to give the whole of ourselves. We owe the martyrs who died for the truth. Along with Bilal, who was thrown into unsupportable torture for countless nights and days, never ceased to say: *"Ahad, Ahad—Allah is One, is One!"* We owe Allah not to be afraid of death and walk on the way of truth performing the duty of the responsibilities of servanthood. We owe Allah to accomplish the features of sincerity and truthfulness. Due to the bloodshed of Abel for the love he offered ourselves, we owe to entrust our friendship to him. All the martyrs of the religion of Islam with their supreme shining examples are enlightening our darkness of unconsciousness. They gave their lives in order for us to see, to wake up, to comprehend and get healed by the light of Divine guidance. Let's play their role, let's walk where they walked, fight where they fought, supplicate where they supplicated, cry where they cried, and take refuge where they took refuge in our Lord of all the worlds. Let's walk and hold hand with the hand with the hand in the chain with the descendants of the descendants up until the seal of all the Prophets, our blessed master Muhammad Mustafa, peace and blessing be upon him.

We have to be aware that when we follow the venerable martyr Abel, we will be in the dangers of Cain. When we follow the Prophets, we will encounter the dangers, threats, attacks of Nimrod, Pharaoh, Abu Yazid, the oppressors, dictators and tyrants of mankind. If we sincerely follow the honor of the universe, the most dignified of all men, Prophet Muhammad, peace and blessings be upon him, we will carry the greatest treasury of his inheritance. There is no greater honor, no greater elevation bestowed by our Majesty for a human being, than to gain the inheritance of the noble character of the Messenger of Allah. As much as the lovers of our noble master are carrying his heritage, to that degree they will receive humiliation, degradation, threats, attacks from the ignorant, the tyrants, the hypocrites, and the unbelievers. As much as they serve humanity in the light of Prophethood, as much as they carry the flag of *tawhid* in their hands, to the same degree they will see poverty, oppression, loss, and martyrdom. The path of Muhammad is plastered with an ocean of his tears of sadness for his community. No other man in this world suffered so much and no other man showed so much compassion for humanity as the honor of the universe. To share his tears of sorrow is the greatest honor and the greatest bliss for his devoted lovers. It means to suffer where he suffered, cry where he cried, supplicate where he supplicated, tremble where he trembled, plead where he pleaded, and take refuge where he took refuge in the Lord of all the worlds.

Thus, whenever believers are threatened by enemies, oppressors and tyrants, let us take refuge in the noblest Surah Al-Fatiha, let us take refuge in the prostration, let us take refuge in the *salawat*, let us take refuge in the *Tahajjud* Prayer, the supererogatory night Prayer, let us take refuge in the pronunciation of the affirmation of unity, let us take refuge in fasting, and let us take refuge in crying tears of sorrow in embracing the poor and sick people on our visits. To carry the treasury of our blessed master's heritage can only mean to become the dust in following his footprints, as it is impossible for any human being living on earth to carry the unimaginable weight of his responsibilities he was capable of. All what the truthful followers can do is trying to adapt some tiny fraction, some small portion of the infinite beauty of his servanthood.

Nevertheless, we should not be afraid of the threats, oppression, and death. But we should fear that the tyrants and unbelievers sully and destroy our consciousness, that they try to deviate ourselves from the straight path. We should fear the secret service of the devil, never ceasing to pull us down with his whisperings into our subconsciousness, into our ears and eyes, penetrating under our skin, enter into the blood of our veins and trying to destroy our mind, our senses, our heart, and our consciousness. We should fear him, as he intends to poison our feelings, intentions, emotions, as he intends to alternate our character into ugliness, trying to wash our brain with evil whisperings. Satan is forever busy to reach closeness to us, although we successfully throw him out, he comes back forever. He whisper, talks, and attacks us continuously, but he is invisible. He plays with us the most condescending games up until we become a play ball in his hands.

There was never any generation who became more perceptive, influenced, and weak towards the whispering of Satan like in our modern societies. The planet earth rarely saw human distortion and ignorance to such degrees. A fighter for the truth named Shandel gives the following statement about today's modern societies: "*The greatest danger for people today lies not in the explosion of an atomic bomb but in the transformation of the very essence of humanity, namely, its dehumanization.*" The description shows that the modern man lives in the danger of becoming like a cadaver, a machine, an animal, an existence without spirit, dehumanized. We can observe that our modern societies fall from the noble feature of excellence, *ikhlas*, sincerity, down into the level of moral bankruptcy. These distortions of human character are all idols of the modern civilization. As we can observe, modern society has much more *shirk* than in previous times. Modern science, political strategies, economic progress, art, education, sports, media, and modern technical innovation have all become idols. In fact the whole world has become an idol. People are, to the furthest degree, morally bankrupted, living a purely materialized life. They worship materialism and capitalism, economic progress like a god. Today, all things of this world become substitutes for our Supreme Creator. Thus, man becomes a compensator, in all actions of his life, he tries to catch up by what he misses. He gets stagnated into the material heaviness of his own life. With his purely materialistic world view, he identifies entirely with the physical reality and therefore compensates his internal loss with his greed and power hunger. Today, people arrived in such terrifying emptiness that they become addicted to the things which surround them. The commercialized world has becomes a drug for people. Therefore, business trade, commerce, making financial profit becomes a religion. What is *shirk*? A worldly religion... One worships the things one loves most. The Holy Qur'an refers: "*Do you ever consider him who has taken his lusts and fancies for his deity?*" (al-Furqan 25:43) The modern man dreams for the fake Paradises.

Today, we can observe that the greatest *shirk* is business trade. We can witness a worldwide corrupted business trade. This means that all levels of life have become perverted for commercial use. Man himself becomes the most wanted article. People get bought and sold. In media, people expose their privacy to attract wide audiences and to make successful business. They sell their most precious intimacy, which is certainly one of the worst sicknesses of modern society. With a terrifying greed and ambition, they invade a whole country; they sell whole tribes and populations. The leaders exploit their people by making financial profit, instead of serving the population with politics, education, science, sports, art, medicine, culture, military, media, and the political establishment. What we see is the eternal problem of this world: the criminal actions against humanity by the leaders; the powerful, the wealthy, who exploited the helpless, the weak, and the poor. Especially in politics and religion, the leaders have lost their credibility. Uncivilized, brutal, dehumanizing, barbarous and corrupt strategies of the leaders dominate the world. The mind games of the political and economic rulers reached the peak of distortion. The degeneration, conspiracy, falseness, hypocrisy of the modern mind reached its peak. Humanity is under the threat of violation, abuse, corruption, exploitation, and terror. They use the distortion of the human mind as a weapon to gain superiority over the world, to secure worldwide control of the financial markets. Their ideologies aim to secure their unrestricted use of worldwide corrupted business trade.

They also manipulate the truths by misconceptions and inaccurate descriptions. Said Nursi states this fact very accurately: "*(In today's world) injustice wears the hat of justice, treason wears the cloak of patriotic zeal, jihad is called aggression and a violation of human rights, and enslavement is presented as emancipation. In short, opposites have exchanged forms.*" These distortions and evil corruptions are all the product of the whisperings of Satan, towards which modern society unfortunately became to the highest degree receptive.

To conclude, people's eternal problem is idolatry, ascribing partners to God. Idols are substitutes for the Almighty. The mother of all idols is the carnal soul. The opposite of *shirk* is *tawhid*, unity. The opposite of *shirk* is dua, supplication. The opposite of *shirk* is the pilgrimage. The opposite of *shirk* is taking refuge in Allah. The opposite of ascribing partners to Allah is the admittance of need and dependence on Allah. So our work and our healing is to continuously supplicate to our Lord of all the worlds in complete need and longing in order to save ourselves from idol worshipping and Satan's whisperings.

The modern man lost the dimensions of inwardness. He suffers from a gradual desacralization of the cosmos, nature, and himself. He lost authenticity and integrity; he lost his own verticality. In order to regain harmony with himself and his environment, the human being has to conform himself to the Divine order. He has to attain a unifying and universal consciousness which sees the interconnectedness of man, the planet earth, and the universe. The fundamental goal of the pilgrimage is to reach peace with oneself, inner harmony, balance, trust, and freedom. Thus, it is a necessity for the pilgrims to reach harmony with one's environment, from the earth towards the skies and the whole universe. The Holy Qur'an states: *"The seven heavens and the earth, and whoever is therein, glorify Him. There is nothing that does not glorify Him with His praise (proclaiming that He alone is God, without peer or partner, and all praise belongs to Him exclusively)"* (al-Isra 17:44). It is the pilgrim's duty to rediscover and reestablish the lost relationship with nature and the cosmos. He has to regain the sensitivity for the spiritual grace of nature. He has to learn to breathe the earth, the stones, the desert, water, mountains, trees, the sky, sun, moon, and stars again. It is the pilgrim and the night, it is him and the desert, it is him and the hills, and it is him and the environment. It is him and his remembrance of what he has lost, what he has forgotten, what is erased from his consciousness, and most important, what is erased from his heart. All of these human values which disappeared in the life of heedlessness and decadence in the world, have to be brought to live again by the pilgrim.

We have an excellent description of the pure nature of man and his position within nature and the universe by Hossein Nasr, the great scholar of our time: "*Man is the channel of grace for nature; through his active participation in the spiritual world he casts light into the world of nature. He is the mouth through which nature breathes and lives. Because of his intimate connection between man and nature, the inner state of man is reflected in the external order. Were there to be no more contemplatives and saints, nature would become deprived of the light that illuminates it and the air which keeps it alive. It explains why, when man's inner being is in darkness and chaos, nature is also turned from harmony and beauty to disequilibrium and disorder.*

Men who live only on the surface of their being can study nature as something to be manipulated and dominate. But only he who has turned toward the inward dimension of his being can see nature as a symbol, as a transparent reality and come to know and understand it in the real sense.

Revelation from the Qur'an to man is inseparable from the cosmic Revelation which is also a book of God. Islam, by refusing to separate man from nature and the study of nature from gnosis or its metaphysical dimension, has preserved an integral view of the universe and sees in the arteries of the cosmic and natural order the flow of Divine grace."

The states of *qabd*, contraction and *bast*, expansion, fear and hope are the constant companions on one's spiritual journey. These are the mysterious changing inner states of the believers. One slides between sufferance, hardship, fear, and the joy of expansion. All is in the Hands of Allah the Almighty. He is the Creator, the All-Hearing, and the All-Knowing. Our noble Messenger says: "*The heart is between the two Fingers of the All-Merciful; He turns it from state to state and gives it whatever form He wishes.*" Nowhere else than on pilgrimage we feel such heightened tremor in our hearts, trembling, hardship, mixed with awe, wonderment, joy, delight, and tears, especially in front of the Ka'ba and on the plain of Arafat. One moment we are awesome, astonished, fearful, trembling in front of God's Majesty and one moment we are melting in loving surrender and joy, overflowing with delight, witnessing His Divine beauty. The constant sliding back and forth is nothing else than sliding between fearing and loving Him, between His Beauty, *Jamal*, and His Might, *Jalal*. We can compare it with the experience of day and night, or life and death, body and spirit, this world and the Hereafter. Especially on the pilgrimage, one slides constantly between life and death, that is to say, between extinction and resurrection, self-sacrifice and rebirth, individuality and unity. It is one's fight for the truth, the greater struggle, *jihad,* where the intellect tries to dominate over the flesh in order to reach the higher levels of the purified soul. It is the experience of fighting between the material realm of the body and its dark desires and the spiritual realms of the soul and its light. In our mundane lives, we feel this struggle to a much lesser degree, but on pilgrimage, we are awakened by the Divine Truth without interruption. We reach a higher spiritual alertness and become receptive for the constant flow of spiritual influences and start to feel Allah's direct supervision. This is the goal of the pilgrimage, to witness Allah's Gaze over oneself at all times and in all places. It represents the exalted state of *ihsan,* sincerity. In our master's words: "*Perfect goodness is that you worship as if seeing God, for even if you do not see Him, He certainly sees you.*" The pilgrims, who inherit the state of sincerity, will feel an overflow of fear and love in their hearts for the One and Only, and the fear and love for the world will be lowered. This station signifies the ultimate spiritual fulfillment for the pilgrims. After these endless years of burning longing for the sacred visit to Mecca and Medina, the pilgrims are finally honored for the greatest privilege, to enter the sacred area of His blessed Presence and feel actually His Gaze. They encounter the One Who continuously supervises themselves, they encounter the One Who is closer to themselves than their jugular vein, they encounter the One Who is with them wherever they are.

The realms of Allah's proximity is the home of the inner pilgrim, the place where he returns, the home of his origin, the place of absolute contentment and peace, the Ka'ba of the heart. To see the Ka'ba of the secret essence and to circumambulate the Ka'ba of the heart is the inner wish of every believer, knowingly or unknowingly. It is the secret essence of all worship activities. These rotations are eternal, never ending. The sacred ritual generates the union of the inner and the outer realities, provided that the lover meets with the Beloved, the desire meets with the Desired, the worshipper meets with the Worshipped. The physical Ka'ba in Mecca meets the inner Ka'ba of the heart. The material garden of Paradise in Medina will meet the Paradise garden of the heart. That is to say, the essence of the believer's heart will meet the essence of the Ka'ba in Mecca. The believer's heart, beating with the pulse of love, will meet the love of his life in Medina, the illuminated city!

The circumambulation of the believers around the Ka'ba on earth is more precious than the angels who circumambulate the Divine Throne in the Heavens, because the believers have to fight an inner struggle with their lower nature and cleanse themselves of egotistical attributes. In order to circumambulate the Ka'ba the pilgrims have to show a firm intention to surrender their particular will to the Divine Will. Allah created angels purely for the sake of performing *tawaf* around His Throne, so their *tawaf* is effortless. But the pilgrims have to apply all their strength in order to leave the world behind them. They left their free will and put on the *ihram,* the shroud of selflessness, and hold on to nothing else than Allah the Almighty. Is not the first command of Allah to the angels to prostrate in front of the first created human being, Adam, a proof of their elevation over the angels? Rumi comments: *"The angel is free because of his knowledge, the beast because of his ignorance. Between the two remains man to struggle."*

Especially the pilgrimage endows us with this ability to discriminate truth from falsehood. The tragedy of modern man is that he has lost the sense to distinguish the right from the wrong, good from the bad, beautiful from the ugly, and misery from happiness. The loss of the power of discrimination arises through neglecting the urgent necessity of man to face himself, to take account, and to make reconciliation. In contrast, the pilgrimage is precisely given to come to terms with oneself, reach peace with oneself, to find inner harmony and tranquility. Furthermore, modern man cannot repent anymore, cannot see his inner world anymore, which results in becoming a stranger to himself. In contrast, the pilgrimage is given to clean the heart of all idols, dirt, trash, bad habits, and heedlessness. Modern man cannot offer himself anymore; he is paralyzed from continuous taking, profiting, corruption, greed, and envy. In contrast, the pilgrimage is given for the sole purpose to trade oneself, to offer one's whole being to one's Lord of all the worlds, the pilgrim gets actually sold and bought by Allah.

Wrapping oneself in a shroud, called *ihram,* the shroud of selflessness, the sacred state of the pilgrim, marks the very essence and the beginning of the pilgrimage. One must abandon, throw away, deny, and reject everything what belongs to the realm of the worldly, the realm of the created. The shroud which is made of two white pieces of cloth signifies the identity of the pilgrim, meaning to remove all signs of worldly identity, sym-

bolizing selflessness and death. Before one is not naked, nullified, negated, one cannot wear the *ihram,* one cannot earn the title of a pilgrim. The
pilgrimage erases all differences of rank and social status. The pilgrim
leaves his family, children, friends, work, homeland, and possessions. He
delivers himself of the heaviness of the worldly cloths and puts on the
cloth of death. He leaves the status of worldly power and earns the status of servanthood. No signs of identity are left. *Ihram* is the robe of
sainthood, the robe of the light of the Divine Attributes of the Almighty.
The shroud is not colorful; it is simple and white without any decoration
or ornaments. The pilgrim's head, arm, and feet have to be bare, simple
and naked. The *ihram* symbolizes the pilgrim's complete internalization
of his personality. His external appearance is completely simple, reduced
up to unrecognizability, in order to beautify his inner self. The body dies
and the spirit shines in full splendor. No cosmetics, no colors are used,
no cloths, socks, shoes, hats are worn in order for the infinite beauty of
the jewels of character to prevail, the light of the Divine Attributes. Therefore the pilgrim has to do the inner work, and peel off the worldly clothes
of artificiality and falseness in order to be able to encounter his real self.
He has to die before dying, that is to say, before dying a natural death,
the pilgrim has to experience the truthful death. He has to deny his egotistical desires, the slavery to his ego and bad habits. The ultimate wisdom for the pilgrim wearing the *ihram,* is to be able to present himself
in complete poverty in order to realize his insufficiency, weakness, and
dependence in front of the Supreme Divinity. The pilgrim shows modesty and need and presents himself in utter humility and loving surrender
in front of the All-Merciful. He enters in a state of desirelessness, wishlessness, with complete submission. Before realizing one's helplessness,
powerlessness, how can the inner eyes of need start to open? Before one
does not have the status of a refuge that is forcefully displaced, the status
of emigration, how can one find the One and Only, how can one become
receptive for the vision of the Creator's Might and Greatness? If one does
not feel ashamed, embarrassed, and bashful in the desert of worldly existence, how can one discover one's true humanity?

The pilgrimage bears the mystery of spiritual poverty. Therefore, it
needs our self-sacrifice. The Divine condition is to sacrifice oneself with
one's own hand. Only then the sacred trade can be realized. We offer ourselves to the Lord of all the worlds, and in return, He will give us eternal

life. In the spiritual world, there is no death without resurrection, no self-sacrifice with new life, no poverty without richness, and no self-extinction without eternity. This is truthful submission expressed in the *talbiyah* of all the pilgrims: "*Here am I, O my great Allah, answering Your call. I am indeed here to Your bidding...*" In order to say the *talbiyah* with one's whole being at the beginning of the pilgrimage, one must be in the state of nothingness, poverty, which is the sacred state of the *ihram*. This implies that one can only say truthfully the *talbiyah,* when one is in the state of selflessness. In order to say the *takbir, Allahu Akbar, God is the Greatest,* with one's whole being before one enters the ritual Prayer, one must be equally in a state of selflessness, nothingness, and poverty. In this respect, the pilgrimage and the ritual Prayer resemble each other. Both the Prayer and the pilgrimage start with the sacred power of this deliberate declaration of *talbiyah* and the *takbir.* With the firm deep-rooted intention, the worshippers are leaving the attachment to the world and enter the plain of the Hereafter.

When Adam resided in Paradise before descending on the Earth, he heard the glorifications, invocations, and remembrance of the angels at the Ka'ba of the heavens, the Oft-Frequented House, *Al-Baytu'l Ma'mur,* doing *tawaf,* and he joined in these Divine recitations. As he had to leave Paradise, he felt deprived of these marvelous hymns of the angels in his worldly life and thus was filled with longing to hear this heavenly sound again. Thus having ordered Prophet Adam, peace be upon him, to build His House on earth, the Ka'ba, the Magnificent realized the fulfillment of Adam's deepest longing for the lost Paradise. That is to say, the Ka'ba is the answer from Allah the Almighty for the profoundest desire of the human being for his beloved Lord. It symbolizes the eternal rendezvous, the meeting place, the reunion of the lover with the Beloved, the seeker with the Sought, the desire with the Desired, after having wandered restlessly in the desert of worldly existence with a burning heart, desperation, dried out lips, heat of search, swollen feet, watered eyes, struggle, affliction, and sufferance. Rumi comments: "*In pain, I breathe easier. The scared child is running from the house, screaming. I hear the gentleness. Under nine layers of illusion, whatever the light, on the face of any object, in the ground itself, I see Your face.*"

Without burning in the desert of worldly existence, one cannot reach the truth of the Ka'ba. Without burning in the fire of the tyrant Nimrod, one cannot earn the rose garden. The Ka'ba represents the absolute object of desire for the human soul, because the Ka'ba bears the symbol of *tawhid*, union. It is the area of absolute peace, trust, and freedom. The Ka'ba is the greatest work of art humanity has ever seen on earth. The miracle is its infinite beauty in its nothingness. The mystery is its irresistible attraction and incomprehensibility. The Ka'ba mirrors the Eternal One. The Ka'ba is the manifestation of absolute power, absolute light, absolute beauty, absolute perfection, and absolute mercy. The Ka'ba is permanent admiration and astonishment, where the intellect, the mind, reasoning get paralyzed. The Ka'ba radiates the light which is neither in the West or the East; it is the light of eternal perfection. The Ka'ba is like a spiritual nuclear power station on earth. The Ka'ba is the ascension of the spirit towards eternity. The Ka'ba is the center of His Thrown on earth, but not the slightest sign of a palace is manifested. No signs of architecture, no signs of art, no signs of building construction. This is the crucial point; the infinite attraction of the Ka'ba is due to its external unattractiveness, its simplicity, and its bareness, in order for the Divine inspiration to rise in the hearts of the pilgrims. The black cover of the Ka'ba is the *ihram* of Allah, simple, no ornament, no color, no decoration, no sign, and no recognition. Nothing to see: the mysterious beauty of the Unseen. The simplicity of the Ka'ba is for the secret Presence of the beauty of His Face. The pilgrims are pulled towards timelessness and spacelessness. Allah has no form, no shape, no color, nothing resembles Him. The Qur'an states: "*In whatever direction you turn, there is the 'Face' of God* (al-Baqarah 2:115). The black cloth of nothingness symbolizes the color of the Truth. It illuminates the face of the spirit. It generates the infinite space of transcendence in order to see wholeness, to see absolute eternity, to breathe and feel the sweet scent of the Hereafter, comprehend the mysterious Divine realms of infinity. Shams al-Tabrizi said: "*Thanks to my Lord, ever since the Ka'ba, the house of God, has been built, God has not made an abode there, but He did dwell in the house of our hearts; and he has never come out of there.*"

Some of the greatest heroes of submission are Prophet Abraham and Prophet Ismail, peace be upon them. Within surrendering to the Divine Will, they did not show the slightest hesitation; on the contrary, they demonstrated the beauty of loving submission to all humanity. They portrait the excellent character features like bravery, straightforwardness, absolute determination, doubtlessness, and wholeheartedness. They followed Allah's orders without fear and doubt, with the belief of certainty. Father Abraham: "*Ismail, I saw that I sacrificed you in my dream.*" The son Ismail: "*Father! Do not show hesitation to obey to our Lord, submit yourself. He will find myself submitted, too, and so God wills, you will find me of the patient!*" In other words, Ismail said in loving surrender to his father: "*Do not hesitate to kill me! Do not hesitate to follow Allah's orders; do not spend for any moment, any doubt to sacrifice myself!*" Like the sheep, soft, willing, giving his neck to the knife... What a heroic generosity at the moment of one's own death. What a miraculous beauty of character. We learn from their excellence of conduct that to be sacrificed, to submit willingly, is the greatest honor. To be sacrificed signifies strength, light, and freedom. It demonstrates such a heroic sacrifice, such a loving submission, that the knife does not cut. We can observe that doubt, hesitation, wondering, insecurity, confusion, indifference, unwillingness, cowardliness are the weaknesses of modern man, the whisperings of Satan. Today we miss the power of determination of one's will, the courage, the straightforwardness, the resolution, that is to say, we miss unconditional submission. Surrendering one's particular will to the Divine Will brings eternal freedom, richness, and power. This is the meaning of a hero, namely to gain the victory of Paradise in the arena of the Divine stage, to gain Allah's good pleasure.

Submission is the highest form of intelligence. Abraham showed us that submission is an act of love. He demonstrated to all his descendants the value and treasury of submitting to the Will of the Lord of all the worlds. His submission is born from his love and his love is born from knowledge. The religion of Islam represents the highest school of thoughts. Thus, submission is the highest form of intelligence. Sacred awareness is born from love, and admiration for the beauty of existence, and for the miracle of creation. This admiration generates sacred awareness for the perfection of creation. Perfection brings Divine love and Divine beauty. Such a sublime love is equal sacred awareness, residing in the beauty of the Divine Presence. This love brings humility, modesty, and surrender. The vision of beauty leads instantly into submission to the One and Only. Abraham showed that unity is never-ending servanthood, it means to offer love within every breath. The Prophet Abraham, peace be upon him, did not fall in love with the transient. He said, as the Qur'anic verse states, "*I love not the things that set"* (al-An'am 6:76), watching the stars, moon in the sky disappearing in the daylight, and watching the sun disappearing at night. Instead he fell in love with permanent, infinite, everlasting, and eternal values. He fell in love with the Omnipresent, the Eternal One, the Ever-Living, the Self-Subsisting. He fell in love with the Divine Essence. He fell in love with the eternal lights of knowledge. Rumi comments: *"If they ask what Love is, say; the sacrifice of will! If you have not left your will behind, you have no will at all. The lover is a king of kings with both worlds beneath him; and a king does not regard what lies at his feet. Only Love and the lover can resurrect beyond time. Give your heart to this; the rest is second-hand. How long will you embrace a lifeless beloved? Embrace that entity to which nothing can cling. What sprouts up every spring will wither by autumn, but the rose garden of Love is always green."*

Sacrifice brings new life, the triumph of the ascension of one's spirit. With submission to God, one saves oneself from the prison of worldly existence. The pilgrimage is the place where knowledge becomes love. In the religion of Islam, there is no torture, no harm, no pain, and no oppression. The way towards Allah is the way towards the eternal direction of His beauty and perfection. On the pilgrimage, the pilgrims try to walk in the footsteps of the Prophets, who brought justice, equality, and peace. This lifelong struggle was made along with their wives. Allah endowed the greatest Prophets with the greatest women, as their wives. These women demonstrated highest elevation of spiritual sublimity, infinite sacred wisdom for all the believers who follow the religion of unity. All the female heroes were chosen by Allah the Almighty to be the heroes of submission, the heroes of true belief, the heroes of self-sacrifice, the heroes of compassion, and the heroes of the fight for the truth. These most honorable women reached the highest standard of morality, wisdom, and love through their total cooperation with their husbands. The All-Merciful chose their wives not only to be their life companions, but their constant supporter, intimate friend, comforter, and helper. They became the servant for the Prophethood of their husband. They showed complete bravery in following, cooperating, fighting for the truth of the religion. All of them regarded as the most heroic women in history because they were helpers in building the foundation of the religion of Divine unity. They fought side by side, shoulders to shoulders, along with their husbands. *"For every great man, there was a great woman."* Starting with

Prophet Abraham, peace be upon him, the destroyer of the idols, the founder of the religion of unity, along with his wife Hajar, one of the greatest women heroes of all time. With the most honored of all men, the noble Prophet, humanity witnessed the most exquisite marriage the world has ever seen. These were the greatest lovers, the greatest wives of all times, Aisha, and Khadija and his most beloved daughter, Fatima who was married with the great Caliph Ali. In a noble tradition, our beloved Prophet says: *"I was made to love three things from your world: women, perfume, and the freshness of my eyes, the Prayer."* This utterance shows the highest form of sacred love for women and this love was perfected and realized in daily life by the exalted personalities, the most remarkable women the world has ever seen. First of all, Aisha, Khadija, and Fatima, may Allah be pleased with them, demonstrated within all their actions, speeches, conduct, and service that women are the jewels of beings and that they are the owners of the first rank within society. They took the greatest pleasure in carrying the heaviest weight of Divine responsibilities for the birth of Islam. The Qur'an states: *"O wives of the Prophet! You are not like any of the other women"* (al-Ahzab 33:32). Khadija represents love, Aisha represents knowledge, and Fatima represents the sacred presence of the Prophet. The Prophet came in the Age of Ignorance and removed the heedlessness. In the Age of Ignorance, the women were not considered as human beings. Thus, his household and the venerable Companions played an essential part in this most powerful spiritual cleaning the world ever witnessed. These first women believers of Islam came at the precise time, in the perfect circumstances, in order to meet the urgent needs of humanity, as the Prophet himself who came in the darkest ages bringing the highest light to all humanity. These women shared their lives with the noble Prophet like no one else; they shared their lives with the one for whom the universe was created. They showed courageousness towards harsh examinations, but showed tenderness and compassion towards the new believers. They never failed to overcome the obstacles, calamities, examinations, and hardship. They are the manifestations of God's all-comprehensive Mercy towards humanity. They are the mother of all believers. They are the queen of all believing hearts. They are the most elevated fruits growing in God's garden. They are the most illuminated stars shining in the heavens.

God's Messenger says: *"The Paradise is at the feet of the mothers."* They attain this station not on the battlefield, but in faith, sincerity, and compassion. They showed us that religion is utter joy, inspiration, and affection. They showed us how to strive on the way of truth for the sake of Allah; although there seemed to be irremovable hindrances, difficulties, obstacles, and hardship; they carried on striving with greater determination. They showed us how to carry the Divine Trust, namely, the sacredness of being a mother, the sacredness of being a wife, and the sacredness of being a woman. There are countless examples of women heroes, like Nasiba, the great lover of our blessed master, who showed total surrender and self-sacrifice. What we learn from Nasiba that the sacred love, struggling with one's lower self, with one's selfishness, in order to achieve the highest character features, is above the love for one's children. Although she experienced the loss of her own children in the battlefield, she was very happy to see her beloved Prophet alive and well.

One of the greatest women saints is Asiya, the Pharaoh's wife, who was tortured and martyred by her own husband for her belief. She showed heroic bravery in the most life threatening situations, highest intelligence in dealing with her husband Pharaoh, one of the greatest tyrants of human history.

One of the most remarkable women is Hajar, not in her achievements or rewards, but in her service. Without her contribution, the ritual of the pilgrimage would not have been completed. She was a black woman slave, left alone in the desert. What a great wisdom! She was left in the desert between life and death. She was left empty-handed, in need of water for her and her son's survival. She was the owner of elevated intention and willpower, firm determination, and perseverance. She used all her strength; she felt the heat of love searching for the water of life.

All the believing men and women of the religion of unity are learning from a black slave woman. We can observe that our blessed master found himself in the same circumstances like Hajar. The noble Prophet was an unlettered orphan, and Allah raised him to be the chief of all imams and he became the mercy for all the worlds. Hajar, a woman slave, became the greatest example for millions of pilgrims until the last day. Due to Hajar's heroic effort in the burning desert, all the uncountable believers who perform the pilgrimage are given to drink the miraculous water of Zamzam until the last day. All believers, who came and will come in later times, can take Hajar as their exalted example for the Sa'y, and will be able to quench their thirst with the holy water of Zamzam.

In the religion of Islam, all men and women carry the fullest responsibility over all the matters of their lives. In Islam, everyone is a shepherd, responsible for his own life and his own flock. Man can achieve knowledge of himself in the sacred mirror, he can receive images of the unseen, and he can receive God's beauty from the mirror of his own existence. Thus man becomes the source of wisdom. Man becomes the hero of his own time. Man becomes the champion conquering his own self. Man becomes the architect building the foundation of unity. He builds his own area of sanctity and gives sacredness to his own time. Man becomes the possessor and the king of his heart and he becomes the lion conquering himself. Rumi says: *"The way that leads to Him is the way of selflessness. True thought is that which opens a way, the true way upon which a king advances. The true king is he who is a king within himself, not with treasures and armies. His kingship remains forever, like the glory of the empire of Muhammad's religion."*

In order to advance in the way of truth we need to play Hajar's role, we have to play Abraham's and Ismail's role, fight where they fought, worship where they worshiped, and supplicate where they supplicated. In return, the pilgrims will receive Zamzam from Hajar, trust and freedom from Abraham, and the beauty of submission from Ismail. We have to become an architect and build the foundation of the Ka'ba, smash the idols of the heart, and build an area of sanctity, and give sacredness to our own time, become a hero of our own time, turn the world into a rose garden, and build the foundation of the house of unity, *tawhid*.

In the religion of Islam, we can learn to become enlightened believers. We have to join the school of mothers, the school of mercy, the school where they teach the knowledge of humility, and the school where we graduate as caliphs, where we graduate as Allah's humble servants. The essence of the religion of Islam is servanthood, *ubudiyah*. The essence of motherhood is servanthood. Therefore it is essential to learn and take example from the mothers of all believers, Fatima, Aisha, and Khadija, and other noble women of faith, Nasiba, Asiya, Maryam, Sumayya, and Hajar, may Allah be pleased with them. They teach us, above everything, that the infinite grace of Divine Mercy is coming from Allah the Almighty. They teach us that the best actions of mankind are the ones done for mankind, for the sake of Allah. Only selflessness can activate the grace of Allah. If we are in search of the exemplary lives of the first women saints in Islam, we have to look for them in our own lives. We have to recognize them inwardly, by their supreme character traits, and externally in our daily life routines.

"*A man came to take leave from Shibli (may Allah sanctify his soul). Shibli asked:*

— Where are you going?

— To the Hajj.

— Take with you two big bags; fill them with Mercy there and bring them to us, so that we will have a share of it, to share with our friends and to offer our guests...

The man took his leave and left to go to Hajj. When he returned, he came to visit Shibli, who asked:

— Did you go to the pilgrimage?

— Yes.

— What did you do first?

— I took a ritual total ablution, put on my pilgrim's garb, made two units of Salah, started reciting the talbiya, and made my intention and decision to do the pilgrimage.

— With your intention and decision to do the Hajj, were you able to cancel all decisions you had taken which were contrary to this decision, since the day you were born?

— No.

— Then you have not made your intention to do the Hajj.

Then you say you took off your ordinary clothes and put on your pilgrim's garb. Have you denuded yourself of all you have done in your ordinary life?

— No.

— Then you have neither taken off your clothes neither have you put on your pilgrim's garb.

When you washed yourself and took your ablution, did you cleanse yourself of all your ills and defects?

— No.

— Then you have not taken your ritual ablution.

When you recited the talbiya and said 'I am present, my Lord, I am here, at Your orders, I am here heedful, there is none like You, all grace is to You, all blessing is from You, all belongs to You, there is no partner with You', did you receive an answer, a call from Allah?

— No.

— Then you have not recited the talbiya.

Did you enter the Harem, the sacred grounds?

— Yes.

- When you entered the Harem, did you vow to leave behind all that is haram and unlawful?

— No.

— Then you have not entered the Harem. Did you visit Mecca?

— Yes.

— When you visited Mecca, did you feel as if you received a different state from Allah?

— No.

— Then you have not been in Mecca.

Did you enter the Sacred Mosque?

— Yes.

— Did you feel closer to Allah in the Sacred Mosque?

— No.

— Then you have not entered the Sacred Mosque. Did you see the Ka'ba?

— Yes.

— In seeing the Ka'ba, did you achieve the goal for which you came?

— No.

— Then you have not seen the Ka'ba.

Did you circumambulate the Ka'ba thrice in fast paces and four times slowly?

— Yes.

— In running thrice around the Ka'ba, did you run away from everything that you were with and in walking four times around did you reach salvation and security and thankfulness?

— No.

— Then you have not left your old self, nor your worldly load; neither have you come closer to your Lord. You have not made your tawaf.

Did you touch and salute the Hajar'ul-aswad (the Black Stone)?

— *Yes.*

— *Pity on you! It is said the one who touches the Black Stone touches the Truth. The one who touches the Truth is in the securest peace. Did you feel this security?*

— *No.*

— *Then you have not touched the Hajar'ul-aswad. Did you make two units of Salah afterwards?*

— *Yes?*

— *In doing so, did you stand in front of your Lord and show Him your intention?*

— *No.*

— *Then you have not made your Salah. Did you stand on the hill of Safa?*

— *Yes.*

— *What did you do there?*

— *I recited the takbir. I declared the Greatness of Allah.*

— *As you stood there, did your soul find purity (saf)? Bid your heart find joy (safa)? As you said 'Allahu Akbar', did the world and the worldly become smaller?*

— *No.*

— *Then you have neither stood on the top of Safa nor did you declare Allah's greatness.*

As you ran between Safa and Marwa, did you run from His Jalal to His Jamal?

— *No.*

— *Then you did not walk seven times between Safa and Marwa. Did you stand on the top of the hill of Marwa?*

— *Yes.*

— *As you stood there, did you feel peace and tranquility descend upon you?*

— *No.*

— *Then you have not been there either.*

— *Did you go to Mina from Mecca?*

— *Yes.*

— *Did you receive your wish?*

— No.

— Then you have not been to Mina.

Have you entered the Masjid al-Hayf?

— Yes.

— When you entered the Masjid al-Hayf, was the fear of Allah refreshed in your heart?

— No.

— Then you did not enter the Masjid al-Hayf. Did you go up to the mountain of Arafat?

— Yes.

— Did you come to know how and why you were created, and where you are going to go? Did you come to know who is your Lord, that Lord who you deny? Has Allah shown you a sign that you were one of the chosen?

— No.

— Then you have not been to Arafat. Have you been to Mash'ar?

— Yes.

— Did you remember Allah at Mash'ar in such a way that you forgot everything else? Did you come to understand there how one is addressed and how one's prayers are answered?

— No.

— Then you have not been to Mash'ar. Did you sacrifice an animal?

— Yes.

— Did you sacrifice your desires and your will for Allah's sake?

— No.

— You have not sacrificed anything. Did you stone the devil at Mina?

— Yes.

— Did you throw away your ignorance? Did you receive wisdom in its place?

— No.

— You have not thrown stones at the devil.

Did you visit the Ka'ba, the Sacred House, after you descended from Arafat?

— Yes.

— What gifts have you received from the Master of that house? For the noble Prophet, peace and blessings be upon him, says: 'The pilgrims are

Allah's visitors; it is right that the Host show honor and give presents to the guests...'

— I have not received any gifts.

— Then you have not done your visitation.

Did you satiate yourself drinking the Zamzam water?

— Yes.

— Did the taste of Zamzam make you promise not to taste anything unlawful, ever?

— No.

— Then you have not drunk the Zamzam water.

Did you make the circumambulation of farewell at the Ka'ba?

— Yes.

— Did you leave all of your ego and all your being behind?

— No.

— Then you have not made your farewell, nor have you made your Hajj. If you wish, you must return and make your Hajj again. If you do, do it the way I told you." (Haqaiq'ut-Tafsir).

Supplications

"I have an eternal rendezvous with my Lord. I have an appointment with my Creator. I have to go to meet Him together with His creatures. I have to emigrate from my home to His house. I have to leave my individuality and join the community of believers. I have to direct myself towards the eternal address of emigration. I have to go straight to Him to regain my humanity. He is the Only One. I have to go to renew my contract with Him. I have to remember what I have forgotten. I have forgotten who I am, this is my shame. I lost my identity as a human being. Alas, I lost the nobility to be His caliph. I lost the great station, the honor, this elevation to be His creature to which all angels prostrate. I lost the ability to carry His trust. I forgot the Divine Names and Attributes which He taught me. I forgot that He blew my soul with His Divine Breath of Mercy. The worst disaster, I forgot to miss Him, to seek Him, to long for Him, to beg with Him, to cry tears for Him, I forgot to love Him! I became a stranger for the Heavens. I lost my very best Friend. I lost the capacity to become a friend. I lost the treasury of a holy friendship. I came here in embarrassment, with tears of regret, trembling for Divine acceptance, burning of shame for my sins, wrongdo-

ings and mistakes. I came here in order to become a stranger to everything except Him and offer my unconditional friendship towards Him. I wish to do the emigration from a life of harm towards a life of beneficence. I wish to deliver myself from a distorted life to a life of unity. I wish to exchange the existence of a stranger into the existence of a friend, I wish to leave ignorance and attain knowledge.

We came here for permanent astonishment. We wish to be shattered by the love we have for You and submerge in the sea of Your Gentleness. We wish to be drunk in love, in the rivers of longing souls, which lead into the ocean of meanings.

Let's melt our individuality away in the innumerable crowds, in the infinite see of white shrouds. Let's embrace each other, let's become one with all. Become one body, have one goal, have one color, have one thought, have one wish, and have one breath! What an excitement, what a comfort for our souls!

O Lord, we are at the source of thousands of holy experiences, we wish to profit from the sounds of eternal sweetness we hear, we wish to taste the heavenly fragrance of the glorious ascension of Your most beloved towards the beauty of Your Majesty. We wish to join the echoes of the voices of Adam and Abraham.

After the return from the pilgrimage, the most precious treasures we are able to bring back, the only thing which we are able to earn at the pilgrimage, are the noble character features of Prophet Muhammad, peace and blessings be upon him. O Lord, we plead You to help us to earn some truthfulness of the Caliph Abu Bakr, some justice of the venerable Umar, some shame and humbleness from the venerable Uthman, some knowledge from the venerable Ali!"

In our modern world, man becomes a slave of his own inventions, whereas man is created to be Your slave! We came with the wish to reverse this truth, namely to live in the way as You meant, to live the beauty of being Your slave. It was the highest inspiration of Your most beloved Prophet, who said: 'Poverty is my pride.'

O Lord, we pulled away with all our strength from the attraction of the world, we cut the attachment to our mundane lives and wish to inhale the perfumes of the Divine! O Lord, we came here to live the atmosphere of Your Divine revelations, to breathe the sweet scent of remembrance every moment. O Lord, we came to renew our faith, to refresh our consciousness, to update *our good behavior, to re-strengthen our belief in You, and to reconstruct our daily agenda into a program of holy sessions of remembrance.*

Our beloved Creator, we need repair, we need repair, we need repair! We came here brokenhearted, full of sorrow, sadness, and destitution. Help us to regain our humanity, to regain our spiritual health, to regain our human conscience, to regain sacred awareness. We came to feel the softness of our hearts.

There was a burned heart knowing his Owner, pleading with his Owner, pleading as his slave, barefooted, poor, naked, never without trembling, never without tears. It was Adam, our forefather. We wish to share the pain of separation with Adam, the first human being You created and the first to leave the Paradise of union with You. O Lord, we wish to share these tears of his heart.

Make us be part in the most beautiful and honorable of all chains, the chain of Your lovers! So that we can become the lovers of the lovers of the lovers of the ones who love You and the ones whom You love!

When will we arrive at a state of having no fear and no grief? If not before Your Sacred House, where else? If not on the plain of Arafat, where else?

We came here to be in continuous admiration. We came to be part of the secret: 'Everything will perish but His Countenance.' We came here to be part of this eternal pleasure, the coolness of our eyes, the bliss of the sacred taste.

You are the All-Benevolent! Here is the place where we have to gain the fruits of the Hereafter. Here is the place where we receive Your bountiful gifts, and live in the Paradise of Your Divine favors and prosperity. Your fruits of sacred wisdom are ever near!

O Lord, make it easy for us! Give us comprehensive guidance, the guidance which heals our spiritual wounds. Offer us the pure drink, to quench our spiritual thirst. O Lord, make it easy for us! We have to show such a little effort, a small action and You give us the greatest rewards, You spoil us with infinite blessings and grace.

O Lord, make it easy for us! We came here and we are embedded by Your light. We came to gaze upon Your beauty unceasingly. We came here to drown in Your ocean of Mercy!

We came to be silent and listen to the silence of our hearts' speech. We came to clean ourselves from false perceptions and direct ourselves to the eternal realms of Your infinite bounty, beauty, and perfection.